AF443089

Megaregions

Megaregions

Globalization's New Urban Form?

Edited by

John Harrison

Department of Geography, School of Social, Political and Geographical Sciences, Loughborough University, UK

Michael Hoyler

Department of Geography, School of Social, Political and Geographical Sciences, Loughborough University, UK

Edward Elgar

Cheltenham, UK • Northampton, MA, USA

Published by
Edward Elgar Publishing Limited
The Lypiatts
15 Lansdown Road
Cheltenham
Glos GL50 2JA
UK

Edward Elgar Publishing, Inc.
William Pratt House
9 Dewey Court
Northampton
Massachusetts 01060
USA

A catalogue record for this book
is available from the British Library

Library of Congress Control Number: 2014947029

This book is available electronically in the ElgarOnline.com
Social and Political Science Subject Collection, E-ISBN 978 1 78254 790 7

ISBN 978 1 78254 789 1

Typeset by Servis Filmsetting Ltd, Stockport, Cheshire
Printed and bound in Great Britain by T.J. International Ltd, Padstow

Contents

Figures

Tables

Contributors

Billy Fleming is a Doctoral Student in City and Regional Planning at the University of Pennsylvania. He is a planner and a landscape architect focusing on the ecological implications for rapid growth, energy demand and water scarcity in the megaregions of the Southern United States. His recent publications have focused on the Texas Triangle and he spent the summer of 2012 working for the White House Domestic Policy Council as a member of the urban affairs team. His work has been funded through the Federal Highway Administration's Dwight D. Eisenhower Graduate Transportation Fellowship program.

Michael R. Glass is a Lecturer of Urban Studies at the University of Pittsburgh, Pennsylvania. His research interests concern the historical and contemporary development of political spaces in American and Southeast Asian city-regions, the practices of trans-urban consultancy networks, and the neoliberalization of housing policy and urban development. He is editor (with Reuben Rose-Redwood) of *Performativity, Politics, and the Production of Social Space* (2014).

John Harrison is a Senior Lecturer in Human Geography at Loughborough University and an Associate Director of the Globalization and World Cities (GaWC) research network. He is a regional geographer interested in how regions and regional space are constructed politically. His recent publications have focused on global urban and regional governance. He is also co-editor of *Planning and Governance of Cities in Globalization* (2013).

Markus Hesse is a Professor of Urban Studies at the University of Luxembourg. His research examines contemporary urban and economic change and its territorial manifestations. His recent publications have focused on cities and regions, economic networks, mobilities and flows, and metropolitan governance, policy and planning. He is also author of *The City as a Terminal* (2008) and a co-editor of *Cities, Regions and Flows* (2013).

Michael Hoyler is a Senior Lecturer in Human Geography at Loughborough University and an Associate Director of the Globalization and World Cities (GaWC) research network. He is an urban geographer interested in the transformation of cities and metropolitan regions in contemporary globalization. His recent publications have focused on the conceptualization and empirical analysis of contemporary (world) city and city-regional network formation. He is also co-editor of *Global Urban Analysis: A Survey of Cities in Globalization* (2011), the *International Handbook of Globalization and World Cities* (Edward Elgar, 2012) and *Cities in Globalization* (2013).

Alex Schafran is a Lecturer in Human Geography at Leeds University. His research focuses on the contemporary restructuring and retrofitting of urban regions, with a particular emphasis on the changing dynamics of race, class and segregation across space and place. His recent publications attempt to fuse critical, historically-rooted and place-based geography with a planner's eye for policy and the future.

Peter Schmitt is an Associate Professor in the Department of Human Geography at Stockholm University and a Senior Research Fellow at the Nordic Centre for Spatial Development (Nordregio). He specializes in urban and regional research, strategic spatial planning and territorial governance, with a geographical focus on Europe and the Baltic Sea Region. His research attempts to understand spatial entities, their dynamics, development paths and socio-cultural and political contexts.

Lukas Smas is a Senior Research Fellow at the Nordic Centre for Spatial Development (Nordregio) in Stockholm, Sweden. He specializes in urban and regional planning, and economic and urban geography. His recent research has focused on multi-scalar inter-city connectivities and knowledge dynamics in Northern Europe.

David Wachsmuth is a Killam Postdoctoral Research Fellow and a Social Sciences and Humanities Research Council Postdoctoral Fellow in the Department of Geography at the University of British Columbia. He holds a PhD in sociology from New York University (2014), where his dissertation research investigated new frontiers in entrepreneurial urban governance and the emergence of competitive multi-city regionalism in the United States. His other research interests include the changing relationship between cities and the environment, critical urban theory, and the politics of urban public space.

Stephen M. Wheeler is an Associate Professor in the Department of Human Ecology at the University of California at Davis. His research focuses on sustainability planning, climate change planning, and urban morphology. He is the author of *Planning for Sustainability* (2nd ed. 2013) and *Climate Change and Social Ecology* (2012), co-editor (with Timothy Beatley) of *The Sustainable Urban Development Reader* (3rd ed., 2014), and a recipient of the Dale Prize for Excellence in Urban and Regional Planning.

Xu Zhang is a PhD candidate in Human Geography and Planning at the University of Amsterdam. He is an urban geographer interested in the transition of Chinese cities and regions under conditions of contemporary globalization. His current research has focused on the economic and spatial restructuring of metropolitan areas in China with the functioning of rising advanced economic activities, as well as the way (national and local) institutional environments filter and shape these changes.

1. Megaregions: foundations, frailties, futures

John Harrison and Michael Hoyler

1.1 INTRODUCTION

> I hope that his own definition will be heeded; for the term is so awe-inspiring, and the phenomenon it describes so dramatic and novel, that it is very easy for misconceptions to take root. (Hecksher, 1964, p. vii)

August Hecksher is a name that is not necessarily instantly recognizable as being pivotal to the intellectual development of research on megaregions. Yet his words offer a profound insight into what lies at the heart of a critical research agenda for those of us whose interest in megaregions has brought us to contribute to this edited collection. When you consider the term Hecksher is alluding to is 'megalopolis', and that his quote appears in the foreword to the paperback edition of Jean Gottmann's classic 20th-century urban geography and planning text *Megalopolis: The Urbanized Northeastern Seaboard of the United States,*[1] the relevance to contemporary work on megaregions starts to become clearer. His words take on added significance when you cast your eye over just some of the many terms that have been used over the last half century by geographers and planners to describe the phenomena of sprawling urbanized landscapes comprising clustered networks of cities: *megalopolis* . . . archipelago economy, galactic city, string city, limitless city, endless city, liquid city, global city-region, world city-region, mega-city region, polycentric metropolis, new megalopolis, megapolitan region, metro region, polynuclear urban region, super urban area, super region . . . *megaregion*.

The first question to consider, then, is why are we focusing on megaregions? After all, if you look back to Peter Taylor and Robert Lang's (2004) list of 50 names given to new metropolitan forms, the term megaregion is not present, while the most recently published 'dictionaries' in human geography both omit megaregion – though interestingly retain entries on 'megalopolis' (Castree et al., 2013; Gregory et al., 2009). Is the term megaregion simply less important than we think it is? Or perhaps the megaregion is as transient as some of the other concepts listed by Taylor and Lang ('cities a la carte', 'servurb' and 'sprinkler city') used to account for current or near-future urban form?

Our starting point is that despite considerable dispute over what the term might mean, an increasing number of commentators seem willing to agree that megaregions are important phenomena in globalization. One widely circulated story is that megaregions constitute globalization's new urban form. Here commentators appear convinced that the expansion of globalizing cities into larger city-regions is being superseded by trans-metropolitan landscapes comprising networked urban centres and their surrounding area. They appear captivated by a perception that what goes on in mega-regions is foreboding our urban futures. And they seem assured that what occurs in megaregions constitutes the leading-edge of capitalist endeav-our, driving competitiveness (Ross, 2009) and determining life opportu-nities (Florida, 2008). From its origins in the United States (Dewar and Epstein, 2007; Lang and Dhavale, 2005; Regional Plan Association, 2006), through to its parallels in European spatial planning (Faludi, 2009), and its spread and application to all manner of different geographical con-texts (Yang, 2009; Pieterse, 2010; UN-Habitat, 2010a, 2010b; Weller and Bolleter, 2013), there can be little doubt as to the importance currently being attached to the megaregion concept by its many advocates.

Nowhere is this intellectual buzz and appetite for megaregions more fervent than in the United States. Inspired by Gottmann's (1961) predic-tion that 'megalopolis' was the antecedent to a new spatial order that would emerge nationwide during the late 20th century, the beginning of the 21st century saw the Regional Plan Association (RPA) consider making their own statement on what they saw as the current and near-future 'megaregional' geography of the United States. Launched in 2005, America 2050 is that vision. It identifies 11 emerging megaregions as prototypes for balanced and sustainable growth across the United States during the first half of the 21st century (Figure 1.1).

The background to America 2050 is significant. It is motivated by both internal and external pressures: internally, by the lack of federal action to identify and bring forward investments to reform the physical infra-structure (transport, energy, water) and secure America's future global economic competitiveness; externally, by what the RPA perceive their 'competitors' in Europe and Asia are already succeeding at by coupling specialized economic functions with integrated transportation modes to enable the efficient movement of workers, goods and information across extended geographical areas. What is compelling about the America 2050 map is it represents a belief that responding to this challenge, first, requires coordination at the megaregion scale, and second, can only be achieved

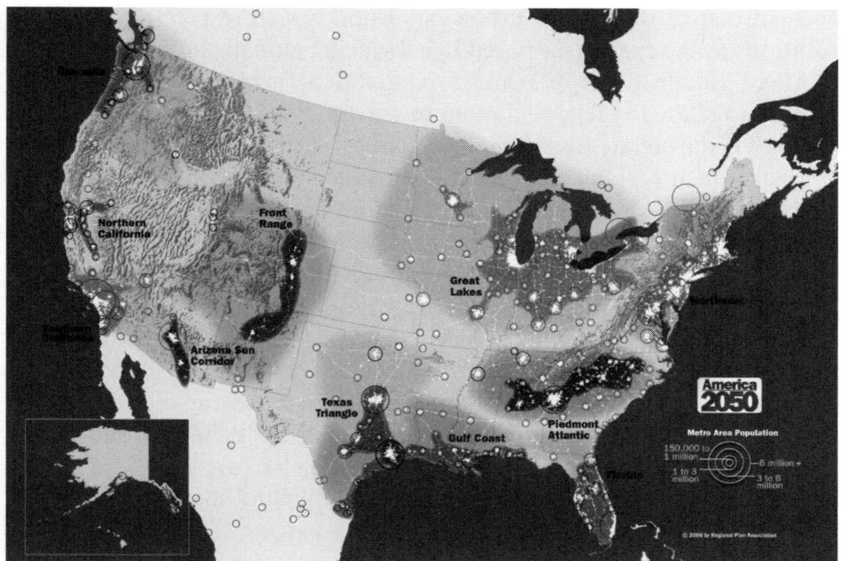

Source: America 2050 (2008). Reproduced by permission of the Regional Plan Association.

Figure 1.1 America 2050's emerging US megaregions with areas of influence

with new investments in infrastructure development in and across these 11 megaregions. It is also an argument constructed from a series of normative assumptions about how our globalizing world is spatially configured.

If you believe the hype, megaregions are the spatial manifestation of economic activity and are fast 'becoming the new engines of global and regional economies' (UN-Habitat, 2010b, p. 1). This argument is undergirded by a now familiar geoeconomic logic that in globalization, the largest and densest clusters of socioeconomic activity are those acting as the most important staging/strategic command posts, and therefore surging ahead, in today's quicksilver global economy. From Florida's (2008) 'spiky world' riposte to Friedman's (2005) 'flat world' thesis, through to Glaeser's (2011) 'triumph of the city' or Brenner's (2013b) 'planetary urbanization', it is impossible to avoid the many reference points to the importance of urban economic processes in globalization. This is ably supported by a geopolitical logic that argues the scale and pace of urbanization in these locations is now so pervasive that new supra-local scales of urbanization are being created, which to function effectively require economic systems and political systems to be geographically aligned. One consequence of this is how urban expansion is seen to preclude localized solutions to the challenges posed by advancing globalization.

All of this leads proponents to claim that 'urban mega-regions are coming to relate to the global economy in much the same way that metropolitan regions relate to national economies' (Florida et al., 2008, p. 460). This statement is significant, bold and challenging in equal measure: significant, because megaregions are the latest episode in the long-running political-economic drama that is the search for a post-national spatial/scalar fix for globalized capital accumulation and organizing (inter) national space economies; bold, because it upholds claims that there is an unbreakable logic linking megaregions (as space) and megaregionality (as process) with the most advanced elements of 21st-century globalization; and challenging, because why should megaregions be any different to the other spatial scale corpses, which, having achieved their own short-lived period of 'new regionalist' orthodoxy, came to be swept away in favour of the latest fashionable and soon-to-be dominant spatial policy tools (Harrison, 2007).

As early as 50 years ago, August Hecksher recognized this very concern. He observed how a spatial concept ('megalopolis') can generate such interest and excitement amongst academics and practitioners that its true value and meaning gets lost among the ensuing euphoria and paraphernalia that is its rise to orthodoxy.[2] It is precisely in the process of becoming a captured concept that Hecksher warns how easy it is for 'misconceptions' to take root. When a concept is captured it is taken away from the foundations upon which it has been constructed to be used in a deeply political way by actors in different contexts who wish to defend or challenge a particular viewpoint. The further a concept is distanced from its foundations, the greater the danger it will be misinterpreted, over-extended and inappropriately used by the actor(s) concerned. Those concepts which do rise to orthodoxy are arguably those at greatest risk of becoming what the social scientist Andrew Sayer (1992) famously categorized as a 'chaotic concept'. In this way, the rise of the megaregion prompts us to confront searching questions about the prospects for megaregionality to achieve the ambitious goals – enhanced competitiveness, accelerating investment in sustainable transportation infrastructure, creating liveable communities, smart planning – its academic and political proponents currently espouse. For within the current body of literature, no meaningful attempts have been made to discuss the foundations, frailties and futures of megaregional research.

This collection aims to instil some coherence into this debate by opening up the megaregion concept for critical scrutiny. Our starting point is that the rhetoric and can-do bravado which currently surrounds megaregions has raced too far ahead of the sustained theoretical and rigorous empirical work needed to support many of the assertions, assumptions, claims and investments being made in the belief that megaregions do constitute globalization's new urban form. In particular, we examine the opportunities and challenges posed by current approaches to conceptualizing megaregions, megaregionality, and planning and governing at this scale. We wish to distinguish between the advances made by new perspectives to analysing megaregions and megaregionality, providing a clear indication of where these advances differ from the spurious claims made elsewhere in relation to megaregions.

To achieve this, the chapter is structured as follows. In the first section we aim to critically examine the foundations upon which the megaregion discourse has been constructed. In so doing, we conceptualize the position occupied by the megaregion in debates prior to the onset of globalization, and then discuss how the concept has been reawakened during globalization. The second section then explores four separate, yet interrelated, lines of argumentation which cut into the megaregional debate as it is currently constructed and form the basis for developing a more critical approach toward megaregional research. We conclude with some cautionary remarks about the challenges and opportunities for near-future megaregional research.

1.2 FOUNDATIONS: FROM MEGALOPOLIS TO MEGAREGIONS – A *NEW* 'LABORATORY FOR URBAN GROWTH'

Despite the recent hype surrounding megaregions, the concept itself – or perhaps more accurately, the foundations upon which it is constructed – has a much longer history, the length of which remains the subject of some significant conjecture (see Baigent, 2004; Zhang, 2014). Nevertheless, for our purposes we are taking the beginning of the 20th century as starting point. This was a time when approximately 7 per cent of the world's population could be considered urban and there were just 16 cities with a population in excess of 1 million people (Harvey, 2000). It was also when the eminent Scottish planner and theorist Patrick Geddes (1915) first considered 'megalopolis', as both a concept and as a place. In this regard, Geddes actually predates Gottmann by almost 50 years in recognizing the potential for an urbanized corridor to extend along the northeastern seaboard of the United States.

In the end Geddes settled on minting the term 'conurbation' to develop his ideas about city evolution and the new urban configurations produced.

In fact it was his contemporary, Lewis Mumford, who was to later pick up the term 'megalopolis' to define the fourth stage of six stages of city evolution (Mumford, 1938). The first three stages – 'eopolis' (village), 'polis' (city) and 'metropolis' (capital city) – chart the rise of the city. The final three stages – 'megalopolis' (a city of exaggerated size), 'tyrannopolis' (overexpansion causing rapid decline) and 'nekropolis' (city abandonment due to war and famine) – chart how great cities fall. For Mumford 'megalopolis' is the last vestige of urban development, the tipping point at which city development becomes over-development and the signal that a city is about to enter a period of (terminal) decline and disintegration.

Uniting Geddes and Mumford was their shared conviction that city expansion became unsustainable once a city reached the size of a megalopolis – though Geddes did stop someway short of Mumford's suggestions that unsustainable equalled irreversible fatality (Meller, 1993). For them and many others writing in the first half of the 20th century, cities were growing too fast and this meant megalopoli were cast in a negative light of the 'city as problem'. Gottmann's (1957, 1961) outlook on the coming megalopolises was the complete antithesis. In this way, Gottmann's labelling of the northeastern seaboard of the United States 'megalopolis' was hugely symbolic. Gottmann makes explicit his referring back over 2000 years to when the ancient Greeks planned for a new city-state (to be called Megalopolis), 'dream[ing] of a great future for it and hop[ing] it would become the largest of the Greek cities' and 'a symbol of the long tradition of human aspirations and endeavor' (Gottmann, 1961, p. 4). While Geddes and Mumford were fiercely critical of urban sprawl, Gottmann actively promoted a ferociously modernist and progressive view of the new urban form. Addressing the still dominant anti-modernist tradition inspired by Geddes and Mumford, Gottmann (1961, p. 13) goes to the length of asking 'Are people both in and out of this extraordinary region united in condemning it?' to emphasize his very different perspective on the emerging urban form.

Gottmann describes late-20th-century urban-economic expansion as promising social and economic fulfilment, enabling the 'masses' to access non-manual jobs, better housing, education and cultural offerings which were seen previously to be the exclusive domain of 'elites'. As a message detailing progress and improvement it quickly gained favour in the United States, particularly with those whose ancestors had left behind the European countryside for the North American city. Alongside this, urban policy elites, so used to hearing anti-urbanist accounts emphasizing the problems associated with the growth of cities, were 'flattered, if not surprised, to find their cities in the van of progress' (Baigent, 2004, p. 690).

Of course, this exposure brought with it a lot of attention. The term 'megalopolis' quickly became shorthand for all that is deemed progressive in (North American) urban planning. While this is not to say that Gottmann did not acknowledge the problems associated with megalopolis, it is noticeable that when so doing the argument veered toward the prophetic: 'Megalopolis stands indeed at the threshold of a new way of life, and upon [the] solution of its problems will rest civilization's ability to survive' (Gottmann, 1961, p. 16). In this way, megalopolis was to provide Gottmann and his contemporaries a 'laboratory for urban growth' as the full effect of globalizing forces began to take hold. Indeed, Gottmann's legacy arguably lives on in the present day focus on megaregions.

Often overlooked in Gottmann's work is the emphasis he placed on both form and function. We say overlooked because while Gottmann's work has traditionally been read for its contribution to informing debates around mapping and planning the evolving urban form, its structure and its anatomy, dig beneath the surface and you will find a putative relational economic geography with incipient ideas about the functioning of the urban system which he went on to develop and expand upon in subsequent works (Gottmann, 1976; Gottmann and Harper, 1990). Yet the dominant reading of Gottmann remains centred on his contribution to debates about the evolving urban form (see Lang and Knox, 2009; Morrill, 2006; Short, 2007; Vicino et al., 2007 for recent re-evaluations of the original megalopolis). This is significant because in the emerging body of work on megaregions, form-dominant approaches to megaregions appear more influential in the United States, whereas European accounts often adopt a more functionally-dominant perspective (see Section 1.3.2). In fact, what we have seen over the past two decades is an attempt to align the functional dominance of the geoeconomic global city (region) literature with the form dominance of traditional planning thought.

Table 1.1 presents key definitions of the major global urban-regional spatial configurations that have been identified in the literature. There are four points we take from this table. The first relates to the geographical context in which these spatial concepts have their intellectual origins and the specific purpose for which they were developed. Spatial concepts are not interchangeable. For us, there is a critical distinction that needs to be made, which helps define and delimit megaregions from other spatial concepts. Broadly speaking we distinguish between three types of urban-regional spatial configurations that relate to the global economy. While global city-regions, mega-city regions and metro(politan) regions relate to one urban system (comprising one or more cities), a megaregion comprises two or more interrelated urban systems, while planetary urbanization represents the reach of the global urban system across all geographic space (Figure 1.2).

Table 1.1 *From megalopolis to megaregions (and beyond)*

Concept	Definition	Minimum population	Maximum population	Geography	Number	Foundational literature
Megalopolis	'[V]ery large polynuclear urbanized systems endowed with enough continuity and internal interconnections for them to be considered a system in itself.' (Gottmann, 1976, p. 162)	25 million	Not specified	Northeastern United States	1	Gottmann (1961)
Global city-region	'[D]ense polarized masses of capital, labour, and social life that are bound up in intricate ways in intensifying and far-flung extra-national relationships. As such, they represent an outgrowth of large metropolitan areas – or contiguous sets of metropolitan areas – together with surrounding hinterlands of variable extent which may themselves be sites of scattered urban settlements.' (Scott, 2001a, p. 814)	1 million	27.9 million	Global	>300	Scott (2001a, 2001b)
Mega-city region	'[A] series of anything between 10 and 50 cities and towns, physically separate but functionally networked, clustered around one or more larger central cities, and drawing enormous economic strength from a new functional division of labour.' (Hall and Pain, 2006, p. 3)	1.6 million	19 million	Western Europe	8	Hall and Pain (2006)
Metro (politan) regions	'[L]arge concentrations of population and economic activity that constitute functional economic areas, typically covering a number of local government	1.5 million	34 million	OECD	78	OECD (2006)

	areas. An economic area in this sense denotes a geographic space within which a number of economic links are concentrated.' (OECD, 2006, p. 31)					
Megaregions	'[I]ntegrated sets of cities and their surrounding suburban hinterlands across which labour and capital can be reallocated at very low cost . . . perform[ing] functions that are somewhat similar to those of the great cities of the past . . . but they do this on a far larger scale.' (Florida et al., 2008, pp. 459–460)	3.7 million	121.6 million[1]	Global	40	Florida et al. (2008)
		20 million	120 million	Global	Not specified	UN-Habitat (2010a, 2010b)
	'[N]etworks of metropolitan centers and their surrounding areas . . . spatially and functionally linked through environmental, economic, and infrastructure interactions.' (Ross, 2009, p. 1)	5 million	54 million	United States	11	Ross (2009)
Planetary urbanization	'[E]ven spaces that lie well beyond the traditional city cores and suburban peripheries – from transoceanic shipping lanes . . . [to] erstwhile "natural" spaces such as the world's oceans, deserts, jungles, mountain ranges, tundra, and atmosphere – have become integral parts of the worldwide urban fabric.' (Brenner and Schmid, 2011, p. 13)	n/a	7 billion +	Global	1	Brenner (2013a, 2013b); Brenner and Schmid (2011)

Note: 1. The largest megaregion of 121.6 million is Pearl River Delta. It is worth noting that back in 2009 it was reported that plans were afoot to expand the region politically so the population of the Pearl River Delta would reach 260 million (Forbes, 2011).

Source: Authors

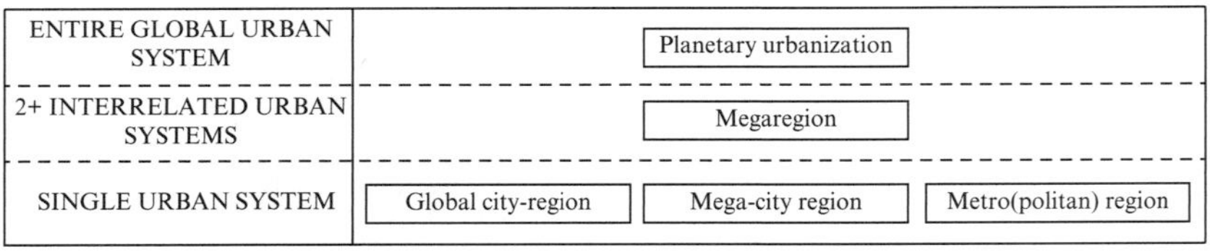

ENTIRE GLOBAL URBAN SYSTEM	Planetary urbanization		
2+ INTERRELATED URBAN SYSTEMS	Megaregion		
SINGLE URBAN SYSTEM	Global city-region	Mega-city region	Metro(politan) region

Source: Authors

Figure 1.2   A typology of global urban-regional spatial configurations

Meanwhile, and somewhat related, second, we would argue there are distinctive North American and European perspectives on researching large-scale urban-regional configurations. American perspectives are still rooted in a form-dominant spatial planning tradition. In contrast, European perspectives, once steeped in discussions about urban spatial form (Dühr, 2007; Faludi, 2009; Kunzmann, 1996), are now more commonly associated with functionally-dominant global-city inspired networked approaches (Hall and Pain, 2006; Hoyler et al., 2008a; Pain and Van Hamme, 2014; Reades and Smith, 2014; Taylor et al., 2009). Distinguishing between these two traditions highlights how the type of megaregion that is constructed varies depending on whether you take rapid urbanization (form) or global economic integration (function) as your starting point for framing globalized urbanization (Harrison and Hoyler, 2014).

Third, the table neatly reflects Florida's (2008, p. 38) assertion that 'bigger and more competitive economic units – megaregions – have superseded cities as the real engines of the global economy'. This prompts us to confront the searching question about whether the newly identified megaregional spaces actually exist as planning, governance and economic spaces. Put bluntly: there has been little or no debate asking if megaregions are internally coherent spaces. One notable exception is the distinction Schafran (2014) makes between 'megaregional space' and 'spaces of the megaregion'. The latter relates to the unevenness of megaregionality within a pre-defined megaregion, drawing particular attention to those more localized spaces where it is actually played out most clearly. This is in stark contrast to the megaregion itself, which is constructed, mobilized and presented as a coherent space in order to achieve certain political outcomes.

This brings us round to our fourth and final point. Deploying the language of Allen et al. (1998, p. 2) 'there is no complete "portrait of a [mega]region". Moreover, "[mega]regions" only exist in relation to particular criteria. They are not "out there" waiting to be discovered, they are our (and others') constructions'. With this in mind, it is important to acknowledge that if the formative work on megaregions has concentrated on identifying *where* megaregional spaces and megaregionality are visible, the questions which are central to future agendas for research are *who* is constructing megaregional spaces, *how* are they constructing megaregional spaces, and *why* are they constructing megaregional spaces. The who and why questions require us to identify the actors involved in constructing megaregions politically, examine their motivations, and ask in whose interest their actions are being directed. It necessitates the need to consider which issues are being brought to the fore, and which are being pushed into the background, within a megaregion framing of development. The how question emphasizes the importance of the actual mechanisms through which megaregional space is constructed politically, in particular, the tactics and strategies employed by actors to advance their essential interests. It is in this way that we concur with the writings of the political geographer John Agnew, who in an intriguingly titled article 'Arguing with regions' reminds us that:

> [W]e should collectively invest in the plural of 'regional logics', tailoring usage to the problems at hand, rather than in a singular logic that simply replaces the romance of the nation-state with an equally simple and one-size-fits-all alternative geographical unit of account such as . . . the global city-region. (Agnew, 2013, p. 15)

While it is not difficult to envisage Agnew now replacing 'global city-region' with 'megaregion', it is what the quote signifies which is of importance here. Megaregions mean different things to different actors in different contexts, each with different goals. There is no one-size-fits-all megaregion. Geography and context matter.

1.3 FRAILTIES: CRITICAL ISSUES IN MEGAREGIONAL RESEARCH

1.3.1 Geographical Excursions: A Spiky World of Megaregions, a Spiky World of Megaregion Interest

> The world's 40 largest mega-regions . . . cover only a tiny fraction of the habitable surface of the earth and are home to less than 18% of the world's population; yet, they are responsible for 66% of global economic activity and about 85% of technological and scientific innovation. (Florida et al., 2008, p. 474)

> The scale and pace of China's urbanization promises to continue at an unprecedented rate. If current trends hold, China's urban population will expand from 572 million in 2005 to 926 million in 2025 and hit the one billion mark by 2030.

> In 20 years, China's cities will have added 350 million people – more than the entire population of the United States today. By 2025, China will have 219 cities with more than one million inhabitants – compared with 35 in Europe today – and 24 cities with more than five million people. (McKinsey Global Institute, 2009, p. 1)

The two quotes refer to the 'spiky world' in which the megaregion debate is often situated. The first, by Richard Florida and his colleagues, provides a global overview – a somewhat placeless idiom of geographical concentration which is often found quoted in the pages of glossy publications produced by prominent national and international organizations to extoll the virtues of megaregional urban growth (see Parsons Brinckerhoff, 2012; UN-Habitat, 2010a, 2010b). With such upbeat endorsements of the potency of large-scale agglomeration economies it is hardly surprising that the next step involves mapping where these megaregional spaces are located globally and providing a snapshot of what a megaregional world/world of megaregions might look like (Florida et al., 2008, 2012).[3] By virtue of being a snapshot in time, this approach masks the dynamism which the second quote alludes to. McKinsey Global Institute show, in population terms, the dynamic geographical gravitation in interest from developments occurring in the United States to the extraordinarily rapid urbanization underway in China. Indeed, this brings us to our second point. As much as there is a spiky world of megaregions, there is also a spiky world of megaregion interest.

If we look back over the past century what we see are some remarkably clear periodizations of megaregional interest. Each periodization is characterized by the particular geographical focus and agenda which precipitated a growing interest in analysing large-scale urban forms. For instance, we have already noted how during the first half of the 20th century the putative megaregional research which emerged from Europe – Geddes and his contemporaries – was heavily influenced by ecological and environmentalist concerns and critiqued urban sprawl; then, during the 1960s, the analytical gaze switched to the United States with Gottmann's modernist and progressive view of the new urban form sparking a North American-dominated interest in the concept of megaregions. We pick the story up in the 1980s with the acceleration of globalization. At this time the focus had returned to Western Europe, and France in particular. France laid the foundations for the European Spatial Development Perspective (ESDP) when it convened a meeting of spatial planning and regional development ministers from across the European Community in 1989 (Faludi and Waterhout, 2002). Alongside this, DATAR[4] commissioned a team of researchers led by a geographer, Roger Brunet, to study the position of French territory in its European context. The study identified a discontinuous urbanized corridor of industrial growth running from northern England to northern Italy which it called the economic *dorsale* ('backbone') of Europe (Brunet, 1989). Bypassing Paris and excluding most of France, what became known as Europe's 'blue banana' provided a clear political statement. The French authors believed that in their national politics there had been excessive centralization of activity and investment in Paris. Their riposte was to argue that in an enlarged Europe, where the political-economic focus was gravitating to the east following the accession of post-socialist countries (see Taylor and Hoyler, 2000), Paris and the majority of French territory could no longer be seen as part of Europe's economic core. Nevertheless, the ESDP revamped the *dorsale* into a 'pentagon' and positioned it as a global economic integration zone – in effect, a megaregion – delimited by the cities of London–Paris–Milan–Munich–Hamburg (Commission of the European Communities, 1999).

The analytical gaze shifted further east in the 1990s in recognition of the rapid urbanization underway in southeast Asia in general, and China in particular (McGee and Robinson, 1995).[5] This was the time when envious eyes were increasingly cast towards the mega-city regional growth economies of the Pearl and Yangtze River Deltas. This is relevant because the 'mega-city region' approach – the 'mega-city' and its 'region' – is a distinctly southeast Asian phenomenon, determined by city population and the sprawling urban form (Hall, 1999; Xu and Yeh, 2011). This is significantly different from a 'global city-region' – 'global city' and its region – where external and internal functional linkages are the determining attribute (Hall, 2001). Megaregions could be read as the attempt to weave the population-inspired mega-city region and functionally-dominated global city-region concepts together. Certainly there is some evidence to suggest this.

Through the work of North American scholars and the RPA's America 2050 initiative the United States is seen as leading the megaregion assault, proactively responding to what they arguably see as the emergence of a megaregional world. Yet we would argue that this work is more reactive than proactive. Citing prominent European writers on European Spatial Development Planning practices – Faludi and Waterhout (2002), Jensen and Richardson (2001) – Ross is clear in the opening salvo to her book *Megaregions – Planning for Global Competitiveness* that 'such planning has set the stage for a more competitive Europe' meaning it is crucial for economic development practitioners in the United States to examine the 'usefulness of the megaregion and spatial planning in an American context' (Ross, 2009, p. 3). Likewise, the RPA is explicit in justifying how their focus on megaregions largely results from what 'our competitors in Asia and Europe' are doing (America 2050, 2013).

What this points towards is significant because it returns us to that fundamental question – why megaregions? Our answer rests in the importance of recognizing that different spatial concepts gained traction in different geographical contexts and at different times. Prominent spatial concepts are those which endure and have salience in a range of contexts. What marks megaregions out from other spatial concepts presently is that for the first time in its history the megaregion has become a truly global concept. Against the backdrop of the European Spatial Development Perspective and rapid urbanization underway in southeast Asia, championing by its North American promoters, and increasing prominence in other contexts (see UN-Habitat, 2010a, 2010b, on the Global South; Pieterse, 2010, on Africa; Weller and Bolleter, 2013, on Australia), what makes the megaregion stand out from other spatial concepts is the enthusiasm it has generated internationally among academics, policymakers and political leaders alike. The broader question this raises is why? More pointedly it encourages us to ask what role globalization is playing, and whether megaregions do constitute globalization's new urban form?

1.3.2 From the Visible to the Invisible: Examining Megaregion Form and Function

A central tenet of megaregional research is the desire and need to define, designate and delimit megaregional space. It cannot be overlooked that 'to govern [or plan] it is necessary to render the visible space over which government is to be exercised. This is not simply a matter of looking: space has to be represented, marked out' (Thrift, 2002, p. 205). Marking out space is a deeply political act and the case of megaregions is no different. Our argument here is that this political act begins when researchers choose to prioritize megaregional form or megaregional function as their entry point. Prioritizing megaregional form leads researchers to start marking out space through observing what is visible in the physical landscape (for example urban sprawl), whereas those who prioritize megaregional function often begin by identifying what is less visible – even invisible –in the physical landscape (for example flows of knowledge and capital). The result is very different mappings of megaregional space and megaregionality. To illustrate this we offer two contrasting examples of how megaregional space is being marked out.

The first approach is adopted by what we might call the 'North American' school of megaregionalists'. Here the approach has been for researchers to consistently mark out megaregional space by taking spatial form as their starting point (Carbonell and Yaro, 2005; Florida et al., 2008; Lang and Knox, 2009; Nelson and Lang, 2011).[6] In each case

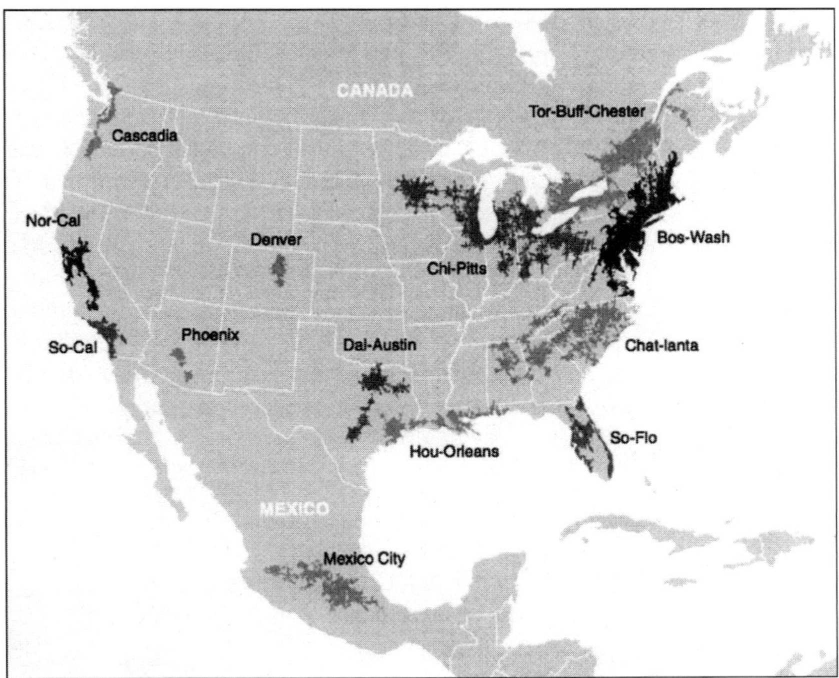

Source: Florida et al. (2008, p. 470). Reproduced by permission of RightsLink/Oxford University Press.

Figure 1.3   A form-dominant cartographic representation of megaregional space

the result has been, first, to designate a smaller number of larger urban-regional economic units as globalization's new urban form. In this way it is a very spatially-selective approach, with only a minority (approximately 15–25 per cent) of the population designated as being included within one of these megaregional spaces. But perhaps more significantly, cartographic representations of megaregional space almost always present these spaces as uniform (Figure 1.3). As a consequence there is an unwitting tendency for form-dominated approaches to infer and/or assume the functional coherence of the megaregional spaces they identify (cf. Burger and Meijers, 2012; Schafran, 2014, 2015).

This brings us to the second group – what we might tentatively call the 'European School' of megaregionalists' – who adopt a function-dominated approach to marking out megaregional space. Following Sassen's (1991) identification of advanced producer service firms as crucial actors and outcomes of deeper globalization and localization processes, the starting point for these researchers is the premise that the economic connections and information flows of business service firms provide 'a strategic lens to examine the intercity relations *within* larger urban regions and *beyond* defined city-regional boundaries, nationally and transnationally' (Hoyler et al., 2008b, p. 1055 original emphasis). This approach is perhaps most synonymous with the research produced as part of the POLYNET project[7] which saw researchers from across Western Europe examine the functional geography of large-scale urban regions. In contrast to form-dominated cartographic representations of megaregional space, function-dominated cartographic representations are able to account for the unevenness of megaregionality processes within the megaregional spaces they identify (Figure 1.4). Moreover, the point we wish to stress is that prioritizing megaregional function over megaregional form has the potential to reveal megaregional spaces which although not appearing to be 'megaregional'

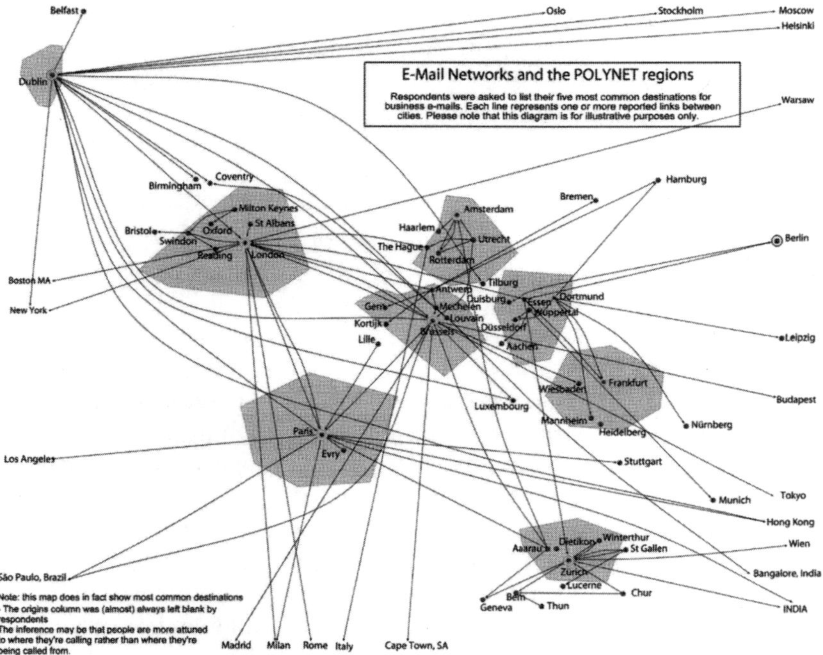

Figure 1.4 A function-dominant cartographic representation of mega-regional space

in their physical manifestation – and by virtue of this automatically closed off from consideration within form-dominant approaches – do actually 'punch above their weight' and act in a way which increasingly resembles processes of megaregionality. For sure these 'imagined' (Nelles, 2012) or *im verborgenen* ('secret' or 'hidden') (Thierstein et al., 2006) megaregional spaces may be small in agglomeration terms but the economic connections and information flows they have engendered through embedding business services firms ensure they are functionally integrated with the global economy (for a prominent example see Thierstein et al., 2008 on northern Switzerland).

We think this prompts the urgent need for megaregional research to examine in which space-times form-dominant and function-dominant megaregional spaces are complementary, overlapping, competing or contradictory. This will require researchers to increasingly confront searching questions around whether form-first and function-first approaches are complementary in specific geographical contexts and to consider what the implications are – both academically, for the explanatory power of the megaregion concept, and practically, for planning and governance at the scale of megaregions – in places where they are (not).

1.3.3 Imagined Megaregions? Megaregional Space, Spaces of the Megaregion

Over the past 15 years the normative assumption that bigger equals more competitive has undoubtedly fuelled a search for a smaller number of larger urban economic units to be championed and lauded as being part of an increasingly exclusive club at the apex of the global urban hierarchy (see Figure 1.2). One way this has been achieved is the emergence of new urban-economic units which aggregate two or more single urban systems into one larger (megaregional) urban system. We only have to look at the names of the emerging megaregions to see examples of this. Of the 40 megaregions identified by Florida et al. (2008), 24 have conjoined names to designate a megaregion constructed from combining two or more urban systems into a larger, single urban system (for example Houston and New Orleans become 'Hou-Orleans'). In this section we seek to extend the discussion about form/functional dominance in megaregion research to begin asking what, if anything, makes these megaregions coherent as economic, but also political, cultural and institutional spaces? To answer this question we suggest two levels of analysis are required.

The first is a macro-level analysis of megaregional space and involves examining which urban systems have been aggregated to form these larger 'megaregional' urban systems and assessing their coherence as a single space. Our own respective research on global city-regions and mega-city regions has highlighted how, on a smaller scale, the evidence suggests that just because two urban systems are located proximate to each other does not mean they can be aggregated up to form a single, larger, more coherent and more competitive urban-economic unit. To take one example, Liverpool and Manchester are UK cities located less than 50 km apart. As single urban systems they do not have the critical mass to register as a global city-region à la Scott (2001a, 2001b) nor compare favourably with international competitors. Yet together they have a population of 6 million, making the single urban-region comparable to the RhineRuhr in Germany (5.3 million), the Rhône-Alpes in France (6.1 million) and the Randstad in the Netherlands (7.5 million). Part and parcel of what Jonas (2013, p. 289) recently referred to as 'internationally-orchestrated city-regionalism', certain policy elites mobilized in the late 2000s to advance the case for bolstering competitiveness by politically constructing a single, globally competitive urban space. Nonetheless, evidence pointed to their being 'no tangible' integration between the two cities and stakeholders failed to 'recognize' the geography (Harrison, 2014). What this alerts us to is a pressing need to assess the functional coherence of megaregional space. While we do not deny that some megaregional spaces are more coherent than others, we do question the coherence of some purported megaregions and mega urban corridors.

The second is a micro-level analysis of megaregional space. We start from a position which acknowledges that there is an unevenness of mega-regionality processes across megaregional space (Sassen, 2007). From the financial district to the suburbs, the parking lot to the shopping mall, the middle-classes to the working-classes, the importance attached to this more localized level of analysis is the need to better understand how processes of megaregionality impact different spaces, places and people unevenly across megaregional space. A guiding question for future megaregional research is (how) does the megaregion concept help in understanding the quite different processes that are played out in these more localized spaces? In this way, Schafran's (2014) distinction between 'megaregional space' and 'spaces of the megaregion' helps us to identify those spaces where megaregionality is more or less important. While we think this is very useful, we would extend this further to include a temporal dimension. This has the advantage of not only providing a snapshot of where mega-regionality is at its strongest or weakest within megaregional space but has the capacity to identify local spaces, places and people for whom processes of megaregionality are a dominant force, a formerly dominant and now declining force, or a newly emerging force.

We think this is particularly important because it provides a starting point for considering what we ultimately believe to be one of the most pressing concerns for megaregional analysis – the geopolitics of mega-regionalism. First and foremost, the two levels of analysis we advocate above are capable of allowing researchers to reveal which areas and social groups are included or excluded from megaregionalism as a geopolitical project. More significantly, it creates the analytical lens necessary to begin to answer the question of megaregionalism, by whom, for whom? For sure, we urgently need more systematic examination of *who* is determining how megaregionalism is constructed politically, *why* – and specifically, in whose interests – megaregionalism is being mobilized, and *how* actors seek to defend and enhance their essential interests through megaregionalism. Ultimately this is a question of governance.

1.3.4   Whose Megaregion Is It?

With all the hysteria surrounding megaregions over the past decade it is perhaps unsurprising to note how few researchers have stopped to ask who is making this noise. This is not to say that researchers have not mentioned the groups involved – in fact, there are few accounts which fail to variously mention America 2050, the Regional Plan Association and the ESDP – rather it is to suggest that this is the extent of their interrogation of who is involved in promoting megaregions. Only a few writers have lingered long enough to consider the critically important questions: Which voices are being heard (the loudest) in the megaregion debate? What do these actors stand to gain from megaregions? Which voices are not being heard? Are certain voices being deliberately excluded (if so, why)? Who decides which voices are heard? These are the key questions we argue need to be at the heart of a more critical analysis of megaregions.

The rise of the megaregion has been underpinned by a strong geoeconomic logic. The rhetoric surrounding megaregions is undeniably one of economic boosterism supported by neoliberal pro-growth models of how economic development and competitiveness is to be achieved in our rapidly changing global economy. In this way it is unsurprising that powerful interest groups – federal and state governments, business and industry leaders, private investment groups, property and real-estate developers – have been prepared to form alliances to extract value from planning at the scale of megaregions. There is a strong argument that powerful actors mobilize in support of the megaregion concept only where they see the potential for planning at this scale to defend and enable their essential interests to be realized. This could be national government decisions on which high-speed rail routes to prioritize for funding, the location and/or expansion of major national infrastructure sites, or the competition between container terminals to be key docking points for post-Panamax cargo vessels. What is significant about this in the context of the megaregion is that at this scale these decisions have moved from the multi-million pound infrastructure investments commonly associated with planning at the metropolitan scale, to the multi-billion investment decisions which were traditionally the sole domain of national politics. Simply put, the stakes are now higher than ever.

One practical illustration of this is the close connection between the Regional Plan Association's America 2050 programme and the US Department of Transportation. It is no secret that much of the support for work on the megaregion concept came from the US Department of Transportation, for whom the megaregion is a vehicle through which they can raise the profile of what they see as the benefits of high-speed rail for economic development. The megaregion concept enables the department to secure the backing of key business leaders, investment groups and state officials to present a stronger business case on the need for more federal investment in high-speed rail and rail passenger capacity. Furthermore, the megaregion framework allows the Department of Transportation to lobby more vociferously on a national scale, therefore increasing the likelihood that they can win (some of) the arguments necessary to deliver one of their key political goals. With this in mind it is not surprising they were prepared to fund the academic research on megaregions necessary to develop this stronger business case for high-speed rail and increased rail passenger capacity. But by virtue of this the focus has been almost exclusively on issues of transportation.[8] Indeed, the only megaregion planning to emerge has related to specific policy spheres: there is no evidence of genuine economic development strategies in the traditional sense.

All of which places the spotlight on what, if anything, megaregions mean for other actors, particularly those whose voice is often not heard so loudly? In other words, what traction does the megaregion concept have among other stakeholder groups? One such area is sustainability, which is currently receiving increased attention. There are those who, on the one hand, see coordinating economic development on the scale of megaregions as presenting opportunities to take a more strategic view on nationally significant planning decisions – land and resource issues, high-speed rail networks, transition to a low-carbon economy through large-scale investment in non-renewables production plants (for example industrial scale wind farms). On the other hand, there are those who oppose planning on the megaregional scale because it is perceived to be the extreme antithesis of the need to move towards more local and sustainable communities. Here the focus is on leading simpler, lower consumption lifestyles, where energy production is decentralized to the scale of the household/community, supporting local business is prioritized over global corporations, and slower-speed modes of transportation (walking, bicycles, public transit) take precedent over the clamour for ever-faster modes (larger freeways, more high-speed rail, greater airport capacity). Research is already beginning to examine the potential contribution of megaregions to economic development *and* the objective of smart, sustainable and inclusive growth (Benner and Pastor, 2011; Fleming, 2015; Marull et al., 2013; Ross et al., 2015; Wheeler, 2009, 2014).

If examining who is involved in promoting megaregions – and what they stand to gain – is one way of moving towards a more critical analysis of megaregions, a second way is to consider which geographical areas are included, on the fringes or excluded from the discursive framing of megaregions. Once again we return to the question of how megaregions are constructed geopolitically. Three examples elucidate our thinking on this point. First, Faludi (2009) points to the geopolitical construction of the ESDPs 'Pentagon' as an example of how policy elites configured this spatial imaginary to ensure a catchy 20–40–50 tagline (20 per cent of EU territory, 40 per cent of the EU population, 50 per cent of EU GDP generated) could be used as a branding and marketing tool for economic boosterism.

Second, the definition used by Lang and Dhavale (2005) to identify 'megapolitan regions' from US Census data is that to be included regions must combine at least two metropolitan areas and have a total population of 10 million residents by 2040. What is interesting to note is that out of the ten megapolitan regions they identify, eight already had over 10 million residents by the year 2000 – so why 2040? Might it be that there was a need to alter the definition to ensure the two remaining regions – Cascadia and Valley of the Suns – which do not currently have 10 million residents, were captured and included within the discursive frame? Off the map by standard criteria, certainly there is a long-standing argument to suggest this might be the case (see Harrison, 2010; Hoyler et al., 2006). Cascadia, for example, has a resident population of 7.5 million but it is arguably the strongest political advocate of large-scale economic cross-border regions. Supported by secession activists who campaign for Cascadian independence, Cascadia has one of the strongest cultural identities and movements (cf. Fleming, 2015), as well as a resident population of over 10 million if you take into account areas located beyond the US national border that are within the cultural region. They therefore represent a powerful political voice and their inclusion within the discursive frame of megaregions has some politico-cultural merits. Similarly for the Valley of the Sun (or Arizona Sun Corridor), which, although only having a resident population of 5 million, is a rapidly expanding regional growth economy. So capturing successful regional economies within the framing of megapolitan regions/megaregions clearly has its merits.

The third example requires us to look at how international organizations such as UN-Habitat (the United Nations Human Settlements Programme) have captured the concept of megaregions to advance their own particular political message and aspirations. UN-Habitat offer a revealing insight into the geopolitical construction of different megaregion discourses because in their annual *State of the World's Cities Report* for 2010–2011 they not only gave prominent billing to megaregions, they constructed a very particular discourse around the development opportunities mega-regions offered countries across the Global South (UN-Habitat, 2010a). What is striking about this report is although their map identifies mega-regions and megaurban corridors in North America and Europe, these spaces were excluded from the narrative. The narrative, reflected most clearly in the press release which accompanied the report's publication, is exclusively constructed around the development potential afforded by megaregions in southeast Asia, South America, and Africa (UN-Habitat, 2010b). From these examples what we see is that understanding how the megaregion concept is constructed to fit particular stories is a crucial, yet somewhat under-researched, dimension of megaregional research.

1.4   FUTURES: MEGAREGIONS AS GLOBALIZATION'S NEW URBAN FORM?

Our ambition for embarking on this project has been to prompt more criti-cal analyses of megaregions, megaregionality and the megaregion concept. By setting out to provide an introduction to what we hope will become a wider debate on megaregions, we have encouraged contributors to be more provocative than they may otherwise be in their academic writing. To facilitate this we asked authors to specifically address three questions in their chapters:

- How robust are the foundations upon which the megaregion concept has been constructed?
- What are the methodological challenges of researching megaregions?
- Do megaregions constitute 'globalization's new urban form'? If not, are there alternative (more suitable) spatial frameworks?

Linking these central themes is the argument that in order to advance intellectual and practical debates on megaregions, attention needs to be focused on the *who*, the *how* and the *why* of megaregions much more than the *what* and the *where* of megaregions. Our aim is to move the debate forward from questions of definition, identification and delimitation to questions of agency (who or what is constructing megaregions), process (how are megaregions being constructed) and specific interests (why are megaregions being constructed); something which, we argue, requires a more political and more historical perspective on megaregions (Harrison and Hoyler, 2015).

NOTES

1. August Hecksher was Director of *The Twentieth Century Fund* who had funded much of Gottmann's research into urbanization of megalopolis.
2. Here we are also reminded of a quote by the English writer G.K. Chesterton, who in his 1905 book *Heretics* commented that 'Nothing more strangely indicates an enormous and silent evil of modern society than the extraordinary use which is made nowadays of the word "orthodoxy" . . . The word "orthodoxy" not only no longer means being right; it practically means being wrong' (pp. 11–12).
3. Here we are making this distinction to emphasize our belief that we live in a world with, not of, megaregions. 'Megaregional world' is where the onus is on the importance of megaregions shaping the world we live in, that is, there is something fundamental connecting megaregions to globalization. We prefer 'world of megaregions' because this recognizes that while we live in a world where there are megaregions and processes of megaregionality this is not to say there is something fundamental connecting megaregions to globalization.
4. DATAR is the French Interministerial Delegation for Regional Planning and Regional Attractiveness. It was set up by President Charles de Gaulle in the 1960s to promote the development of French regions as a counterbalance to Paris. When Jacques Chirac, a former mayor of Paris, became Prime Minister, then later President of France, DATAR's raison d'être lost its political influence. Its future existence was founded on conceptualizing French territory in the fast evolving European context (Faludi, 2009).
5. It would be remiss not to acknowledge that this mega-city regional literature extended beyond southeast Asia to include many accounts of similar processes occurring across parts of Latin America and Africa.
6. This is not to say there is a uniform approach – one only has to look in the United States at the epistemological differences between megaregionalists, who concentrate on traditional urban-regional planning concerns, and megapolitanists, whose focus is on interpreting US Census data (Fleming, 2015) – rather it is to highlight how this approach is qualitatively different from the more functionally-dominant approach which has been central within European debate.
7. POLYNET (or 'POLYNET: Sustainable Management of European Polycentric Mega-City Regions' to give its full title) was a €2.4 million research project funded by the European Regional Development Fund under the INTERREG IIIB North West Europe programme between 2003 and 2006. The aim was to examine changes in functional connections and information flows (physical/transportation and virtual/ICT) in eight major urban regions across North West Europe: South East England, the Paris Region, Central Belgium, the Randstad, Rhine-Main, RhineRuhr, Northern Switzerland and Greater Dublin. The principal project outcomes are reported in Hall and Pain (2006), Halbert et al. (2006) and Hoyler et al. (2008a).
8. You only have to look at the America 2050 website (http://www.america2050.org/) to see the predominance of transportation issues in the debate over megaregions in the United States.

REFERENCES

Agnew, J. (2013), 'Arguing with regions', *Regional Studies*, **47** (1), 6–17.
Allen, J., D. Massey and A. Cochrane (1998), *Rethinking the Region*, London: Routledge.
America 2050 (2008), 'U.S. megaregions with areas of incluence', available at http://www.america2050.org/pdf/2050_Map_Megaregions_Influence.pdf (accessed 25 September 2013).
America 2050 (2013), 'Megaregions', available at http://www.america2050.org/content/megaregions.html (accessed 25 September 2013).
Baigent, E. (2004), 'Patrick Geddes, Lewis Mumford and Jean Gottmann: divisions over "megalopolis"', *Progress in Human Geography*, **28** (6), 687–700.
Benner, C. and M. Pastor (2011), 'Moving on up: regions, megaregions, and the changing geography of social equity organizing', *Urban Affairs Review*, **47** (3), 315–348.
Brenner, N. (2013a), 'Theses on urbanization', *Public Culture*, **25** (1), 85–114.
Brenner, N. (ed.) (2013b), *Implosions/Explosions: Towards a Study of Planetary Urbanization*, Berlin: Jovis.
Brenner, N. and C. Schmid (2011), 'Planetary urbanisation', in M. Gandy (ed.), *Urban Constellations*, Berlin: Jovis, pp. 10–13.
Brunet, R. (1989), *Les Villes Europeénnes: Rapport pour la DATAR*, Paris: La Documentation Française.
Burger, M. and E. Meijers (2012), 'Form follows function? Linking morphological and functional polycentricity', *Urban Studies*, **49** (5), 1127–1149.
Carbonell, A. and R.D. Yaro (2005), 'American spatial development and the new megalopolis', *Land Lines*, **17** (3), 1–4.
Castree, N., R. Kitchin and A. Rogers (2013), *A Dictionary of Human Geography*, Oxford: Oxford University Press.
Chesterton, G.K. (1905), *Heretics*, London: Lane.
Commission of the European Communities (1999), *European Spatial Development Perspective: Towards Balanced and Sustainable Development of the Territory of the EU*, Luxembourg: Office for Official Publications of the European Communities.
Dewar, M. and D. Epstein (2007), 'Planning for "megaregions" in the United States', *Journal of Planning Literature*, **22** (2), 108–124.
Dühr, S. (2007), *The Visual Language of Spatial Planning: Exploring Cartographic Representations for Spatial Planning in Europe*, London: Routledge.
Faludi, A. (2009), 'The megalopolis, the blue banana, and global economic integration zones in European planning thought', in C.L. Ross (ed.), *Megaregions: Planning for Global Competitiveness*, Washington, DC: Island Press, pp. 18–34.
Faludi, A. and B. Waterhout (2002), *The Making of the European Spatial Development Perspective: No Masterplan*, London: Routledge.
Fleming, B. (2015), 'Towards a megaregional future: analysing progress, assessing priorities in the US megaregion project', in J. Harrison and M. Hoyler (eds), *Megaregions: Globalization's New Urban Form?* Cheltenham, UK and Northampton, MA, USA: Edward Elgar, pp. 200–229.
Florida, R. (2008), *Who's Your City? How the Creative Economy is Making Where to Live the Most Important Decision of Your Life*, New York: Basic Books.
Florida, R., T. Gulden and C. Mellander (2008), 'The rise of the mega-region', *Cambridge Journal of Regions, Economy and Society*, **1** (3), 459–476.

Florida, R., C. Mellander and T. Gulden (2012), 'Global metropolis: assessing economic activity in urban centers based on nighttime satellite images', *The Professional Geographer*, **64** (2), 178–187.

Forbes (2011), 'A city of 260 million – where else but China?' *Forbes* [online], 4 November, available at http://www.forbes.com/sites/megacities/2011/04/11/a-city-of-260-million-where-else-but-china/ (accessed 24 September 2013).

Friedman, T. (2005), *The World is Flat*, New York: Farrar, Straus and Giroux.

Geddes, P. (1915), *Cities in Evolution: An Introduction to the Town Planning Movement and to the Study of Civics*, London: Williams & Norgate.

Glaeser, E. (2011), *Triumph of the City*, Oxford: Pan Books.

Gottmann, J. (1957), 'Megalopolis or the urbanization of the Northeastern Seaboard', *Economic Geography*, **33** (3), 189–200.

Gottmann, J. (1961), *Megalopolis: The Urbanized Northeastern Seaboard of the United States*, New York: Twentieth Century Fund.

Gottmann, J. (1976), 'Megalopolitan systems around the world', *Ekistics*, **41** (243), 109–113.

Gottmann, J. and R. Harper (eds) (1990), *Since Megalopolis: The Urban Writings of Jean Gottmann*, Baltimore, MD: Johns Hopkins University Press.

Gregory, D., R. Johnston, G. Pratt, M. Watts and S. Whatmore (eds) (2009), *The Dictionary of Human Geography* (5th edition), Chichester: Wiley-Blackwell.

Halbert, L., F.J. Convery and A. Thierstein (eds) (2006), 'Special issue: Reflections on the polycentric metropolis', *Built Environment*, **32** (2), 109–218.

Hall, P. (1999), 'Planning for the mega-city: a new eastern Asian urban form?', in J. Brotchie, P. Newton, P. Hall and J. Dickey (eds), *East West Perspectives on 21st Century Urban Development: Sustainable Eastern and Western Cities in the New Millennium*, Aldershot: Ashgate, pp. 3–36.

Hall, P. (2001), 'Global city-regions in the twenty-first century', in A.J. Scott (ed.), *Global City-Regions: Trends, Theory, Policy*, Oxford: Oxford University Press, pp. 59–77.

Hall, P. and K. Pain (eds) (2006), *The Polycentric Metropolis: Learning from Mega-City Regions in Europe*, London: Earthscan.

Harrison, J. (2007), 'From competitive regions to competitive city-regions: a new orthodoxy, but some old mistakes', *Journal of Economic Geography*, **7** (3), 311–332.

Harrison, J. (2010), 'Networks of connectivity, territorial fragmentation, uneven development: the new politics of city-regionalism', *Political Geography*, **29** (1), 17–27.

Harrison, J. (2014), 'Rethinking city-regionalism as the production of new non-state spatial strategies: the case of Peel Holdings Atlantic Gateway strategy', *Urban Studies*, **51** (11), 2315–2335.

Harrison, J. and M. Hoyler (2014), 'Governing the new metropolis', *Urban Studies* **51** (11), 2249–2266.

Harrison, J. and M. Hoyler (2015), 'Megaregions reconsidered: urban futures and the future of the urban', in J. Harrison and M. Hoyler (eds), *Megaregions: Globalization's New Urban Form?* Cheltenham, UK and Northampton, MA, USA: Edward Elgar, pp. 230–255.

Harvey, D. (2000), *Megacities Lecture 4: Possible Urban Worlds*, Amersfoort: Twynstra Gudde Management Consultants.

Hecksher, A. (1964), 'Foreword', in J. Gottmann, *Megalopolis: The Urbanized*

Northeastern Seaboard of the United States, Cambridge, MA: MIT Press, pp. vii–viii.

Hoyler, M., T. Freytag and C. Mager (2006), 'Advantageous fragmentation? Reimagining metropolitan governance and spatial planning in Rhine-Main', *Built Environment*, **32** (2), 124–136.

Hoyler, M., R.C. Kloosterman and M. Sokol (eds) (2008a), 'Special issue: Globalization, city-regions and polycentricity in north-west Europe', *Regional Studies*, **42** (8), 1055–1217.

Hoyler, M., R.C. Kloosterman and M. Sokol (2008b), 'Polycentric puzzles – emerging mega-city regions seen through the lens of advanced producer services', *Regional Studies*, **42** (8), 1055–1064.

Jensen, O. and T. Richardson (2001), 'Nested visions: new rationalities of space in European spatial planning', *Regional Studies*, **35** (8), 703–717.

Jonas, A.E.G. (2013), 'City-regionalism as a contingent "geopolitics of capitalism"', *Geopolitics*, **18** (2), 284–298.

Kunzmann, K. (1996), 'Euro-megalopolis or themepark Europe? Scenarios for European spatial development', *International Planning Studies*, **1** (2), 143–163.

Lang, R.E. and D. Dhavale (2005), 'Beyond Megalopolis: exploring America's new megapolitan geography', *Metropolitan Institute Census Report Series*, 05:01, Alexandria, VA: The Metropolitan Institute at Virginia Tech.

Lang, R.E. and P.L. Knox (2009), 'The new metropolis: rethinking megalopolis', *Regional Studies*, **43** (6), 789–802.

McGee, T.G. and I.M. Robinson (eds) (1995), *The Mega-Urban Regions of Southeast Asia*, Vancouver: UBC Press.

McKinsey Global Institute (2009), *Preparing for China's Urban Billion – Summary of Findings*, McKinsey & Company.

Marull, J., V. Galletto, E. Domene and J. Trullén (2013), 'Emerging megaregions: a new spatial scale to explore urban sustainability', *Land Use Policy*, **34** (1), 353–366.

Meller, H. (1993), 'Some reflections on the concept of megalopolis and its use by Patrick Geddes and Lewis Mumford', in T. Barker and A. Sutcliffe (eds), *Megalopolis: The Giant City in History*, New York: St. Martin's Press, pp. 116–129.

Morrill, R. (2006), 'Classic map revisited: the growth of megalopolis', *The Professional Geographer*, **58** (2), 155–160.

Mumford, L. (1938), *The Culture of Cities*, New York: Harcourt.

Nelles, J. (2012), *Metropolitan Governance and Policy: Governing Beyond Local Boundaries in the Imagined Metropolis*, London: Routledge.

Nelson, A.C. and R.E. Lang (2011), *Megapolitan America: A New Vision for Understanding America's Metropolitan Geography*, Chicago, IL: APA Planners Press.

OECD (2006), *Competitive Cities in the Global Economy*, OECD Territorial Reviews, Paris: Organisation for Economic Co-operation and Development.

Pain, K. and G. Van Hamme (eds) (2014), *Changing Urban and Regional Relations in a Globalizing World: Europe as a Global Macro-Region*, Cheltenham, UK and Northampton, MA, USA: Edward Elgar.

Parsons Brinckerhoff (2012), *The Future of Cities and Urban Infrastructure*, New York: Parsons Brinckerhoff.

Pieterse, E. (2010), 'The mega-regions of Africa in global perspective', *The Global Urbanist*, 24 March 2010, available at http://globalurbanist.com/2010/03/24/the-mega-regions-of-africa-in-global-perspective (accessed 25 September 2013).

Reades, J. and D.A. Smith (2014), 'Mapping the "space of flows": the geography of global business telecommunications and employment specialization in the London mega-city-region', *Regional Studies*, **48** (1), 105–126.

Regional Plan Association (2006), *America 2050: A Prospectus*, New York: RPA.

Ross, C.L. (ed.) (2009), *Megaregions: Planning for Global Competitiveness*, Washington, DC: Island Press.

Ross, C.L., D. Lee, E. Meijers and T. Welch (2015), *Megaregions, Prosperity and Sustainability*, London: Routledge.

Sassen, S. (1991), *The Global City: New York, London, Tokyo*, Princeton, NJ: Princeton University Press.

Sassen, S. (2007), 'Megaregions: benefits beyond sharing trains and parking lots?', in K.S. Goldfeld (ed.), *The Economic Geography of Megaregions*, Princeton, NJ: The Policy Research Institute for the Region, pp. 59–83.

Sayer, A. (1992), *Method in Social Science: A Realist Approach*, London: Routledge.

Schafran, A. (2014), 'Rethinking mega-regions: sub-regional politics in a fragmented metropolis', *Regional Studies*, **48** (4), 587–602.

Schafran, A. (2015), 'Beyond globalization: a historical urban development approach to understanding megaregions', in J. Harrison and M. Hoyler (eds), *Megaregions: Globalization's New Urban Form?* Cheltenham, UK and Northampton, MA, USA: Edward Elgar, pp. 75–96.

Scott, A.J. (2001a), 'Globalization and the rise of city-regions', *European Planning Studies*, **9** (7), 813–826.

Scott, A.J. (ed.) (2001b), *Global City-Regions: Trends, Theory, Policy*, Oxford: Oxford University Press.

Short, J.R. (2007), *Liquid City: Megalopolis and the Contemporary Northeast*, Washington, DC: Resources for the Future.

Taylor, P.J. and M. Hoyler (2000), 'The spatial order of European cities under conditions of contemporary globalisation', *Tijdschrift voor Economische en Sociale Geografie*, **91** (2), 176–189.

Taylor, P.J. and R.E. Lang (2004), 'The shock of the new: 100 concepts describing recent urban change', *Environment and Planning A*, **36** (6), 951–958.

Taylor, P.J., D.M. Evans, M. Hoyler, B. Derudder and K. Pain (2009), 'The UK space economy as practised by advanced producer service firms: identifying two distinctive polycentric city-regional processes in contemporary Britain', *International Journal of Urban and Regional Research*, **33** (3), 700–718.

Thierstein, A., C. Kruse, L. Glanzmann, S. Gabi and N. Grillon (2006), *Raumentwicklung im Verborgenen: Die Entwicklung der Metropolregion Nordschweiz*, Zürich: Verlag Neue Zürcher Zeitung.

Thierstein, A., S. Lüthi, C. Kruse, S. Gabi and L. Glanzmann (2008), 'Changing value chain of the Swiss knowledge economy: spatial impact of intra-firm and inter-firm networks within the emerging mega-city region of northern Switzerland', *Regional Studies*, **42** (8), 1113–1131.

Thrift, N. (2002), 'Performing cultures in the new economy', in P. Du Gay and M. Pryke (eds), *Cultural Economy*, London: Sage, pp. 201–234.

UN-Habitat (2010a), *State of the World's Cities 2010/2011: Bridging the Urban Divide*, Nairobi: UN-Habitat.

UN-Habitat (2010b), 'Urban trends: urban corridors – shape of things to come?', UN-Habitat Press Release, 13 March, Nairobi: UN-Habitat.

Vicino, T., B. Hanlon and J.R. Short (2007), 'Megalopolis, 50 years on: the transformation of a city region', *International Journal of Urban and Regional Research*, **31** (2), 344–367.

Weller, R. and J. Bolleter (2013), *Made in Australia: The Future of Australian Cities*, Perth: University of Western Australia Publishing.

Wheeler, S.M. (2009), 'Regions, megaregions, and sustainability', *Regional Studies*, **43** (6), 863–876.

Wheeler, S.M. (2015), 'Five reasons why megaregional planning works against sustainability', in J. Harrison and M. Hoyler (eds), *Megaregions: Globalization's New Urban Form?* Cheltenham, UK and Northampton, MA, USA: Edward Elgar, pp. 97–118.

Xu, J. and A.G.O. Yeh (eds) (2011), *Governance and Planning of Mega-City Regions: An International Comparative Perspective*, London: Routledge.

Yang, J. (2009), 'Spatial planning in Asia: planning and developing megacities and megaregions', in C.L. Ross (ed.), *Megaregions: Planning for Global Competitiveness*, Washington, DC: Island Press, pp. 35–52.

Zhang, X. (2015), 'Globalization and the megaregion: investigating the evolution of the Pearl River Delta in a historical perspective', in J. Harrison and M. Hoyler (eds), *Megaregions: Globalization's New Urban Form?* Cheltenham, UK and Northampton, MA, USA: Edward Elgar, pp. 175–199.

2. *Mega*urban regions: epistemology, discourse patterns, big urban business

Markus Hesse

2.1 INTRODUCTION

Recent debates have placed the concept of megaregions at the forefront of urban and economic geography, trying to make sense of the growth of ever larger metropolitan areas and addressing related urban forms, functions and settings (Ross, 2009). This line of thought is based on a largely empirical and political-economic perspective applied to a specific set of contents (data) and associated territory (for example, Hall and Pain, 2006). Thus it responds to well-known developments in urban growth and urban regional form once described by Gottmann's (1957) famous treatise on the 'Megalopolis' more than five decades ago. Later on, colleagues from the US and Europe coined further urban-regional labels and signifiers, such as polycentric urban region, post-metropolis, metapolis, edge city or edgeless city (see, for example, Soja, 2000; Ascher, 1995). Whereas these urban-regional classifications tend to be mostly analytic, the mega-regional narrative looks somewhat different: it also refers to competition between these regions, and it relies heavily on the language of boosterism (Todorovich, 2009). Moreover, there is an inherent notion of 'policy boosterism' behind it, that is the everyday comparative practice of city governments and mayors claiming to know what the big, important city-regions are about and how these machines can be steered, in order to provide growth and prosperity (cf. McCann, 2013). If the premier league of global city-regions or megaregions is about to emerge, what metropolitan mayor would not like to be part of this?

By exploring the most recent case of metropolitan classification – the megaregion – this chapter seeks to explore the discursive or epistemological nature of the concept behind. It critically discusses epistemology, language and the prescribed role these terms may play for what one could also call 'communicative urbanization'. The chapter thus aims at deciphering certain associations that, either intended or not, explicit or implicit, seem to be part of the common sense that is exchanged within professional communities. Quite often, these professionals do represent epistemic communities as well, in the sense that they share common beliefs on a certain subject, make use of a joint repertoire of terms, ideas and concepts, and do assign certain meanings to the matter they are talking about – without necessarily questioning these terms too much or too often (see for example Miller and Fox, 2001; Zollman, 2007). My suspicion is that this is also the case with megaregions. The more popular this term and the associated concept is becoming, the more it seems useful to explore the question of where it comes from, what its meanings are, and whether it brings urban-regional policies forward or not. Consequently, it is the purpose of this chapter to address such questions of terminology and epistemology, of discourse and meaning of the megaregion.

Against this background, the chapter is structured as follows. First, I will briefly explore the origins of the mega prefix and its appearance in urban and regional studies. In so doing, I am making particular reference to Jean Gottmann's 'Megalopolis', but also to related authors and other subjects where mega applies. Secondly, I will explore the soundtrack of positivism, the great and the big, borrowing from John Naisbitt's euphemistic futurology once applied to more or less inevitable megatrends that are likely to transform our lives. A discourse analysis of the language of megatrends complements this critical view. The chapter will then, thirdly, explain why for me megaurban regions also fit perfectly into the emerging, homogenizing discourses of the triumphant city (Glaeser, 2011), of the urban age (Gleeson, 2012, 2013) and planetary urbanization (Merrifield, 2013). Fourthly, I will address the specific way matter and meaning are bundled together in megaregions – revealing also an essentialist notion underlying this concept, where regions are reconstructed as a bounded territory – despite the claim that regions have to be considered as unbound, relational and fluid (Amin, 2004; Lagendijk, 2007). The chapter concludes by seeking appropriate terms and concepts that can be helpful in order to address these issues properly.

2.2 MEGA-THINKING AND ITS APPLICATION IN URBAN AND REGIONAL STUDIES

What does *mega* mean, where does it come from and how has it been applied so far? According to the third edition of the *Oxford English Dictionary* (published in 2001 by Oxford University Press), 'mega' is actually defined as a prefix in the metric system that denotes a factor of a million (10 to the power of 6, or 10^6), as confirmed by the standardized International System of Units (SI). Going further back, the etymology of the word stems from the Greek term μέγας, which literally means great. Megalopolis was once the 'name given to a city in Peloponnese founded by Epaminondas around 371–368 BCE' (Short, 2007, p. 1). Greatness, the celebration of size, is core to any ancient or modern meaning of megalopolis. To a certain extent, this also applies to metropolis, given the emerging processes of 'metropolization' observed by urban researchers more recently (Decoville, 2008), or the interest on the part of urban policymakers in seeing their city or region being officially labelled as metropolitan (Hesse and Leick, 2013). This search for significance is even visible in culture and society, taking account, for example, of Fritz Lang's movie 'Metropolis' (1927), the futurist urban utopia that helped to popularize the idea of a metropolis – mother city – quite substantially. As growth can be considered one of the penultimate drivers and consequences of modernization processes, this may explain why terms such as megalopolis or metropolis are still in use and obviously attractive to researchers and policymakers today.

The attractiveness of prefixes such as *metro* or *mega* applies particularly to urban and regional studies, with most recent attention being paid to the megaregion. Although the notion of the megaregion seems to be something more recent, the mega prefix has variously been applied in earlier urban and regional studies. At least three different concepts seem to be relevant here. Firstly, mega-cities referred to the rise of urban agglomerations in developing countries, particularly in Africa, Asia and Latin America (van der Ploeg and Poelhekke, 2008). These mega-cities were viewed extremely specifically in terms of size and numbers, with regard to growth rates, speed of development, levels of social inequality, and so on. Depending on the definition applied, the threshold of population that one unit has to exceed in order to qualify for this prefix is 5 to 8 million (Pacione, 2009; United Nations, 2011). The emergence of mega-cities is considered one of the most visible consequences of globalization for urban areas, not only due to size but also characterized by rapid growth and a lack of order, resulting in big challenges for planning and organizing these huge areas. Perhaps it is more justified to use the mega prefix in this particular case than in any other, in relation to size, growth rates and planning challenges.

The second use of the concept concerns megaprojects. These are large-scale (urban) building or infrastructure projects, such as airports, railway stations, big shopping centres, museums or office towns. Large-scale urban projects are not only important parts of contemporary urban development, but in the 1980s and 1990s they also became emblematic for urban planning and policy processes as such (Priemus, 2010). They are termed megaprojects as they tend to be quite big, and so are the problems they contribute to: they are often difficult to integrate into the urban fabric, and they face substantial risks such as rising costs, delays in realization, planning and governance problems (Swyngedouw et al., 2002). Also, as a result of size and complexity, they are difficult to steer; a situation exacerbated by the power of private agents and concomitant lack of effective public control. The variety of existing definitions of megaprojects tends to be excessive, and there seems to be a common sense only in that such megaprojects are extraordinary, representing special cases rather than the norm of urban and regional development. This, however, does not diminish their popularity among policymakers and developers.

The third application now concerns the megaregion or megaurban region, which is the focus here. Urban and regional researchers placed the megaurban region prominently on the agenda during the mid and late 2000s (Ross, 2009). Megaregion is the label for 'networks of metropolitan centers and their surrounding areas', used particularly in the case of areas that comprise more than one major city or metropolitan region (Ross, 2009, p. 9). In this sense, megaregion is only the most recent in a whole series of attempts to make sense of contemporary developments, most notably of globalization, information technologies and their urban-economic imprint, and to understand the related changes in the urban system. Starting with an analysis of both quantitative growth and qualitative changes in single city-regions, the mega prefix is increasingly being used in order to characterize the shift from what started out as global cities to global city-regions or megaregions. This was also the context of the POLYNET research network, dedicated to studying the 'polycentric metropolis' (Hall and Pain, 2006). Besides the fact that the project applied mega even to city-regions of rather modest size (such as Dublin, Ireland, central Belgium or Frankfurt/Rhine-Main, Germany), this work obviously grappled with terminology as well: the authors actually needed the book's cover and one chapter title just to introduce three or four different terms for pointing at one single issue – emerging large city-regions – by using or introducing labels such as mega-city region, polycentric metropolis and polyopolis. The great variety, if not fuzziness, of contemporary urban and regional developments seems perfectly reflected by this sort of terminological confusion. It confirms that the question of how to label these large agglomerations is far from trivial, and the epistemology behind such concepts seems to be quite important when assigning a particular meaning to a certain matter. This sort of confusion remains even in the case where one makes a clear distinction between a megaregion (addressing at least two major city- or metro-regions in conjunction) and a mega-city or megaurban region, which consists of a large agglomeration with one pre-dominant core area (see Harrison and Hoyler, 2015).

The most meaningful and also most famous concept of mega in an urban or regional context is usually traced back to Jean Gottmann's pioneering study titled *Megalopolis: The Urbanized Northeastern Seaboard of the United States* (Gottmann, 1961). The assumption that a new type of agglomeration was emerging was first presented by Gottmann in an article in the journal *Economic Geography* a few years earlier (Gottmann, 1957). *Megalopolis* quickly became one of the most prominent studies of urban-regional form. It reflected the growing, increasingly interdependent, and wide-reaching urbanized corridor that had evolved (even then) on the northeastern seaboard of the United States, between Boston and Washington, DC (see Figure 2.1). From the perspective of an urban-regional analyst, 'Megalopolis' was approached as follows: 'We have felt it appropriate to describe a unique geographical region, characterized more than any other by enormous urban and metropolitan growth, and to assess the present status of a vast region in the northeastern seaboard section of the United States' (Gottmann, 1957, p. 189). Simply put, Megalopolis was the big one, archetypical in terms of size, mass and exceptional growth, but then it was also considered to be unique, nothing that could be generalized. This seems to be rather different from today, where the proponents of megaregions tend to see this as the ultimate urban-regional form under conditions of globalization and technological change. Nevertheless, Gottmann then assumed that Megalopolis would be a laboratory for studying urbanization, rather than a general blueprint for urban development: 'In this sense Megalopolis is a pioneer area: the processes which develop therein will help toward an understanding of, and will forecast ways and obstacles to, urban growth in various other parts' (Gottmann, 1957, pp. 190–191).

Vicino et al. (2007) and Short (2007) have taken a retrospective look at *Megalopolis* 50 years on, and provided a detailed analysis of the current shape of the region. This followed an earlier, 25-year retrospective account that Gottmann himself had published in 1987, where he considered Megalopolis (as a unique place) becoming megalopolis (a generic concept) (Gottmann, 1987). Looking at the seaboard corridor from today's perspective, it has changed from an industrial, edged and centred place to a post-industrial, edgeless and de-centred agglomeration, driven by processes such as growth, internal differentiation (for example, segregation) and immigration (Short, 2007). By positioning the eastern seaboard region against the case of Los Angeles, the authors also discuss the possible paradigmatic role of the north-eastern Megalopolis in comparison with Southern California. While the analysis of this concrete region then

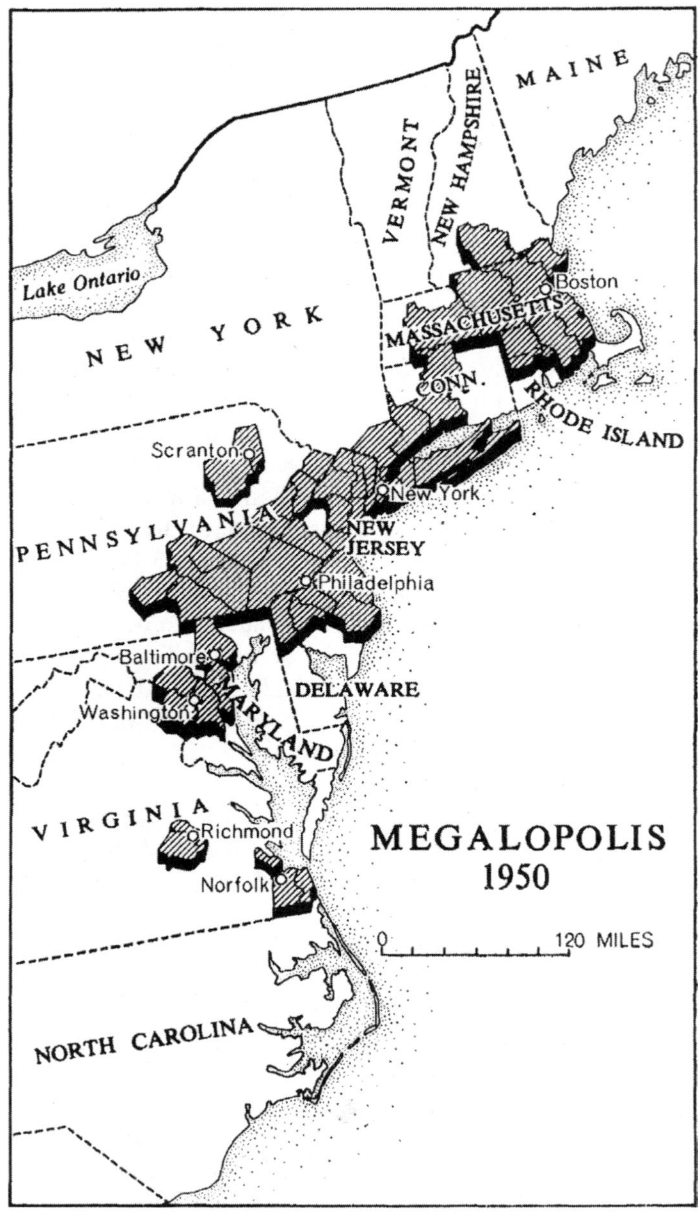

Source: Gottmann (1957, p. 191). Reproduced by permission of Wiley-Blackwell Publishers, UK.

Figure 2.1   Gottmann's 'Megalopolis'

and now is interesting in empirical terms, the authors' reflection on its scientific constitution, by way of assigning a certain meaning to a certain region, is most useful for discussing today's urban-regional discourses. This applies both to the generic conceptual framework underlying megalopolis and to its normative assessment. Firstly, critics were even then questioning whether the idea of a megalopolis is consistent, given the complexity of spatial interactions happening within the region and beyond its borders, on various spatial scales. For example, 'Peter Hall questioned whether the term was a "convenient fiction, a tool for analysis or has it a deeper function or physical reality?"' (Short, 2007, p. 8, referring to Hall (1973) on urban containment in England). Secondly, various voices are rather critical of the urban outcome of megalopolitan growth and size. Scientific reports and journalists' work tend to speak of megalopolis when pointing out their 'unappealing' consequences, such as land take, transport demand and uncontrolled sprawl. Quoting an unpublished paper written by Robert Lake in 2003, Short points out Gottmann's inherent celebration of size, bigness and growth, the sense of inevitability, and a stunning belief in entrepreneurialism and consumer choice – a megaurban utopia that has obviously overlooked the problems arising in exactly the same region (Short, 2007).

In both works discussed here, the authors nonetheless recognized that 'Gottmann's work was enormously influential and ... the term Megalopolis entered the lexicon of urban studies' (Vicino et al., 2007, p. 345; Short, 2007). While this might be true as far as the related disciplines of geography and planning are concerned, it seems different when one looks at general reference works, encyclopaedias and so on. This is evident from the very instructive account by Baigent (2004), who examined historical works that had emphasized the megalopolis even before Gottmann did. Furthermore, Baigent went on to observe that terms such as metropolis and megalopolis did not receive an entry in the *Oxford English Dictionary* before 1976, and once they were included in this and other reference works, they were presented inconsistently concerning term, author and sources. Baigent (2004) also recalled that the origins of such thoughts (as a general framework, not a regional case study, and mostly critical) had already been laid down by authors such as Patrick Geddes and Lewis Mumford in the early 20th century. According to Baigent (2004), Geddes developed a trajectory, starting with the city as polis, and metro-polis, the capital, before ending up as megalo-polis, the city overgrown and characterized by megalomania. Degeneration then ensues, bringing about parasito-polis, before the aggregation of diseases forms patholo-polis and necro-polis. It is important to note, as Baigent did, that Geddes had sketched these terms as theoretical possibilities of urban and regional development, yet did not consider this as his own opinion on such issues. In more political terms, Geddes rejected any fatalism in 'evolutionary environmentalism', but had a certain trust in the motivation of people to respond actively to their environment.

The most profound commentator and critic of growth and size as an outcome of megalopolitan development, however, was Lewis Mumford. Both books, *The Culture of Cities* (Mumford, 1937) and *The City in History* (Mumford, 1961), had separate chapters devoted to megalopolis, addressing harsh criticism at the various societal and spatial outcomes of the very large city. In the chapter 'A brief outline of Hell', Mumford (1937) bundles this criticism in a rather crisp manner, and inspired by Geddes' work, he also developed a stage model of urban and metropolitan growth that eventually leads to disintegration and destruction (see Table 2.1). Using a vocabulary that borrows from apocalyptic notions and cultural pessimism, Mumford made reference to doom-laden scenarios from authors such as Oswald Spengler (*Der Untergang des Abendlandes*, 1922) or James Joyce's *Ulysses* (also 1922), characterizing the novel's hero Leopold Bloom as 'a dissociated mind in a disintegrated city: perhaps the normal mind of the world metropolis' (Mumford, 1937, p. 271). Thus Mumford sees the urban cycle inevitably ending up in pathology: 'Every overgrown megalopolitan centre today, and every province outside that its life touches, exhibits the same symptoms of disorganization, accompanied by no less pathological symptoms of violence and demoralization' (cited in Baigent, 2004, p. 690). Mumford's overly pessimistic approach stands in contrast to the euphoric appreciation of today's megaregions.

2.3   MEGA-SPEAKING: JOHN NAISBITT'S FUTURISM AS A DISCOURSE TEMPLATE

What made today's speaking of mega so popular, given not only the critical voices from the past, but also the complexity of contemporary societal organization and its urban-regional outcomes? How did the mega prefix not only enter the lexicon of urban and regional studies, but also general vocabulary? I want to argue it was neither urban and regional discourse nor megaprojects and their technological fashion pushing the envelope in this respect. It was a particular mix of forecasting, business and economics literature and reference that helped to popularize the idea of mega, most notably by promoting mega*trends*. Megatrends received significant attention in the 1980s and 1990s, and it is probably fair to say that this term might have pushed more attention towards mega than anything else. Megatrends were proclaimed in order to describe overarching

Table 2.1   Stages of megalopolitan development

Stages	Signifier	Description
First stage	Eopolis	Rise of the village community, development of a permanent habitation, cultivation and domestication of animals, establishment of utilities.
Second stage	Polis	Association of villages or blood groups having a common site that lends itself to defence against others; systematic division of labour.
Third stage	Metropolis	Within the region, one city emerges from the less differentiated villages and country towns. Taking advantage of strategic location and infrastructure, it attracts a large number of inhabitants and becomes 'mother city'. Surplus of regional production, emergence of a specialized trading class.
Fourth stage	Megalopolis	Beginning of the decline: the city concentrates on bigness and power, for the wellbeing of the rich. Dominance through physical conquest (military), finance, tendency to aggressive enterprise and enterprising aggression. Overinvestment in the material apparatus of bigness. The city as a means of association, as a haven of culture, becomes a means of dissociation.
Fifth stage	Tyrannopolis	Extensions of parasitism throughout the economic and social scene. Politics becomes competition for the exploitation of the municipal and state exchequer by this or that class or group. Development of predatory means as a substitute for trade and give-and-take. Widening of the gap between producing classes and spending classes. Uncertainty hangs over every prospect of the future. Beginnings of megalopolitan exodus.
Sixth stage	Necropolis	War and famine and disease rack both city and countryside. The physical towns become mere shells. Those who remain in them are unable to carry on the old municipal services or maintain the old civic life. The names persist, the reality vanishes. Relapse into the more primitive rural occupations. In short: Necropolis, the city of the dead: flesh turned to ashes: life turned into a meaningless pillar of salt.

Source: Own compilation based on Mumford (1937, pp. 285–292).

socioeconomic and technological developments. This sort of thinking was, if not created, at least popularized by management guru John Naisbitt. He brought this term to the non-fiction shelves in every bookstore and helped to make mega part of everyday speech. His 1982 volume *Megatrends* remains one of the most successful non-fiction books published in the US (14 million copies, according to his own website). He identified mega-trends triggered by changes in technology, by globalization and religion, and certainly by scientific progress (for example in biology or life sciences). Among the ten most important megatrends identified in the 2000 edition of the book were – focusing in particular on economics and labour markets – the move from centralization to decentralization, bringing business operations to small and home offices; the move away from institutionalized education to self-help and continuing education in many places; the abandonment of hierarchical bureaucratic networking for information and decision-making; and the emergence of multiple-option solutions and job definitions.

This looks like rather under-complex creative forecasting that actually requires little more than reading newspapers and some imagination to speculate about the future. Two benefits may be associated with this sort of mega talk: on the one hand, the sounds of megatrends as the ultimate drivers of society and economy in the present and the future is promising and affirmative; on the other hand, they are vague enough that they are not easily debunked as pure speculation, opening various avenues for deriving related political responses, for example. However, one is tempted to argue that megatrends are mostly based on speculation, brought forward by a strange mix of business vocabulary and positivistic future scenario writing. Also, megatrends appear to 'happen' somehow inevitably. So the unspoken message associated with megatrends is that it seems wise for everybody, most notably corporations and institutions, to adapt to them – while not asking whether this makes sense, whether such trends will inevitably come about or whether they offer any alternative development path. Despite its commercial success, the book and its approach also received hefty criticism – such as 'mega hype, mega bad' by educational scientist Louis Goldman (1983). He called it 'conceptually indefensible' and 'statistically unreliable' (p. 55), besides referring to the lurid tone and 'faddish jargon' that characterized most of Naisbitt's writings. Goldman also criticizes the author's reification of constructs such as industrial society and information society, both set in contrast to each other, as if one trend would follow the other in a model of subsequent stages. Considering the two stages as mutually exclusive would be nothing but 'pernicious nonsense', according to Goldman (p. 56). The astonishing thing, however, is neither Naisbitt's commercial success, nor the sheer number of followers who, even today, occupy the management and organization literatures with the rather obscure science of forecasting trends. One may wonder why trend studies have so rarely come under critical scrutiny, even though the underlying soundtrack is highly questionable. Like the inevitability of free markets, trends are considered to be God-given and falling from heaven; they appear inevitable in likelihood and reach, and thus they do not leave much room for alternatives (properties that make scenarios being essentially distinct from trends).

Beyond this, trend writing reveals that there is a distinction to be drawn between obvious matters and contents on the one hand, and also more obscure, sometimes unspoken but important meanings conveyed on the other hand. Thus both megatrends and megaregions seem to be an ideal subject of discourse analyses. Discourse analyses can be traced back to recent developments in cultural studies and social sciences which have emphasized a certain turn from a rather material, objectivistic perspective towards a more interpretative, subjectivist view of the world (see Bachmann-Medick, 2006). Such approaches have discarded the traditional positivistic approach of scientific inquiry. Instead, they allow quite different perspectives to be developed, particularly by putting a strong emphasis on language, communication and discursive interaction (Glasze and Mattissek, 2009). This literature also seems helpful when exploring the role of cities and space as the subject of constructivist analysis and discursive practices. As Raco (2003, p. 38) pointed out in his discourse analysis of urban regeneration projects in the UK, the form and the nature of discourses of urban development are key to reflecting and (re)producing unequal social and economic geographies. Thus analysing spatial discourses against the background of constructivist thinking aids a better understanding of the nature of places as socially constructed, by linking discourses and practices, and helps to overcome essentialist ideas of space, regions and cities. As places must be competitive in 'real or imagined hierarchies' (Raco, 2003, p. 39), otherwise they would be left out by investors and public spending, urban discourses and narratives are also important frameworks for allowing the contours of associated policies to materialize.

Thus the increasingly popular usage of mega offers significant potential for a critical discourse analysis. In a recent paper published in Elsevier's *Futures*, a discourse analysis was undertaken concerning megatrends, inspired by the discourse theory of Ernesto Laclau and Chantal Mouffe (von Groddek and Schwarz, 2013, p. 32). In this study, megatrends were seen as empty signifiers, a particular form of emptiness. This means that megatrends are bundling too broad a range of discursive elements – with the effect that they are so overloaded with meaning that they can no longer convey clear information. Instead, they provide both an

over- and under-determined abstract form of meaning that lacks a connection between the signifier and the signified. They address discourses,
but cannot convey concrete meaning (von Groddek and Schwarz, 2013,
p. 33). Following the authors further: 'Megatrends, in parallel to empty
signifiers, are a semantic form that works as an abstract bracket for
heterogeneous societal changes, which leads to an overdetermination of
meaning. Consequently, working with megatrends may limit the capacity
of organizations to develop foresight' (p. 32). Thus the authors argue that
megatrends tend to describe a certain discursive phenomenon only in an
imaginary manner:

> [F]irstly because a discourse can never be fixed, and secondly – and more
> importantly – an empty signifier always has to be meaningless up to a certain
> point or else it would not be possible to address the discourse at all. The empty
> signifier can therefore be perceived as a paradoxical form within the discourse
> that fixes meaning by the emptiness of meaning. (p. 32)

For illustrative purposes, the authors discuss the case of the German firm
Siemens (p. 33). In 2006, Siemens had decided to engage in urban issues,
based on the identification of urbanization and demographic change as
major megatrends that were considered relevant for the company's future
business and strategy. Consequently, Siemens founded the business sector
'Infrastructure and Cities'. Even today, this is explicitly legitimized by
the assumption that megatrends can be observed, such as urbanization,
climate change, globalization and demographics (Siemens Homepage,
www.siemens.com/en, accessed 12 September 2013). However, without
a deeper understanding of what such apparent megatrends may mean
in concrete terms, not least economically, these fields may remain
empty, or, more precisely, empty signifiers: they are merely imaginary,
yet unable to convey concrete meaning. It is probably no surprise that
the Infrastructure and Cities business of Siemens has developed rather
poorly since then, and it is currently subject to various cost-cutting and
reorganization strategies within the corporation (*Wirtschaftswoche*, no.
15, 8 April 2013, pp. 54–55).

2.4 WHETHER MEGA OR NOT: RETHINKING THE REGION

Besides the rhetoric of hype and boosterism and its implicit determinism,
another important question that has to be addressed in the megaregion
discourse concerns contemporary understandings of 'region'. In this
context, the mega prefix in urban and regional studies must be viewed as

part of a broader social construction of the city and the urban. This means that the traditional imagination of the world located in a kind of container space is challenged once again. Territory and region are, firstly, no longer considered as given, fixed entities of physical and material properties to be located on a certain segment of the Earth's surface. However, they are viewed as different parts within a broader system, a wide network of socio-economic and ecological interrelations (Gregory, 1993). In that sense, the relational character of the region can also be treated as something 'accidental', rather than considered a fixed, constitutive matter (Lagendijk, 2007). Secondly, in this context there are no clear endings and beginnings, in both temporal and territorial regards. The contemporary region is unbound, discontinuous and increasingly difficult to demarcate, delineate and thus to determine based on spatial terminology (Amin, 2004).

This point has previously been made by John Allen and colleagues in their related call to 'rethink' the region (Allen et al., 1998). By exploring spatial transformations in the UK, they were asking questions such as 'when was' and 'where is' the south-east region? – thus discussing the enormous degree of external connectivity that has shaped this particular part of the country once again, and noting that the underlying dynamics could no longer be assigned to a clearly demarcated, delineated territory. There are hardly exact endings and beginnings of the contemporary region to be identified, so that one could consider particular large city-regions becoming the penultimate shape and scale for development. In a similar vein, Agnew (2013) viewed regions as a classification device. In order to reflect such properties also in the case of his reassessment of the northeastern Megalopolis in the US, Short (2007) introduced the notion of the 'liquid city'. With particular reference to the work of sociologist Zygmunt Bauman and his elaborations on late-modern, 'liquid' life, the term relates to the various forms of mobilities and destabilization that constitute megaregional space: 'Megalopolis is a large liquid metropolis whose boundary demarcation is always provisional' (Short, 2007, p. 15). Furthermore:

> The end result of myriad individual actions, investment decisions, and political choices is the collective, unforeseen creation of a giant urban region larger than our capacity to humanize it and greater than our imagination to conceptualize it. Megalopolis stands as a testimony to the unplanned, collective end point of individual everyday decisions. (Short, 2007, pp. 18–19)

This line of thought corresponds with critical interrogations of categories such as space and place, scale and region, which have been developed quite substantially in geography and planning discourses more recently (see, for example, the reviews in Elden, 2010; MacKinnon, 2010; Jonas, 2012a,

2012b, 2013). Geographers and planners engaged in apparent megaurban regional issues are called upon to take these debates and developments into account, rather than falling into the trap of boosterism, policy hype and megaurban speculation.

The fundamental challenge in this respect is twofold. Firstly, how to do justice to these complex settings and properties in methodological terms when exploring social practices and spatial relations with respect to territory and region. Second, how to avoid the essentialist trap of re-delineating regions and assigning content to a fixed territory, where settlement structures, demographic or socioeconomic contents and the normative ambitions of policy and planning are put together, thus constructing the region. One example here is the labelling of city-regions by policy and politics as officially acknowledged 'metropolitan' regions (cf. Hesse and Leick, 2013). Another case refers to border regions, where internal borders are conceived of as having vanished, yet, paradoxically, new outer frontiers are simultaneously created in order to constitute the border regions themselves, on the basis of strategies of regionalization (Hesse, 2012). Although some attention has indeed been paid to issues of definition, delineation and designing megaregions (see the typology developed by Banerjee, 2009; also Lang and Nelson, 2009), the challenge of the critical approaches named above remains largely unaddressed in the mainstream of megaregion research.

Secondly, the case of policy and planning makes this issue even more complex: the asymmetries between distanced, if not global interactions on the one hand, and the institutional spaces of cities and regions on the other hand, are well known. And even if the megaregion may fit as a tool or category in analytical regards, nothing is yet said about the question of whether and how it can be governed. It even seems unclear whether the concept as such is basically normative, 'or is it just a projection from the present?' (Banerjee, 2009, p. 84). Given that it makes sense to conceive of the modern large urban region as something distinct, based on size, growth, global significance and internal differentiation, there is an obvious shadow side to megaregional growth. One must not necessarily take on Mumford's apparatus of doom and apocalypse to be sensitive to these problems. However, within the epistemic community of those who are engaged in megaregional issues and analyses, critical comments are relatively rare and hard to detect, representing a few islands in an ocean of boosterism (see, however, Fainstein and Fainstein, 2009; Benner and Pastor, 2011). That said some attempts have been made to approach megaurban regions from the perspective of governance (see Orfield and Luce, 2009; Todorovich, 2009; Innes et al., 2010). As to now, the recipes presented do not sound totally distinct from what was discussed in earlier cases; that is, concerning the 'metropolitics' agenda (see Orfield and Luce, 2009). Making the case for establishing regional not local institutions, which in Orfield and Luce's case referred to the experience gained from the Twin Cities Metropolitan Council and Portland's Metro, might be difficult to organize in the case of megaregions. Understanding them as a distinct system of at least two major metropolitan regions, the challenge is enormous. If a clear, consistent and politically effective system of governing single metro areas is still missing, who would be seriously willing and able to tame the tiger of megaregional development?

Hence it can be argued that according to rising degrees of size, speed of growth and complexity, the difficulties of steering megaurban regions remain prevalent, being as 'wicked' as previous policies tended to be at metropolitan levels. This applies particularly to the issue of scale, to the ways in which the governance of cities and urban regions has been constituted and constructed, as a relation between the territory of the city on the one hand, and something hard to define 'out there' on the other hand (Cox, 2010, p. 216). Given the complex concurrence of vertical and horizontal power issues, governance institutions and political processes, the belief that an upward extension of the planning and policy space to the scale of the megaregion would create appropriate solutions is unrealistic at best, if not naïve. Planning discourses have tried to escape from these obvious difficulties by creating 'soft spaces' (Allmendinger and Haughton, 2009), reflecting the 'variable geometries' of late-modern spaces. And yes, there is good reason to give up a generalized notion of the region through the bounds of traditional geographical thought (and thus to clearly defined political-administrative boundaries), and to develop regional constructs alongside these variegated geometries, in order to avoid essentialist regionalism. However, the debate on soft spaces and related constructs needs to be concerned with the materiality of real-world problems, and if it is to advance policy and planning, it needs to go beyond the production of further urban and megaregional constructs.

2.5   PLANETARY URBANIZATION?

This chapter has provided a critical examination of the mega prefix as a popular term that is applied in both socioeconomic diagnostics and in urban-regional studies. Putting these various thoughts and developments together, there is a striking association that can be made between (1) the general 'hype and boost' rhetoric of mega-speak, (2) the inevitability of broader mega-developments happening and (3) the constructed nature of the megaregion. My first conclusion derived from this analysis was to question the logics behind megaregional thought and practices, and to comment critically on its constructed scalar nature. The second consequence, not least connected to the globalization rationale that underlies the concept of the megaregion, is to look at the global scale. Variegated forms of interrelation, interdependence and conflict have already been discussed in order to better understand today's relation between the global and the local (see Cox, 1995; Gaffikin and Perry, 2012; Sassen, 2013; Taylor et al., 2013). However, given the notion of growth, size and urbanization carried forward by the debate on megaregions, there are also striking conceptual associations and semantic analogies with these more recent discourses. Among them, the idea of a possible planetary course towards urbanization is gaining the most traction. In some ways it indicates that the megaregion urban discourse is subject to discursive upscaling processes, where the proclamation of megatrends, the assumption of their apparent inevitability and the related urban-regional manifestations seamlessly fit into an overarching paradigm concerning urbanization at the global level (see Bettencourt and West, 2010; Glaeser, 2011). It is probably no coincidence that the rise of megaurban regions as a spatial classification on the one hand, and the hypothesis of secular if not planetary urbanization on the other hand, have jointly hit the ground in the late 2000s and early 2010s. Both issues, however, deserve a critical reflection of their basic assumptions and propositions (see Gleeson, 2012, 2013; Tomaney, 2014).

Megaurban thinking fits perfectly into this sort of ultimate and inevitable global urbanization theory as a kind of all-encompassing, planetary process nobody can escape from. So megatrend and megaurban obviously have a lot in common with regard to a newly emerging, truly global grand narrative. Notable in this respect is also the fact that this sort of new paradigm has been framed by big urban business from both academia and corporations. In these two different worlds, cities and urbanization seem to be key for understanding the 21st century. Big firms such as Siemens or IBM have founded departments specialized in urban business. Science, business and big politics have agreed upon urbanization as a major paradigm, claiming an almost secular power of explanation. This notion is clearly behind the assumption of an *urban age* to come, behind Glaeser's (2011) claim of the *Triumph of the City*, or the 'urban equation' as presented in *Nature* (Anon., 2010a, 2010b). These works approach the increasing degree of differentiation in the urban fabric through an analytical lens defined by homogenizing terms and models. Since 2007, this thinking has become particularly popular after the United Nations revealed that for the first time a majority of the world's population lived in cities. Despite the questionable validity of global databases, the potential for statistical bias and inaccuracy and alike, such claims present the urban age as a sort of totalitarian, naturalized construction. As Gleeson (2012, p. 933) states: 'Within a totalising, law-bound view of urbanisation, it is not hard to sense the spectre of naturalism. The overall cast is urbanisation as an inevitable form of species drive, or at least the only sensible response to the sirens of urban destiny'.

In this context, Tomaney (2014) also commented critically on the neo-orthodoxy of leadership and local development that is being addressed by the proponents of the triumph of the city and the advent of the urban age, as lacking sensitivity to the extreme degree of inequality that characterizes the large, heterogeneous agglomerations they are effectively talking about. It seems evident that this naturalized, politically polished construction of the 'new urban world' (Kourtit et al., 2013) has been discursively framed with the particular help of academics and urban consultants. Knowledge brokers from institutions such as the Brookings Metro Center, New York's Regional Plan Association, LSE's Urban Age Consortium or Ed Glaeser with his column in the *New York Times* (not to forget the master-mind of the creative city, Richard Florida (for example Florida, 2002) and his writing for *The Atlantic City*) were essential for mobilizing and circulating the new urban orthodoxy. In this respect, both related publications and even more so global conference series and seminars were instrumental in pushing the universalized idea of urbanization into the orbit of big politics. Thus the knowledge brokers were quite successful not only in selling economic development recipes to governments and metropolitan mayors, receiving an enormous degree of recognition at the interface of science and policy, but also in creating new epistemic formations. *Mega*, with its specific semantic underpinnings of the great, the important and the inevitable, is part of this orchestration of city and region, or of communicative urbanization.

2.6 CONCLUSION

In concluding this journey across various fields of developments, discourses and associations, this chapter has taken a critical look at the mega prefix in societal, regional and – last but not least – global forms of development and urbanization. It seems in a way representative for creating a new understanding of what cities and the urban are about. However, to my mind, speaking of both megaregions as the larger system and also of mega-city regions as single metropolitan areas does not move the debate forward, for various reasons. The mega term borrows from hype and speculative trend-framing, fits into the somewhat totalitarian, at least naturalist view of the world, where difference, choice and politics do not apply, and it conveys a clearly essentialist or naturalist understanding of city and region, by delineating territory and assigning certain contents to space. The case of megaregions also reveals how a constructed entity has been successfully placed on the political agenda by academics and consultants from big urban business, captivated by large-scale urban rhetoric and the like. My argument is that mega, the language of the big and thus the discourse of megaurban regions being *the* essential urban-regional form of the future, conveys a positivistic, (natural) science-based view of the urban world. It is close to related assumptions of urbanization happening not only on a planetary level but also being 'triumphant'. This line of thought remains inadequate and one-dimensional, and leaves no space for alternative ideas of the urban. Consequently, it challenges what recent geographical theory has thought about space, as it is close to natural science in terms of proposing an 'urban equation' (as *Nature* did), and maybe planetary urbanization will one day be married up to the Anthropocene, ending up with a new kind of meta-theory of the urban-regional world. Ironically, certain biologisms that are inherent in the language of mega and of universal urbanization can already be found as early as in Mumford's writings on necro-polis and the demise of the city that is too big.

What does all this mean for our debate? What could be an appropriate lesson to be derived from these thoughts? In the light of the above criticism, there are three consequences that could be taken into account in further exploration of this issue. Firstly, one could ask whether we need such a 'one size fits all' label for regions at all, and if so, what this could be. Whilst being fully aware of the fluid, expanded and constructed nature of the late-modern region, I would argue that it is still sufficient to approach these territorial units as metropolitan regions, avoiding the rather contested or contaminated meaning of the mega prefix. Secondly, against the desire of politics and big urban business to demarcate, to label and thus to sell regions, it seems to be more important to emphasize process against product, to seek for explanation and appropriate interpretation of contemporary urban and metropolitan change, rather than to assign fixed properties to bounded territories. Thirdly, it makes sense to reflect on the 'murky' waters of policy studies in geography and other disciplines (Woods and Gardner, 2011), and to avoid unhealthy proximity to decision-makers, big business and big politics. This is far from making a case against public engagement. Yet one should remain both careful and critical when seeking apparently clear terms and concepts for addressing rather complex issues. If megalopolis must be considered an 'enduring enigma' (Platt, 2010), and there is good reason to believe so, this might even more apply to the mega-region. So urban researchers might be well advised to resist the language of the big, the great, the ultimate, and discard policy boosterism. It is exactly this critical political-economic and scientific environment in which the thoughts outlined above are embedded, thus hopefully contributing to a more reflective use of mega speak and a more cautious approach to megaregions.

ACKNOWLEDGEMENTS

My sincere thanks go to Professor Robert Krueger, Worcester Polytechnic Institute (WPI) in Worcester, Massachusetts (USA), for commenting on an earlier draft of this paper, and to Margret Vince, Nottingham (UK), for careful proofreading.

REFERENCES

Agnew, J.A. (2013), 'Arguing with regions', *Regional Studies*, **47** (1), 6–17.
Allen, J., D. Massey and A. Cochrane (1998), *Rethinking the Region*, London: Routledge.
Allmendinger, P. and G. Haughton (2009), 'Soft spaces, fuzzy boundaries, and metagovernance: the new spatial planning in the "Thames Gateway"', *Environment and Planning* A, **41** (3), 617–633.
Amin, A. (2004), 'Regions unbound: towards a new politics of place', *Geografisker Annaler*, **86** B (1), 33–44.
Anon. (2010a), 'The urban equation', *Nature*, **467** (7318), 899.
Anon. (2010b), 'The century of the city', *Nature*, **467** (7318), 900–901.
Ascher, F. (1995), *Métapolis ou l'avenir des villes*, Paris: Editions Odile Jacob.
Bachmann-Medick, D. (2006), *Cultural Turns: Neuorientierungen in den Kulturwissenschaften*, Reinbek: Rowohlt.
Baigent, E. (2004), 'Patrick Geddes, Lewis Mumford and Jean Gottmann: divisions over "megalopolis"', *Progress in Human Geography*, **28** (6), 687–700.
Banerjee, T. (2009), 'Megaregions or megasprawls? Issues of density, urban design and quality growth', in C.L. Ross (ed.), *Megaregions: Planning for Global Competitiveness*, Washington, DC: Island Press, pp. 83–106.
Benner, C. and M. Pastor (2011), 'Moving on up? Regions, megaregions, and the changing geography of social equity organizing', *Urban Affairs Review*, **47** (3), 315–348.
Bettencourt, L. and G. West (2010), 'A unified theory of urban living', *Nature*, **467** (7318), 912–913.
Cox, K. (1995), 'Globalisation, competition and the politics of local economic development', *Urban Studies*, **32** (2), 213–224.
Cox, K. (2010), 'The problem of metropolitan governance and the politics of scale', *Regional Studies*, **44** (2), 215–222.
Decoville, A. (2008), 'Métropolisation et résistance des territoires: l'exemple luxembourgeois', *L'Espace Politique*, **4** (2008–1), available at http://espacepolitique.revues.org/694 (accessed 12 September 2013).
Elden, S. (2010), 'Land, terrain, territory', *Progress in Human Geography*, **34** (6), 799–817.
Fainstein, N. and S.S. Fainstein (2009), 'Social equity and the challenge of

distressed places', in C.L. Ross (ed.), *Megaregions: Planning for Global Competitiveness*, Washington, DC: Island Press, pp. 191–215.

Florida, R. (2002), *The Rise of the Creative Class: And How It's Transforming Work, Leisure, Community and Everyday Life*, New York: Basic Books.

Gaffikin, F. and D.C. Perry (2012), 'The contemporary urban condition: understanding the globalizing city as informal, contested, and anchored', *Urban Affairs Review*, **48** (5), 701–730.

Glasze, G. and A. Matissek (eds) (2009), *Handbuch Diskurs und Raum: Theorien und Methoden für die Humangeographie sowie die sozial- und kulturwissenschaftliche Raumforschung*, Bielefeld: Transcript.

Glaeser, E. (2011), *Triumph of the City: How Our Greatest Invention Makes Us Richer, Smarter, Greener, Healthier, and Happier*, New York: Penguin.

Gleeson, B. (2012), 'The urban age: paradox and prospect', *Urban Studies*, **49** (5), 933–943.

Gleeson, B. (2013), 'What role for social science in the urban age?', *International Journal of Urban and Regional Research*, **37** (5), 1839–1851.

Goldman, L. (1983), 'Megatrends: megahype, megabad', *Educational Leadership*, September, 55–57.

Gottmann, J. (1957), 'Megalopolis or the urbanization of the northeastern seaboard', *Economic Geography*, **33** (3), 189–200.

Gottmann, J. (1961), *Megalopolis: The Urbanized Northeastern Seaboard of the United States*, New York: Twentieth Century Fund.

Gottmann, J. (1987), *Megalopolis Revisited: 25 Years Later*, College Park, MD: University of Maryland Institute for Urban Studies.

Gregory, D. (1993), *Geographical Imaginations*, Oxford: Blackwell.

Hall, P. (1973), *The Containment of Urban England* (two volumes), London: Allen and Unwin.

Hall, P. and K. Pain (eds) (2006), *The Polycentric Metropolis: Learning from Mega-City Regions in Europe*, London: Earthscan.

Harrison, J. and M. Hoyler (2015), 'Megaregions: foundations, frailties, futures', in J. Harrison and M. Hoyler (eds), *Megaregions: Globalization's New Urban Form?* Cheltenham, UK and Northampton, MA, USA: Edward Elgar, pp. 1–28.

Hesse, M., with S. Kmec, R. Reckinger and C. Wille (2012), 'Regionalisation processes as practices of borderisation', *IDENT2-Working Papers*, 1, Luxembourg: Université du Luxembourg.

Hesse, M. and A. Leick (2013), 'Wachstum, Innovation, Metropolregionen: Zur Rekonstruktion des jüngeren Leitbildwandels in der deutschen Raumentwicklungspolitik', *Raumforschung und Raumordnung*, **71** (4), 343–359.

Innes, J.E., D.E. Booher and S. Di Vittorio (2010), 'Strategies for megaregion governance: collaborative dialogue, networks, and self-organization', *Journal of the American Planning Association*, **77** (1), 55–67.

Jonas, A.E.G. (2012a), 'Region and place: regionalism in question', *Progress in Human Geography*, **36** (2), 263–272.

Jonas, A.E.G. (2012b), 'City-regionalism: questions of distribution and politics', *Progress in Human Geography*, **36** (6), 822–829.

Jonas, A.E.G. (2013), 'Place and region III: alternative regionalisms', *Progress in Human Geography*, **37** (6), 822–828.

Kourtit, K., P. Nijkamp and M.D. Partridge (2013), 'The new urban world', *European Planning Studies*, **21** (3), 285–290.

Lagendijk, A. (2007), 'The accident of the region: a strategic relational

perspective on the construction of the region's significance', *Regional Studies*, **41** (9), 1193–1207.
Lang, R.E. and A.C. Nelson (2009), 'Megapolitan America: defining and applying a new geography', in C.L. Ross (ed.), *Megaregions: Planning for Global Competitiveness*, Washington, DC: Island Press, pp. 107–126.
MacKinnon, D. (2010), 'Reconstructing scale: towards a new scalar politics', *Progress in Human Geography*, **35** (1), 21–36.
McCann, E. (2013), 'Policy boosterism, policy mobilities, and the extrospective city', *Urban Geography*, **34** (1), 5–29.
Merrifield, A. (2013), 'The urban question under planetary urbanization', *International Journal of Urban and Regional Research*, **37** (3), 909–922.
Miller, H.T. and C.J. Fox (2001), 'The epistemic community', *Administration & Society*, **32** (6), 668–685.
Mumford, L. (1937), *The Culture of Cities*, London: Secker and Warburg.
Mumford, L. (1961), *The City in History: Its Origins, Its Transformations, and Its Prospects*, London: Secker and Warburg.
Naisbitt, J. (1982), *Megatrends: Ten New Directions Transforming Our Lives*, New York: Warner Books.
Orfield, M. and T.F. Luce (2009), 'Governing American metropolitan areas: spatial policy and regional governance', in C.L. Ross (ed.), *Megaregions: Planning for Global Competitiveness*, Washington, DC: Island Press, pp. 250–279.
Pacione, M. (2009), *Urban Geography: A Global Perspective*, New York: Routledge.
Platt, R.H. (2010), 'Megalopolis: an enduring enigma', *Technology and Culture*, **51** (1), 223–226.
Priemus, H. (2010), 'Megaprojects: dealing with pitfalls', *European Planning Studies*, **18** (7), 1023–1039.
Raco, M. (2003), 'Assessing the discourses and practices of urban regeneration in a growing region', *Geoforum*, **34** (1), 37–55.
Ross, C.L. (ed.) (2009), *Megaregions: Planning for Global Competitiveness*, Washington, DC: Island Press.
Sassen, S. (2013), 'When the center no longer holds: cities as frontier zones', *Cities*, **34**, 67–70.
Short, J.R. (2007), *Liquid City: Megalopolis and the Contemporary Northeast*, Washington, DC: Resources for the Future.
Soja, E.W. (2000), *Postmetropolis: Critical Studies of Cities and Regions*, Oxford: Blackwell.
Swyngedouw, E., F. Moulaert and A. Rodriguez (2002), 'Neoliberal urbanization in Europe: large-scale urban development projects and the new urban policy', *Antipode*, **34** (3), 542–577.
Taylor, P.J., B. Derudder, M. Hoyler and P. Ni (2013), 'New regional geographies of the world as practised by leading advanced producer service firms in 2010', *Transactions of the Institute of British Geographers*, **38** (3), 497–511.
Todorovich, P. (2009), 'America's emerging megaregions and implications for a national growth strategy', *International Journal of Public Sector Management*, **22** (3), 221–234.
Tomaney, J. (2014), 'Region and place I: institutions', *Progress in Human Geography*, **38** (1), 131–140.
United Nations (2011), 'World urbanization prospects – the 2011 revisions', available at http://esa.un.org/unup/ (accessed 26 April 2013).

Van der Ploeg, F. and S. Poelhekke (2008), 'Globalization and the rise of mega-
-cities in the developing world', *Cambridge Journal of Regions, Economy and
Society*, **1** (3), 477–501.
Vicino, T.J., B. Hanlon and J.R. Short (2007), 'Megalopolis 50 years on: the
transformation of a city region', *International Journal of Urban and Regional
Research*, **31** (2), 344–367.
von Groddek, J. and J.O. Schwarz (2013), 'Perceiving megatrends as empty signi-
fiers: a discourse-theoretical interpretation of trend management', *Futures*, **47**
(1), 28–37.
Woods, M. and G. Gardner (2011), 'Applied policy research and critical human
geography: some reflections on swimming in murky waters', *Dialogues in
Human Geography*, **1** (2), 198–214.
Zollman, K.J.S. (2007), 'The communication structure of epistemic communities',
Philosophy of Science, **74** (5), 574–587.

3. Megaregions and the urban question: the new strategic terrain for US urban competitiveness

David Wachsmuth

3.1 INTRODUCTION

We live, so the refrain goes, in an era of global urbanization where new urban forms and new economic processes intermingle in complex and perhaps unprecedented ways. As Taylor and Lang (2004) argue, urban studies confronts the 'shock of the new'. Indeed, Taylor and Lang offer a helpful starting point for evaluating the question of what would it mean, in an era of global urbanization, for megaregions to be globalization's new urban form. They provide a list of 100 concepts describing recent urban change, which, they point out, was by no means exhaustive when it was compiled. It is difficult to imagine that in the decade that has passed since its release this figure will not, at a minimum, have doubled. Of the 50 concepts Taylor and Lang single out as describing new intercity relations, 48 include some variant of 'global', 'world', 'international', 'transnational' or 'planetary'. In other words, if megaregions are indeed globalization's new urban form, they have plenty of company in that role.

The connection between urban form and economic process is of course not a new scholarly concern. Since Manuel Castells (1977) first posed the 'urban question' four decades ago, critical urban studies have debated the relationship between processes of capitalist accumulation and governance and the production of urban space. Accordingly in this chapter I wish to draw on some old insights to advance some new claims about contemporary urbanization processes. The aim of the chapter is to historicize and critically reinterpret recent US scholarly and policy interest in megaregions. Successive periods of urbanization have produced both new urban forms and new urban networks. I argue that the historical specificity of the megaregion is such that it is simultaneously both city and urban network. The fragmentation and dispersal of metropolitan regions and the simultaneous interconnection of multiple such regions mean that commuting, social reproduction and everyday life (traditionally seen as proper to the city or metropolitan area) increasingly occur within a space defined by the megaregional built environment, which also is the space defining regional production and circulation possibilities (traditionally seen as proper to the region). I apply this conceptualization to reinterpret the growing scholarly and policy emphasis on the economic competitiveness of megaregions (Halbert et al., 2006; Florida et al., 2008; Xu and Yeh, 2011). Nowhere has this emphasis on megaregions as competitive economic units been more prevalent than in the US (Dewar and Epstein, 2007; Ross, 2009). However, and contrary to the new prevailing wisdom, I argue that US megaregions are not emerging as competitive actors in the global economy, but rather are better understood as strategic terrains upon which a multitude of differently scaled competitiveness strategies are being enacted.

To develop this argument, I proceed as follows. Section 3.2 contrasts 1960s and 1970s scholarship on megalopolis with contemporary scholarship on megaregions. I then situate this contrast within debates over the 'urban question' in Section 3.3. In the next section, I periodize US capitalist urbanization through changing transportation technologies. I argue that megaregions are characteristic of a third, 'regional' period, in which functionally integrated metropolitan areas have begun to give way to a more heterogeneous, 'hybrid' urban landscape in which cities and urban networks are to some extent spatially coexistent. Finally, Section 3.5 provides evidence that the political economic result of this hybrid landscape is not the emergence of megaregions as competitive units in the global economy, but rather an intensification of competitiveness policies and discourses at multiple spatial scales.

3.2   HISTORICAL APPROACHES TO ENORMOUS URBAN AREAS, IN THEORY AND POLICY

The majority of recent scholarly work on large-scale urban regions in the US has either assumed or has argued the proposition that these regions are becoming an important new territorial unit of economic activity. However, the novelty of this proposition is worth subjecting to some scrutiny, since a generation ago there was a wave of scholarly interest in enormous urban areas that paralleled today's scholarship in many respects, along with a wave of policy interest that has not yet been equalled in the present moment. Before providing my own analysis, I therefore begin by briefly reviewing and contrasting the scholarship on 'megalopolis' and 'megaregions'.

Patrick Geddes coined the term 'megalopolis' (Geddes, 1915), but it was his student Lewis Mumford who used it most influentially by speculating on the new urban form it represented (Meller, 1993). For Mumford, megalopolis was nothing more than the phenomenon of cities grown monstrous and out of control, 'not in fact a new sort of city, but an anti-city' (Mumford, 1961, p. 505). Although Mumford disapproved of the new emerging form, he saw it as a qualitative transformation in the urbanization process, which contrasted with contemporary 'metropolitanist' arguments that the basic central-city-plus-suburb form established in the 19th century – in the 'great' cities such as New York and Chicago – would persist indefinitely, even as these metropolitan areas grew larger and larger (Fishman, 2000).

Jean Gottmann (1961), who agreed with Mumford that a qualitative transformation was afoot, had a more optimistic interpretation of the same phenomenon. He argued that 'Megalopolis' – the urbanized northeastern seaboard of the US from Boston to Washington – was not simply a set of overgrown cities, but rather a historically novel concentration of population, economic power and social diversity that was potentially on the verge of generalizing into a new urban species. Unlike Mumford's form-centric analysis, Gottmann stressed the economic specificity of megalopolis. He argued that the Boston–Washington megalopolis performed a 'hinge' function, connecting a national economic space to the west with an international one to the east – via the seaboard. Gottmann was thus the first to make the argument that the megalopolis (or megaregion) is an inherently global phenomenon, a claim which he initially articulated with respect to the unique urban form of the Boston–Washington megalopolis, but which was subsequently generalized. Later work by Gottmann (1976) and Constantinos Doxiadis (1966, 1967, 1968, 1970, 1974) applied the concept of 'megalopolis' to various urban areas in the US – most prominently the Great Lakes region (see Glass, 2015) – and beyond. Doxiadis, who was a futurist as well as an urbanist, used the Great Lakes Megalopolis as a stepping stone to prospectively analyse a completely urbanized planet, which he called 'ecumenopolis'. The result is that, over the course of the 1960s and early 1970s, the concept of megalopolis shifted in the writings of its key proponents from a novel and exceptional urban form to a prototypical urban form (Brenner, 2003). What had previously been 'Megalopolis' – a historically unique urban agglomeration in the northeast US – became 'megalopolis', a generalized pattern of polycentric urban development expected to become increasingly common across the globe.

Gottmann's and Doxiadis's megalopolis concept saw a modest uptake in the North American urban policy environment. Rhode Island Senator Claiborne Pell wrote a public policy book entitled *Megalopolis Unbound* in 1966, focusing on the transportation challenges facing the

Boston–Washington corridor, and sponsored federal legislation (the High-Speed Ground-Transportation Act of 1965) to help alleviate these challenges (Pell, 1966). In 1975, the Canadian Department of State and Doxiadis's *World Society for Ekistics* held a conference in Toronto on the Great Lakes Megalopolis, whose findings were later published as a book (Leman and Leman, 1976). The aim was to identify the implications of transborder urban development in the Great Lakes for Canadian governance, and to contribute to the 1976 Habitat I conference in Vancouver (which established UN-Habitat, the United Nations agency charged with ensuring sustainable urban development on a global scale). Both Gottmann and Doxiadis participated, along with luminaries such as Buckminster Fuller, Marshall McLuhan and Margaret Mead. The policy impact of the conference was minimal, however. In part this was for exactly the same reason that Doxiadis's ambitious study of the Great Lakes Megalopolis quickly became irrelevant – namely, the crisis of Fordism and its negative impact on urban growth in the region. The actual governance challenges that confronted the Great Lakes from the mid-1970s onward were those of decline and crisis, not growth. The Great Lakes conference was the last significant megalopolitan policy initiative, and by the mid-1970s the North American scholarly and policy interest in megalopolis had largely dissipated. While research continued to be conducted on large-scale urbanization processes throughout the 1980s and 1990s, these efforts generally occurred at sub-megalopolitan scales – perhaps best illustrated by the 'post-metropolis' thesis put forward by the Los Angeles school of urbanism (Scott, 1988; Soja, 1989; Davis, 1990; Dear, 1991).

When the concept of megalopolis resurfaced 20 years later, it did so in the context of East Asia, under the headings 'mega-city', 'mega-city region' and 'megaregion'. While some scholars have sought to draw connections between the East Asian mega-city and the paradigmatic Los Angeles post-metropolis (Webster, 1995; Soja, 2011), most have seen the East Asian mega-city as a phenomenon emerging distinctively within the Global South. Indeed, these polycentric, production- and trade-focused regions are widely interpreted as being counterparts to the global city phenomenon (Friedmann and Wolff, 1982; Sassen, 2001) – part of the development of a new international division of labour, which has seen the global core–periphery arrangement of manufacturing in the core and resource extraction in the periphery replaced by one in which manufacturing occurs in the Global South while finance and other advanced producer services cluster in key urban centres across both Global North and South.

Recent approaches to megaregions have thus stressed their relationship to global circuits of production, trade and power. Peter Hall (1999), for example, emphasizes the East Asian provenance of the mega-city, its distinctive polycentrality and its co-development with economic globalization. Manuel Castells (2000), meanwhile, argues that the distinctive aspect of mega-cities is their global connection and local disconnection – their articulation within the global space of flows that allows them to decouple themselves from and to some extent transcend entirely the local relations of proximity that were defining aspects of megalopolis for Mumford and Gottmann. While stressing the importance of territorial continuity and thereby implicitly disagreeing with Castells on that particular point, Richard Florida agrees with him about the new role megaregions are playing in the global economy. Specifically he argues that 'Urban mega-regions are coming to relate to the global economy in much the same way that metropolitan regions relate to national economies' (Florida et al., 2008, p. 460). Florida's claim (along with his work mapping megaregions worldwide by using night-time satellite imagery) is worth emphasizing because it captures a new trend in the literature: the generalization of the megaregion as a truly global form of urban development, one that spans Global North and Global South. It is within this context that the concept of megalopolis has returned to prominence in the US, 50 years after Gottmann first proposed it.

An emerging body of mainly North American scholarship, mostly in urban planning (Lang and Dhavale, 2005; Dewar and Epstein, 2007; Vega and Penne, 2008; Ross, 2009; Nelson and Lang, 2011) and geography (Florida et al., 2008; Florida, 2010), but also in sociology (Sassen, 2009; Benner and Pastor, 2011), economics (Glaeser, 2007) and environmental studies (Wheeler, 2009, 2015), has begun to explore large-scale urban areas in the US under the heading of the megaregion. The US megaregions literature adopts two key assumptions about its research object. First, megaregions in the US – as a territorial form or settlement type – are fundamentally similar to large urban areas in other parts of the world, and in particular East Asia and Western Europe. Thus urban researchers and policymakers in the US can better understand US megaregions by studying them in an international comparative perspective. Second, megaregions in the US are a product of economic globalization to the same extent as East Asian mega-cities and, more generally, the megaregion is emerging as a key competitive territorial unit in the global economy.

The result is that, in epistemological terms, the new 'megaregion' closely resembles the old 'megalopolis' – an upscaled form of the traditional city (Wachsmuth, 2014) with a novel connection to the global economy. But whereas Gottmann and Doxiadis understood megalopolis as a prototypical urban form – the harbinger of a new, globalizing urban future – contemporary scholarship on megaregions treats them as something closer to a stereotype (Brenner, 2003), that is, a generic, globalized form common to a wide variety of geographical contexts.

3.3 THE URBAN QUESTION

Having established this historical transition within the literature on enormous urban areas, I now offer some critical observations. The premise of this chapter is that contemporary debates over megaregions – their specificity as a phenomenon, their scope and extent, and their relationship to globalization and other macroeconomic processes – can be more fruitfully advanced if we embed them within what Castells (1977) characterized as the 'urban question'. By this term I refer to the historical and geographical specificity of urban processes and urban forms within the structures of capitalism.[1] The urban question thus encompasses debates over the nature of cities, urban–rural relations and processes of urban change which date back to the Chicago school of sociology – and earlier – but roots such debates firmly in political-economic soil.

When Castells first posed the urban question, he did so as a critique of the Chicago school. The latter, he claimed, treated urban environments as a causal force in the social transformations wrought by the onset of capitalist modernity, when the true relationship was the opposite. Castells argued that the city is a spatial expression of capitalism, corresponding to the reproduction of labour power, particularly in its large-scale, state-mediated form, which Castells would subsequently term 'collective consumption'. For Castells, other social processes may occur within cities, but they do not stand in any necessary relationship to them and thus are not properly the domain of urban analysis. This functionalist interpretation of the urban question has not withstood the test of time (indeed, Castells's own repudiation of these arguments began almost immediately after he published them), but the broader analytical strategy of linking urban form and function to dynamics of capital accumulation and struggle has proven to be a powerful one. In this spirit, I turn to two aspects of the urban question which Castells did not address, but which will be useful for decoding contemporary discourses on megaregions: (1) periodization as an analytical procedure within urban studies; and (2) the distinction between *intraurban* and *interurban* aspects of the urban question.

Castells's apparently general analysis of capitalist urbanization was tightly – and not always reflexively – tied to the Fordist–Keynesian era. So just as Doxiadis's Fordist-era predictions about endless growth in the Detroit-centred Great Lakes Megalopolis ran aground after the crisis of 1973, the neoliberal transformation of state-economy relations ushered in from the mid-1970s onward surely played a role in Castells's retreat from the positions staked out in *The Urban Question*. Subsequent critical urban scholarship explicitly periodized the urban question in both epistemological (Brenner, 2000) and functional terms (Harvey, 1989b). In both cases, the historical-geographical specificity of urbanization under Fordist advanced capitalism was made explicit. More generally, periodization addresses the prospect that urban processes and urban forms can take on radically different relationships to processes of capitalist accumulation and social struggle at different points in history. For this reason, it is arguably indispensable for undertaking the kind of meso-level analysis prompted by the urban question. We thus arrive at the proposition, posed as a question in this book's subtitle but assumed or argued by numerous scholars, that the megaregion stands in some sort of necessary relationship with processes of economic globalization. There are many examples, but I will highlight two by way of illustration. First, Hall (1999, p. 13) describes the mega-city region as 'the spatial expression of a new form of economic development on a transnational scale', while second, Florida et al. (2008, p. 460), quoted above, argue that 'urban mega-regions are coming to relate to the global economy in much the same way that metropolitan regions relate to national economies'. Effectively, these propositions are periodizations of the urban question, with the megaregion joining or even displacing the city and metropolitan region as a characteristic urban form within globalizing neoliberal capitalism.

But what kind of urban form is the megaregion? There is a long tradition in urban studies – especially in geography and to a lesser extent in sociology – of situating the analysis of individual cities within larger urban networks. We can thus distinguish between the 'internal' and 'external' dimensions of the urban question – a distinction captured best by Brian Berry's (1964) memorable phrase 'cities as systems within systems of cities'. Castells's investigation of the urban question was effectively limited to the city as a system: the functional role and internal organization of cities within the larger context of the capitalist mode of production. But, just as any individual city or local urban form should be located, as Castells argued, within a broader political-economic context, it can also be located within a broader interurban context. To take two prominent examples from contemporary urban studies: the study of gentrification and neighbourhood change has largely been a study of the internal dimensions of the urban question – the causes and impacts of changing flows of capital and populations within metropolitan areas[2] – while the study of global cities and world city networks has, meanwhile, largely been a study of the external dimensions of the urban question – changing divisions of labour within interurban networks. Even where global city research has examined, for example, sociospatial polarization within individual global cities, the explanatory framework of such research is generally the interurban network rather than the individual city or metropolitan area. This distinction between the internal and external relations of cities has been a central meta-theoretical line of demarcation for urban studies up to now. Returning to Taylor and Lang's (2004) list of 100 concepts for describing recent urban change, these authors supply 50 concepts under each of the twin headings of 'new metropolitan form' and 'new intercity relations'. Of course, the distinction is an abstraction. Any concrete urban phenomenon will in practice implicate both intra-urban and inter-urban relations. But it is a useful heuristic for theory-building, not least to begin untangling the relationship between megaregions and globalization.

3.4   PERIODIZING REGIONAL URBANIZATION: EXURBAN GROWTH WITHOUT DAILY TRANSPORTATION INTEGRATION

In this section I situate megaregions – as specific urban morphologies – within a more general historical phase of US urbanization, which, following Soja (2011), I call here 'regional urbanization'. I understand this as the third major period of capitalist urban development in the US, following an industrial and then a metropolitan period. This periodization is not particularly controversial in general terms (although it is described with a variety of names; see for example, Gordon, 1978; Walker, 1981; Harvey, 1989a; Scott, 2011; Soja, 2011), but the brief built-environment-theoretical account I give here emphasizes more than others the importance of periodic transformations of transportation technology in driving urban political economies.

The analytical framework I use to perform this periodization rests on the interaction between two stylized facts: (1) ongoing demographic-driven expansion of urban populations and built environments; and (2) periodic systemic transformations in transportation and communications technologies that have allowed larger and larger urban areas to be internally integrated and to be connected in new ways to external economic spaces and to the natural environment. The first point is a simple empirical observation about population growth, rural–urban migration and immigration. The proportion of the US population living in urban areas has increased steadily and with no significant regressions across all areas and throughout the entire history of the country. In the first decade of the 21st century alone, the amount of urbanized land increased by 15 per cent in the US.[3]

The second stylized fact – repeated transformations of transportation and communication technologies – is derived from Schumpeterian and Marxian theories of 'long waves' in the capitalist economy (Mandel, 1980; Freeman and Louça, 2001; Perez, 2002). These hold that periodic cycles of innovation and diffusion drive economic growth in repeating cycles of boom and bust. Each cycle pivots around the development of some key technology characterized by a low and steadily declining cost curve, ready availability, and amenability to many different applications (Freeman and Louça, 2001). The details of the various long-wave theories are beyond the scope of this chapter, as are their points of disagreement (but see Day, 1976). However, the key observation here is simply that each cycle of technological development has led to the diffusion of new transportation and communication technologies which have enabled new modes of intra-urban or inter-urban development, changing cities or changing the relations between cities and other urban or rural spaces by promoting some accumulation pathways while devaluing others. Long waves of capitalist development are thus also fundamentally long waves of urbanization:

- The coal- and iron-driven development of railroads in the second half of the 19th century enabled extended city–farmland economies to develop, most prominently in the Midwest (Cronon, 1991).
- The electrification at the turn of the century enabled efficient intra-urban commuting via streetcars and tramways that allowed the modern division of the living space from the work space and thus the basic urban/suburban city form. The accompanying development of steel allowed much larger long-distance shipments of goods via steel ships.
- The oil-driven motorization of the economy following the Great Depression, in combination with the subsequent development of the interstate highway system and its metropolitan equivalents, laid the basis for downtown disinvestment, the expanding Fordist suburban city and its incorporation within a relatively unified national economic space.
- The IT revolution beginning in the 1970s and the subsequent logistics revolution helped facilitate the new international division of labour and its corresponding global city form (Sassen, 2001).

Emphasizing the fundamentally technological character of these major changes in US urbanization processes should not be taken as implying that the processes were deterministic or somehow asocial. Quite the opposite in fact: each of these techno-economic paradigms has been the site of intense sociospatial struggles – both within different factions of elites and between capitalist and popular classes – over the particular development pathways to be followed and how the economic returns generated should be distributed. Goddard (1994) shows, for instance, the constitutively political character of the national transition from rail to highways as the dominant mode of interurban transportation from the 1920s onward, with an emerging cross-class 'highway-industrial complex' facing off against entrenched railroad monopolists. More recently and on a smaller scale, De Lara (2013) argues that the logistics revolution has enabled new forms of racialized and class-based urban restructuring in coastal urban areas, with port distribution facilities relocated from inner-city (near-dock) areas where organized labour is strong to exurban (inland) areas where precarious and non-unionized labour can instead be exploited.

The first two of the technological revolutions collectively enabled industrial urbanization, a 'structured coherence' (Harvey, 1989b) defined most succinctly by a city internally differentiated between industry and residence, and externally differentiated vis-à-vis the agricultural country-side within a regional division of labour. While this pattern held in the US and formed the basis for the urban sociology of the Chicago School (Park et al., 1925), it is more paradigmatically associated with England following the Industrial Revolution (Williams, 1973).

The motorization revolution and its associated social developments enabled metropolitan urbanization, and the larger-scale, suburbanized urban areas now generally referred to as 'metropolitan areas'. Fordist metropolitan areas encompassed unprecedented physical area and popu-lations, but were able to remain economically integrated (as labour markets and housing markets) because of the development of metro-politan highway systems. A faster general transportation system allowed a larger area to remain functionally a city. While post-war suburbanization transformed the US most thoroughly, it was a common process to varying extents throughout the advanced capitalist world.

The third and present phase of US urbanization is regional urbani-zation. This phase corresponds to the IT revolution and the round of economic globalization it has facilitated. Indeed, information technology demonstrates the potential unity of transportation technologies for accom-plishing the 'annihilation of space by time' (Marx, 1973; Harvey, 1989c). Whereas previous technological revolutions enabled new space economies through new modes of transportation, the IT revolution has had its impact by rendering existing modes of transportation feasible at new scales and degrees of complexity through ubiquitous and effectively instantaneous global telecommunications. They key developments here are 'just-in-time' production networks and containerization, and the domain of business logistics which they comprise – a domain, Cowen (2010, p. 602) argues, which has 'quietly put the cold calculation of cost at the center of a vital form of the production of space'.

The IT and logistics revolution has indeed transformed the global economy and the position of certain city-regions within that economy – significantly port cities and global cities. But, contrary to early predictions about telecommuting, for example, it has not significantly transformed the internal spatial organization of the city. Commuting occurs via the same highway systems that undergirded Fordist suburbanization, but ongoing population growth and the universalization of automobility have increased the scale of urban built environments well beyond the limits of a daily commute (Sheller and Urry, 2000). So, like the industrial and metropolitan periods of urban development, the regional period has seen greatly expanded urban areas. But unlike those previous periods there has not been a transformation in transportation practice to allow the larger urban areas to be integrated as single labour and property markets.

As they expand into contact with each other along interstate highways these new 'splintering' (Graham and Marvin, 2001) urban areas form megaregions. In an important sense, then, megaregions are simultaneously city and urban network – in Berry's (1964) phrasing they are both systems of cities and the cities themselves. In schematic terms, critical urban studies has tended to map social reproduction onto the scale of the city, and production and circulation onto the scale of the region (Castells, 1977; Harvey, 1989b; Storper and Walker, 1989; Smith, 2008). But megaregions combine elements of both these functions. The fragmentation and dispersal of metropolitan regions and the simultaneous interconnection of multiple such regions mean that commuting, social reproduction and everyday life occur not within bounded cities, but increasingly within overlapping and splintered spaces defined by the megaregional built environment.[4] At the same time, however, megaregions are not easily 'represented' as spaces of everyday life the way the city is (Wachsmuth, 2014) – an important consideration given the centrality of place branding and boosterism to contemporary urban governance (Logan and Molotch, 2007; Boyle, 1999; Short, 1999). Meanwhile, thanks to the logistics revolution, the megaregional built environment which loosely circumscribes the space of social reproduction is also the space defining regional production and circulation possibilities (Sassen, 2009). The result is vast urban areas which are internally integrated in some but not all of the ways that the industrial and metropolitan cities were, and which have some but not all of the characteristics of larger interurban networks.

This periodization, summarized in Table 3.1, suggests two conclusions – one historical, one geographical – with respect to the specificity of the US megaregion. The first is that, to the extent that the megaregion represents a generalization of the prototypical form of megalopolis, it is a decidedly

Table 3.1   A built-environment-theoretical periodization of US urbanization

Period	Approximate dates	Transportation and communication technology	Internal relations	External relations
Industrial urbanization	1850–1940	Railroads, streetcars, steel ships	*Cities*: differentiated between industry and residence	Cities and agricultural hinterlands
Metropolitan urbanization	1940–1980	Highways	*Metropolitan areas*: comprising central city and extended suburbs	National interstate highway system
Regional urbanization	1980–present	Information technology and logistics	*Megaregions*: not functionally integrated	Globalization, but also megaregions

Source: Author

partial generalization. Gottmann's megalopolis had two key features: an enormous, polycentric morphology and an articulating function between local and global economic space. The former is certainly present in what are now referred to as megaregions, but the latter is not. As Gottmann (1976, p. 110) argued in his own preliminary generalization of the megalopolis concept, 'a necessary condition of a megalopolis is a hinge articulating two or more networks, one of them a national internal network, and another an international and overseas network'. Notwithstanding the Fordist-era centrality of the nation-state in this claim, which arguably no longer obtains in the neoliberal era, Gottmann identifies a specific, globalizing economic role played by the original northeast US megalopolis and a handful of other huge urban areas around the world. Attempting to apply the same standard to the Regional Plan Association's (2008) 11 US megaregions would be an absurdity. For example, the Piedmont Atlantic region, centred on the I-85 corridor connecting Atlanta and Charlotte, has the population size, overlapping commuting zones and economic interconnectedness to make it a plausible megalopolis according to Gottmann's criteria. But there is no hinge function, no privileged articulation of local or national economic space to the global economy. In fact, it may be that the very conditions that have given rise to regional urbanization as I have defined it here – the failure, in the face of relentless expansion of urban areas, of information and communications technology to transform the internal relations of cities as it has done with the global interurban network – have also rendered Gottmann's hinge function unnecessary or obsolete.

The second, related conclusion is that morphological similarities underlying very large urban areas worldwide do not necessarily imply any functional or economic similarities. The contemporary US urban growth pattern of constantly expanding urban areas without new transportation technology integrating these spaces is both productive of a distinctive political economy and cannot be assumed to be present in other historical and geographical contexts (see Section 3.5). Analyses which assume a correspondence between megaregional form and function, such as the consistent delineation of large urban areas through nighttime-light mapping (Florida et al., 2008), offer suggestive imagery but potentially obscure more than they reveal (see Harrison and Hoyler, 2015). In fact, the relationship between morphological and functional polycentrality is a fraught one (for example, Meijers, 2005; Cowell, 2010; Oort et al., 2010; Burger and Meijers, 2012; Vasanen, 2012), and morphology on its own says little except when placed in economic and institutional context.

3.5   COMPETITIVE URBAN POLICY, COMPETITIVE MEGAREGIONAL POLICY?

The megaregion's hybridity – city and urban network – sheds light on a major divergence between the actually existing political economy of US megaregions and a key assumption or prediction of megaregion scholars. The latter is the idea that megaregions are, or are becoming, competitive actors in the global economy. This proposition informs much of the US megaregions literature, including its orientation towards how megaregions interact with the global economy, current governance deficits, economic development strategies and proposed coordination mechanisms. The signal research statement so far is the recent edited volume *Megaregions: Planning for Global Competitiveness* (Ross, 2009).

In contrast to this policy-driven literature on megaregional competitiveness, though, the reality is that there are remarkably few instances of elites or policymakers undertaking competitiveness-oriented strategies at the megaregional scale in the US. The megaregions literature explains this fact via the governance challenges associated with making megaregions competitive. The preponderance of these challenges is identified as relating to either connectivity and the built environment – in particular transportation systems (Vega and Penne, 2008) and urban sustainable growth (Dewar and Epstein, 2007) – or economic development. These challenges are contextualized with respect to developments in Europe and Asia, which are generally presented as possessing more effectively coordinated and governed megaregional economies, and thus are held up as best practices for US policymakers.

While the governance and regulatory challenges associated with coordination at the megaregional scale are no doubt formidable, they are not the whole story. Here a comparison with the discourse on megalopolis 50 years ago is instructive. Megalopolis, after all, was also the subject of considerable public policy concern with respect to governance challenges. But the public policy response to megalopolis, both its initial uptake in the northeast US and then in the binational Great Lakes region, was predominantly one of service provision: how to adequately deliver and redistribute resources across an urban landscape of unprecedented size. The Twentieth Century Fund, the publisher of Gottmann's (1961) *Megalopolis: The Urbanized Northeastern Seaboard of the United States*, followed up on the success of the book a few years later with a short volume called *The Challenge of Megalopolis* (Von Eckardt, 1964). The latter identified in a digestible, graphic-heavy format the (generally redistributive) policy implications of Gottmann's study.

The contrast with contemporary policy discourse on megaregions is stark. While some US-based scholars (for example Benner and Pastor, 2011) and policy actors (for example Morrison Institute, 2011) have approached megaregions through an equity, redistribution or service-provision lens, the preponderance of research and policy has been firmly oriented around megaregions as economic competitiveness concerns (see Wheeler, 2015). It is therefore useful to add a regulatory dimension to the built environment periodization presented in the previous section. For megaregions are not only a product of a hybrid city/network built environment, but also of a neoliberal policy environment which has fundamentally transformed the aims and objects of urban governance. The post-1980s urban economic policy consensus can be summarized as follows:

- Enhancing economic competitiveness within global inter-urban competition is the basic goal of urban policy, as opposed to redressing national or regional sociospatial inequalities (Brenner, 2004). Cities are engines of economic advantage, not sites of economic disadvantage, and public investment should be leveraged to support the former rather than diminish the latter (Jessop, 2002; Theodore and Peck, 2012).
- The specific advantage of cities and regions is their capacity for innovation: this advantage must be nurtured through attracting talent and encouraging investment in 'creative' sectors of the economy (Florida, 2002).
- Traditional forms of municipal government are insufficient to properly encourage innovation and increase competitiveness: collaborative governance is needed between sectors and between individual jurisdictions within the larger urban region.
- Flexible policy circuits – ad hoc and project-oriented partnerships – are preferable to formal ones (Peck, 2011).

In the US, this neoliberal policy ideal has been promoted by prominent non-governmental institutions such as the US Chamber, the Brookings Institution and the Council on Competitiveness (2010), and globally by the OECD (Theodore and Peck, 2012) and the World Bank. Its major operationalization is through the discourse of urban competitiveness. The concept of competitiveness as applied to territories has been defined in countless ways (*inter alia* Frohberg and Hartmann, 1997; Begg, 1999; Budd and Hirmis, 2004; Turok, 2004; Delgado et al., 2012). Conceptualizations variously emphasize labour force skill, productivity, innovation and broader notions of well-being. Correspondingly, policies undertaken to improve competitiveness can be differentiated among a number of different axes (Brenner and Wachsmuth, 2012). They may follow a low-road strategy oriented towards lowering costs for capital, or a high-road strategy oriented towards innovation and new economic possibilities (Storper and Walker, 1989; Eisenschitz and Gough, 1996). They may target specific industries or sectors of the economy, and hence specific networks of regional, national or global competitors. However, policymakers understand this heightened need to compete, the basic assumption underlying competitiveness policy is that something can and should be done – that a locality's economic performance relative to national or global competitors can be significantly affected by policy, and that it is the role of governance actors to implement such policy.

This is precisely how scholars and policymakers have approached megaregions: as the units of competitiveness within a global space of competition. But, in practice, the outcome of the hybrid urban development which has given megaregions their distinctive spatial character has been to increase the prospects for interurban competition *within* megaregions. In other words, contrary to the assumptions of the literature, I argue here that megaregions are not becoming competitive actors within the global economy but rather are becoming a new space of competition. Megaregions represent a heightening of the imperative towards interurban competition but at a new spatial scale.

This argument can be substantiated empirically through an examination of the recent US trend toward 'competitive multi-city regionalism'. For many decades now, institutions of local elite economic governance in the US have been consolidating at the metropolitan scale. Chambers of commerce are now routinely metropolitan in scope, as are economic development organizations and the wide array of civic partnerships characteristic of neoliberal urban governance. However, a more recent trend – thus far unnoticed in the scholarly literature – has been the establishment of economic development partnerships between metropolitan areas. In 1973 there were only 12 such partnerships in the US; now there are 171. They range from coalitions of small towns, such as the East Central Illinois Super Region, to partnerships covering multiple cities containing millions of people, such as the Florida High Tech Corridor Council. Competitive multi-city regionalism is squarely a product of the era of regional urbanization. But while these partnerships are proliferating within US megaregions, they are not megaregional in scale.

As a brief example to substantiate this claim, Figure 3.1 shows the multi-city economic development partnerships at work in the state of Indiana. A few points can be made about this list. First, competitive multi-city regionalism has proliferated incredibly in recent years. Indiana (the 16th largest state by both population and urban density) contains 13 multi-city partnerships. Ten were founded since 2000, including six since

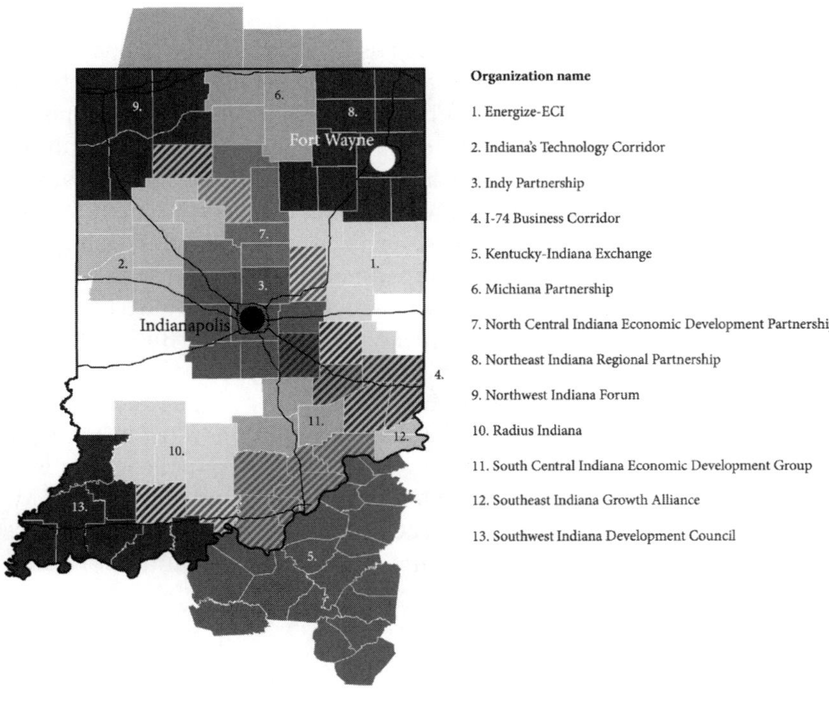

Source: Author

Figure 3.1 Multi-city regional economic development partnerships in Indiana

2008. Second, multi-city economic development partnerships are by no means mutually exclusive; the same organizations or city elites may well participate in several distinct but spatially overlapping regional projects. Third, the institutional capacities and strategic orientations of these partnerships vary widely, from marketing partnerships with no dedicated staff to large organizations with boards of directors and independent budgets. And finally, fourth, none of these partnerships looks like a megaregional partnership. Indiana's urban areas are generally considered to be part of the Great Lakes megaregion, and while there is a business alliance operating at that scale (the Great Lakes Metro Chambers Coalition, of which three of Indiana's chambers of commerce are members), elite activity is focused far more intently on the multi-city regional scale.

The situation in Indiana is a reasonable proxy for the rest of the country. In the era of regional urbanization, new forms of greater-than-metropolitan-scale economic strategies have proliferated. A full explanation for this phenomenon is far beyond the scope of this chapter, but I can point briefly to two important factors germane to the analysis I have been advancing. First, multi-city economic development partnerships have proliferated due to the increasing blurring of metropolitan labour and property markets, which has facilitated an endemic instability in local growth coalition formation. Second, they have proliferated due to the regional scope of key industries enabled by information technology and valorized under the neoliberal urban policy ideal – particularly logistics, higher education, and advanced manufacturing – which has introduced a centrifugal tendency into economic governance. But while these strategies have proliferated within megaregions, they are not megaregional strategies *per se*. In other words, US megaregions do not appear to be emerging as competitive actors in the global economy, as much scholarship and nearly the entirety of the megaregional policy literature suggests is or should be occurring. Instead, and in line with the arguments about the city/urban-network hybridity I have been advancing, megaregions appear to be emerging as variegated strategic terrains, upon which a multitude of differently scaled competitiveness strategies are being enacted.

3.6 CONCLUSION: DO MEGAREGIONS IMPLY MEGAREGIONALISM?

The preceding analysis is meant simultaneously to affirm the importance of the urbanization trend now frequently described with the term 'megaregion', and to cast significant doubt on the dominant interpretation of that trend within the US scholarly and policy literature. Much of the thrust of that literature suggests that the ongoing growth of US megaregions will lead to (or necessitates) megaregionalism as a policy project. But, given the overwhelming orientation of contemporary urban policy discourse towards economic competitiveness as the key object of urban governance, megaregionalism is only sensible to the extent that megaregions approximate or can be made to approximate strategic actors in the global economy.

By contrast, in stressing the essentially hybrid character of megaregions as both city and urban network, this chapter suggests that megaregions as strategic actors are unlikely to emerge. Instead, megaregions – sprawling, polycentric urban areas connected externally to new global economic spaces but not internally integrated in the manner of cities and metropolitan areas – have been encouraging and are likely to continue to encourage a wide range of local economic strategies at a variety of scales. Closer theoretical and empirical attention to those new forms of strategic action may indeed be the most fruitful way of identifying the multiple articulations between the megaregion as urban form and globalization as economic process.

NOTES

1. The standard synthetic reference points on the urban question are Saunders (1986) and Gottdiener (1994). More recently, for a scale-theoretical perspective, see Brenner (2000).
2. Although see Smith (2002) and subsequent work on globalization and gentrification for an exception.
3. The US Census Bureau recently redefined its measures of urban place, making longer-term comparisons difficult.
4. The well-documented increase in commuting flows across US metropolitan boundaries (Pisarski, 2006), alongside Moss and Qing's (2012) recent examination of the emergence of 'super commuting' across groups of metropolitan areas, provides important empirical evidence for this proposition, as well as confirmation of the basic parameters of the megaregions defined by the Regional Plan Association (2008) and others.

REFERENCES

Begg, I. (1999), Cities and competitiveness, *Urban Studies*, **36** (5–6), 795–809.

Benner, C. and M. Pastor (2011), 'Moving on up? Regions, megaregions, and the changing geography of social equity organizing', *Urban Affairs Review*, **47** (3), 315–348.

Berry, B.J.L. (1964), 'Cities as systems within systems of cities', *Papers in Regional Science*, **13** (1), 147–163.

Boyle, M. (1999), 'Growth machines and propaganda projects: a review of readings of the role of civic boosterism in the politics of local economic development', in A.E.G. Jonas and D. Wilson (eds), *The Urban Growth Machine: Critical Perspectives, Two Decades Later*, Albany, NY: State University of New York Press, pp. 55–70.

Brenner, N. (2000), 'The urban question as a scale question: reflections on Henri Lefebvre, urban theory and the politics of scale', *International Journal of Urban and Regional Research*, **24** (2), 361–378.

Brenner, N. (2003), 'Stereotypes, archetypes, and prototypes: three uses of superlatives in contemporary urban studies', *City & Community*, **2** (3), 205–216.

Brenner, N. (2004), 'Urban governance and the production of new state spaces in Western Europe, 1960–2000', *Review of International Political Economy*, **11** (3), 447–488.

Brenner, N. and D. Wachsmuth (2012), 'Territorial competitiveness: lineages, practices, ideologies', in S. Bishwapriya, L.J. Vale and C. Rosan (eds), *Planning Ideas That Matter: Livability, Territoriality, Governance and Reflective Practice*, Cambridge, MA: MIT Press, pp. 179–204.

Budd, L. and A. Hirmis (2004), 'Conceptual framework for regional competitiveness', *Regional Studies*, **38** (9), 1015–1028.

Burger, M. and E. Meijers (2012), 'Form follows function? Linking morphological and functional polycentricity', *Urban Studies*, **49** (5), 1127–1149.

Castells, M. (1977), *The Urban Question: A Marxist Approach*, translated by A. Sheridan, Cambridge, MA: MIT Press.

Castells, M. (2000), *The Rise of the Network Society: The Information Age, Volume 1*, 2nd edition, Malden, MA: Blackwell.

Council on Competitiveness (2010), *Collaborate: Leading Regional Innovation Clusters*, Washington, DC: CoC.

Cowell, M. (2010), 'Polycentric regions: comparing complementarity and institutional governance in the San Francisco Bay Area, the Randstad and Emilia-Romagna', *Urban Studies*, **47** (5), 945–965.

Cowen, D. (2010), 'A geography of logistics: market authority and the security of supply chains', *Annals of the Association of American Geographers*, **100** (3), 600–620.

Cronon, W. (1991), *Nature's Metropolis: Chicago and the Great West*, New York: W.W. Norton & Co.

Davis, M. (1990), *City of Quartz: Excavating the Future in Los Angeles*, New York: Verso.

Day, R.B. (1976), 'The theory of the long cycle: Kondratiev, Trotsky, Mandel', *New Left Review*, **99**, 67–82.

Dear, M.J. (1991), *The Postmodern Urban Condition*, London: Wiley & Sons.

De Lara, J.D. (2013), 'Goods movement and metropolitan inequality: global restructuring, commodity flows, and metropolitan development', in P.V. Hall and M. Hesse (eds), *Cities, Regions and Flows*, London: Routledge, pp. 75–91.

Delgado, M., C. Ketels, M.E. Porter and S. Stern (2012), 'The determinants of national competitiveness', *National Bureau of Economic Research Working Paper*, 18249, Cambridge, MA: National Bureau of Economic Research.

Dewar, M. and D. Epstein (2007), 'Planning for "megaregions" in the United States', *Journal of Planning Literature*, **22** (2), 108–124.

Doxiadis, C.A. (1966), *Emergence and Growth of an Urban Region: The Developing Detroit Area, Volume 1: Analysis*, Detroit, MI: Detroit Edison Company.

Doxiadis, C.A. (1967), *Emergence and Growth of an Urban Region: The Developing Detroit Area, Volume 2: Future Alternatives*, Detroit, MI: Detroit Edison Company.

Doxiadis, C.A. (1968), 'The emerging Great Lakes megalopolis', *Proceedings of the Institute of Electrical and Electronics Engineers*, **56** (4), 402–424.

Doxiadis, C.A. (1970), *Emergence and Growth of an Urban Region: The Developing Detroit Area, Volume 3: A Concept for Future Development*, Detroit, MI: Detroit Edison Company.

Doxiadis, C.A. (1974), *Ecumenopolis: The Inevitable City of the Future*, New York: W.W. Norton & Co.

Eisenschitz, A. and J. Gough (1996), 'The contradictions of neo-Keynesian local economic strategy', *Review of International Political Economy*, **3** (3), 434–458.

Fishman, R. (2000), 'The American planning tradition: an introduction and interpretation', in R. Fishman (ed.), *The American Planning Tradition: Culture and Policy*, Washington, DC: Woodrow Wilson Center Press, pp. 1–29.

Florida, R. (2002), *The Rise of the Creative Class: And How It's Transforming Work, Leisure, Community, and Everyday Life*, New York: Basic Books.

Florida, R. (2010), *The Great Reset: How the Post-Crash Economy Will Change the Way We Live and Work*, New York: Harper.

Florida, R., T. Gulden and C. Mellander (2008), 'The rise of the mega-region', *Cambridge Journal of Regions, Economy and Society*, **1** (3), 459–476.

Freeman, C. and F. Louçã (2001), *As Time Goes By: From the Industrial Revolutions to the Information Revolution*, New York: Oxford University Press.

Friedmann, J. and G. Wolff (1982), 'World city formation: an agenda for research and action', *International Journal of Urban and Regional Research*, **6** (2), 319–344.

Frohberg, K. and M. Hartmann (1997), 'Comparing measures of competitiveness', *Institute of Agricultural Development in Central and Eastern Europe – Discussion Paper*, No. 2, Halle: IAMO.

Geddes, P. (1915), *Cities in Evolution: An Introduction to the Town Planning Movement and to the Study of Civics*, London: Williams & Norgate.

Glass, M.R. (2015), 'Conflicting spaces of governance in the imagined Great Lakes megaregion', in J. Harrison and M. Hoyler (eds), *Megaregions: Globalization's New Urban Form?* Cheltenham, UK and Northampton, MA, USA: Edward Elgar, pp. 119–145.

Glaeser, E.L. (2007), 'Do regional economies need regional coordination?' in K.S. Goldfield (ed.), *The Economic Geography of Megaregions*, Princeton, NJ: Princeton University Press, pp. 11–57.

Goddard, S.B. (1994), *Getting There: The Epic Struggle Between Road and Rail in the American Century*, Chicago, IL: University of Chicago Press.

Gordon, D. (1978), 'Capitalist development and the history of American cities', in W.K. Tabb and L. Sawers (eds), *Marxism and the Metropolis*, New York: Oxford University Press, pp. 25–63.

Gottdiener, M. (1994), *The Social Production of Urban Space*, 2nd edition, Austin, TX: University of Texas Press.

Gottmann, J. (1961), *Megalopolis: The Urbanized Northeastern Seaboard of the United States*, New York: Twentieth Century Fund.

Gottmann, J. (1976), 'Megapolitan systems around the world', *Ekistics*, **41** (243), 109–113.

Graham, S. and S. Marvin (2001), *Splintering Urbanism: Networked Infrastructures, Technological Mobilities and the Urban Condition*, New York: Routledge.

Halbert, L., K. Pain and A. Thierstein (2006), 'European polycentricity and emerging mega-city regions: "one size fits all" policy?' *Built Environment*, **32** (2), 206–218.

Hall, P. (1999), 'Planning for the mega-city: a new eastern Asian urban form?', in J. Brotchie, P. Newton, P. Hall and J. Dickey (eds), *East West Perspectives on 21st Century Urban Development: Sustainable Eastern and Western Cities in the New Millennium*, Aldershot: Ashgate, pp. 3–36.

Harrison, J. and M. Hoyler (2015), 'Megaregions: foundations, frailties, futures', in J. Harrison and M. Hoyler (eds), *Megaregions: Globalization's New Urban Form?* Cheltenham, UK and Northampton, MA, USA: Edward Elgar, pp. 1–28.

Harvey, D. (1989a), 'From managerialism to entrepreneurialism: the transformation in urban governance in late capitalism', *Geografiska Annaler B*, **71** (1), 3–17.

Harvey, D. (1989b), *The Urban Experience*, Baltimore, MD: Johns Hopkins University Press.

Harvey, D. (1989c), *The Condition of Postmodernity: An Enquiry Into the Origins of Cultural Change*. Cambridge, MA and Oxford: Blackwell.

Jessop, B. (2002), 'Liberalism, neoliberalism, and urban governance: a state-theoretical perspective', *Antipode*, **34** (3), 452–472.

Lang, R.E. and D. Dhavale (2005), 'Beyond Megalopolis: exploring America's new megapolitan geography', *Metropolitan Institute Census Report Series*, 05:01, Alexandria, VA: The Metropolitan Institute at Virginia Tech.

Leman, A.B. and I.A. Leman (eds) (1976), *Great Lakes Megalopolis: From Civilization to Ecumenization*, Ottawa: Urban Affairs Canada.

Logan, J. and H. Molotch (2007), *Urban Fortunes: The Political Economy of Place*, 2nd edition, Los Angeles and Berkeley, CA: University of California Press.

Mandel, E. (1980), *Long Waves of Capitalist Development*, Cambridge: Cambridge University Press.

Marx, K. (1973), *Grundrisse*, translated by M. Nicolaus, New York: Vintage Books.

Meijers, E. (2005), 'Polycentric urban regions and the quest for synergy: is a network of cities more than the sum of the parts?', *Urban Studies*, **42** (4), 765–781.

Meller, H. (1993), 'Some reflections on the concept of megalopolis and its use by Patrick Geddes and Lewis Mumford', in T. Barker and A. Sutcliffe (eds), *Megalopolis: The Giant City in History*, London: St. Martin's Press, pp. 116–129.

Morrison Institute (2011), *Watering the Sun Corridor: Managing Choices in Arizona's Megapolitan Area*, Arizona: Morrison Institute for Public Policy.

Moss, M.L. and C. Qing (2012), *The Emergence of the 'Super-Commuter'*, New York: Rudin Center for Transportation.

Mumford, L. (1961), *The City in History: Its Origins, Its Transformations, and Its Prospects*, New York: Harcourt, Brace & World.

Nelson, A.C. and R.E. Lang (2011), *Megapolitan America: A New Vision for Understanding America's Metropolitan Geography*, Chicago, IL: APA Planners Press.

Oort, F.v., M. Burger and O. Raspe (2010), 'On the economic foundation of the urban network paradigm: spatial integration, functional integration and economic complementarities within the Dutch Randstad', *Urban Studies*, **47** (4), 725–748.

Park, R.E., E.W. Burgess and R.D. McKenzie (1925), *The City*, Chicago, IL: University of Chicago Press.

Peck, J. (2011), 'Geographies of policy: from transfer-diffusion to mobility-mutation', *Progress in Human Geography*, **35** (6), 773–797.

Pell, C. (1966), *Megalopolis Unbound: The Supercity and the Transportation of Tomorrow*, New York: Frederick A. Praeger.

Perez, C. (2002), *Technological Revolutions and Financial Capital: The Dynamics of Bubbles and Golden Ages*, Cheltenham, UK and Northampton, MA, USA: Edward Elgar.

Pisarski, A.E. (2006), *Commuting in America III: The Third National Report on Commuting Patterns and Trends*, NCHRP Report 550, TCRP Report 110, Washington, DC: Transportation Research Board.

Regional Plan Association (2008), *America 2050: An Infrastructure Vision for 21st Century America*, New York: RPA.

Ross, C.L. (ed.) (2009), *Megaregions: Planning for Global Competitiveness*, Washington, DC: Island Press.

Sassen, S. (2001), *The Global City: New York, London, Tokyo*, 2nd edition, Princeton, NJ: Princeton University Press.

Sassen, S. (2009), 'Novel spatial formats: megaregions and global intercity geographies', in C.L. Ross (ed.), *Megaregions: Planning for Global Competitiveness*, Washington, DC: Island Press, pp. 219–249.

Saunders, P. (1986), *Social Theory and the Urban Question*, 2nd edition, New York: Routledge.

Scott, A.J. (1988), *Metropolis: From the Division of Labor to Urban Form*, Berkeley and Los Angeles, CA: University of California Press.

Scott, A.J. (2011), 'Emerging cities of the third wave', *City*, **15** (3–4), 289–321.

Sheller, M. and J. Urry (2000), 'The city and the car', *International Journal of Urban and Regional Research*, **24** (4), 737–757.

Short, J.R. (1999), 'Urban imagineers: boosterism and the representation of cities', in A.E.G. Jonas and D. Wilson (eds), *The Urban Growth Machine: Critical Perspectives, Two Decades Later*, Albany, NY: State University of New York Press, pp. 37–54.

Smith, N. (2002), 'New globalism, new urbanism: gentrification as global urban strategy', *Antipode*, **34** (3), 427–450.

Smith, N. (2008), *Uneven Development: Nature, Capital, and the Production of Space*, 3rd edition, Athens, GA: University of Georgia Press.

Soja, E.W. (1989), *Postmodern Geographies: The Reassertion of Space in Critical Social Theory*, New York: Verso.

Soja, E.W. (2011), 'Regional urbanization and the end of the metropolis era', in G. Bridge and S. Watson (eds), *The New Blackwell Companion to the City*, Oxford: Wiley-Blackwell.

Storper, M. and R. Walker (1989), *The Capitalist Imperative: Territory, Technology, and Industrial Growth*, Cambridge, MA: Blackwell.

Taylor, P.J. and R.E. Lang (2004), 'The shock of the new: 100 concepts describing recent urban change', *Environment and Planning A*, **36** (6), 951–958.

Theodore, N. and J. Peck (2012), 'Framing neoliberal urbanism: translating "commonsense" urban policy across the OECD zone', *European Urban and Regional Studies*, **19** (1), 20–41.

Turok, I. (2004), 'Cities, regions and competitiveness', *Regional Studies*, **38** (9), 1069–1083.

Vasanen, A. (2012), 'Functional polycentricity: examining metropolitan spatial structure through the connectivity of urban sub-centres', *Urban Studies*, **49** (16), 3627–3644.

Vega, H.L. and L. Penne (2008), 'Governance and institutions of transportation investments in U.S. mega-regions', *Transport*, **23** (3), 279–286.

Von Eckardt, W. (1964), *The Challenge of Megalopolis*, New York: Twentieth Century Fund.

Wachsmuth, D. (2014), 'City as ideology: reconciling the explosion of the city form with the tenacity of the city concept', *Environment and Planning D*, **32** (1), 75–90.

Walker, R. (1981), 'A theory of suburbanization: capitalism and the construction of urban space in the United States', in M. Dear and A.J. Scott (eds), *Urbanization and Urban Planning in Capitalist Society*, New York: Methuen, pp. 383–429.

Webster, D. (1995), 'Mega-urbanization in ASEAN: new phenomenon or transitional phase to the "Los Angeles World City"'? in T.G. McGee and I.M. Robinson (eds), *The Mega-Urban Regions of Southeast Asia*, Vancouver: University of British Columbia Press, pp. 27–41.

Wheeler, S.M. (2009), 'Regions, megaregions, and sustainability', *Regional Studies*, **43** (6), 863–876.

Wheeler, S.M. (2015), 'Five reasons why megaregional planning works against sustainability', in J. Harrison and M. Hoyler (eds), *Megaregions: Globalization's New Urban Form?* Cheltenham, UK and Northampton, MA, USA: Edward Elgar, pp. 97–118.

Williams, R. (1973), *The Country and the City*, Oxford: Oxford University Press.

Xu, J. and A.G.O. Yeh (eds) (2011), *Governance and Planning of Mega-City Regions: An International Comparative Perspective*, New York: Routledge.

4. Beyond globalization: a historical urban development approach to understanding megaregions

Alex Schafran

4.1 INTRODUCTION

Geographers are no more insusceptible to the cult of newness than fashion designers or gadget heads. Especially for those of us who follow the movements of economic activity or chart changes in urban growth patterns and linkages between places, there is constant temptation to look upon the horizon and declare a particular phenomenon 'new'. Few phenomena have engendered such wide-eyed hysteria, and produced so many tangled neologisms, as globalization; a generally ill-defined über-force which has somehow made very smart people forget their history. For as the geographer Richard Walker (1996, p. 60) noted during an earlier wave of 'obsession with globalization', not only does a focus on the 'new' often ignore history, it 'runs the risk of erasing geography, setting back the clock to the days of featureless plains in location theory'.

The study of megaregions and its variants – from Gottmann's (1961) 'megalopolis' to 'mega-city regions' (Hall and Pain, 2006) and 'megapolitan areas' (Lang and Dhavale, 2005) – is not immune to the conceit of newness either. There is little doubt that the current size and scope of intertwined urbanization is unprecedented – these urban regions are undoubtedly larger than at any time in history, no doubt more complex and have a greater quantity and variety of movements, networks, connections and intertwined spaces. Yet the idea that either large conurbations of interconnected urban activity or sizable polycentric metropolitan regions are somehow *entirely* new is to ignore more than a century of urban history.

In fitting with the aim of this book, which is to bring a more critical eye to megaregional scholarship than has at times been the case over the past decade, the goal of this chapter is to assert a more historicized perspective in megaregional research – one that sees the size of megaregions as new but which interprets their form, their processes of formation and their existence as a geographic scale through the more jaded eyes of urban and regional history. The megaregion is, after all, a critically important scale of analysis for contemporary geography, but to maintain its analytical power we must use it more critically and more historically to properly harness its power for both understanding and intervention. This means focusing on the broader process of megaregional formation as *an urban process* – a process which is not entirely new, nor is it entirely linked to either globalization or pure economic geography, or to the movements of major firms. This is also about transportation, housing, infrastructure development, race and class segregation, and so on. In short, all of the pieces which are part of the urban puzzle are part of the megaregional phenomenon, and this being the case they must be built into our analyses.

To develop this argument, I begin by examining basic contemporary definitions of megaregions, focusing in particular on a group of under-standings dominated by economic geographers concerned with globalization – in particular, the idea of 'global cities' and urban hierarchies – which I argue helps drive this largely ahistorical narrative. One key thread of recent megaregional research has been dominated by an economic geography concerned with post-industrial hierarchy, rendering megaregions not only ahistorical but as places where the majority of the population and institutions are not considered economic or political actors. Yet in one of the many ironies of megaregional research, it is from a generally ignored piece by two of global cities theory's greatest proponents, Peter Taylor and Kathy Pain, that I pull a simple but historically rooted distinction between two major types of megaregions – a theoretical framing which is developed in the second section of the chapter. I want to argue that their idea of a megaregionality informed by two different urbanization processes – one based around an expansionist primate city, the other based around the fusion of more equal smaller cities – deserves to become an operational foundation for megaregional research (Taylor and Pain, 2007).

I then attempt to illustrate this framework using examples from Northern California, Northern England and Greater Paris, taking a whirl-wind tour through their historical development as megaregions. These examples help demonstrate the utility of this process-based understanding of megaregions and my assertion of both history and the functional components of urban development – transportation, housing, power politics, and so on – as methodological pillars of megaregional analysis. They also point us toward what I argue is a more satisfying and more useful definition of megaregionality as an urbanization process. This is particularly important given the longstanding concern with political intervention at this new urban scale – intervention whose difficulty is not just a question of scale, but one of complex power relations, inequalities and imbalances, and political divisions which have roots going back centuries. Finally, I conclude with a brief discussion of why this chapter is necessary, which, I argue, has everything to do with the long and unfortunate shadow of Chicago and Los Angeles.

4.2   DEFINING MEGAREGIONS

> Megaregions are networks of metropolitan centers and their surrounding areas. (Ross, 2009, p. 1)

> Mega-regions are integrated sets of cities and their surrounding suburban hinterlands across which labour and capital can be reallocated at very low cost. (Florida et al., 2008, p. 459)

For a concept which has grown significantly as an analytical tool over the past decade, there is little consensus as to the definition of megaregions. Part of this can be attributed to a mish-mash of related terms – megapolitan region, polycentric mega-city region – and to the geographic and disciplinary diversity of megaregional scholarship. From its origins in the United States (Gottmann, 1961) through the European 'blue banana' (Brunet, 1989) and the rise of Asian megaurban areas (McGee and Robinson, 1995; Xue-qiang and Si-ming, 1990), there is now a diverse and highly globalized set of writings about these rapidly expanding urban spaces.

As I have argued elsewhere, the overwhelming common thread – a fact which may seem tautological – is an obsession with bigness. Megaregions are generally defined as massive urban spaces, 'an ever expanding totality' (Schafran, 2014, p. 588). In some definitions, this results in megaregions the size of an entire country (see Italy in Florida et al., 2008), or vast regions of the United States which previously were named the Midwest (see America 2050, 2008).

A second critical thread is the idea of networks and flows, the forces which are driving certain forms of megaregionality. This is generally the domain of economic geographers, often focusing on the growth of information economies and global cities – whether from the American perspective of Ross and Florida (quoted above) or the more European perspective of Peter Hall, Peter Taylor and Kathy Pain. This is a literature heavily intertwined with urban transformation under conditions of globalization and it should come as no surprise that the writings of Allen Scott (2001; Scott and Storper, 2003), Saskia Sassen (1991, 2001) and Manuel Castells (2000) factor heavily in these discussions. Much of the empirical analysis, for instance in Hall and Pain's (2006) influential collection on polycentricity in Europe,[1] examines advanced producer services (APS). Observing their location in close proximity to one another they argue this is resulting in clusters of knowledge-centric economies becoming 'a central feature of the new post-industrial economy' (Hall and Pain, 2006, p. 4).

Like Florida, Hall and Pain (2006, p. 3) define megaregions, in part, based on 'a new functional division of labour'. Their focus is on the 'functional networks' which bind places together, whether it is low-cost airlines, certain forms of business services, or other movements of the wealthy, the powerful, or the 'creative'. Unsurprisingly, this approach leads to a constant discussion of megaregions in the language of hierarchies and globality. The problem with these post-industrial economy/ globalization definitions of megaregions is not that they are incorrect, but that they only offer a partial explanation of the phenomena of megaregionality. Moreover, they often overshadow other components of megaregionality which are just as critical to understanding what is happening on the ground. Crucially they tend to prioritize a narrow geoeconomic logic (based on firms and the qualities of this movement or that movement) for their explanation, over and above considering other aspects which fit within a broader geohistorical and/or geopolitical explanatory framework. Even though many of the economic geographers would argue that they focus on 'process', they tend to focus only on a few economic processes, rather than the deeper and broader question of the urbanization process in general. Surely globalization and the growing power of APS firms are critical to the formation of large, interconnected urban spaces, but this is certainly not the only important process. The differences between and within megaregions – a central concern for another major theme in the literature, which is political and policy intervention at this megascale – are often lost amidst a hail of numbers, rankings and schematic maps.

Ironically, a clearer understanding of the historical process of megaregional urbanization – as opposed to simply the economic processes which help but do not exclusively drive this process – is buried in a contribution by two of the aforementioned European global city theorists to one of the foundational contemporary American texts on the process (Regional Plan Association and Lincoln Institute of Land Policy, 2007) – Kathy Pain and Peter Taylor. Perhaps something got lost on the way across the Atlantic, and in the remaining text, I attempt to explain their idea and illustrate in more depth its practical use in advancing megaregional research.

4.3   TWO PROCESSES OF MEGAREGIONAL FORMATION

In 2007, two influential American urban think tanks, the Regional Plan Association (RPA) and the Lincoln Institute of Land Policy, gathered a group of urban scholars in Northern California for a meeting on megaregions. The meeting included papers by scholars and policy experts relating to specific megaregions in the United States, with one invited contribution from Europe – a paper by Peter Taylor and Kathy Pain.

The paper 'Polycentric mega-city regions: exploratory research from Western Europe' was seemingly a summary of some efforts of the POLYNET research group which produced the aforementioned Hall and Pain edited book on polycentric mega-city regions. Yet towards the end of the text, Taylor and Pain depart from the economic geography of their original work on the POLYNET project and instead wedge in a section entitled 'Making sense of mega-city regions as a theory of process'. Building on ideas from the original POLYNET report which were not fleshed out (Taylor et al., 2006), they identify two types of megaregional formation – one, which they consider a form of Jacobsian regional growth (Jacobs, 1984), essentially relies on an expanding primate city, á la Paris or London: 'The new scale of expansion in this process', they write, 'means that the city-region is enveloping previously separate cities as well as promoting growth in settlements not previously deemed to be "cities"' (Taylor and Pain, 2007, p. 65). The second process – eschewing the postmodern love for neologisms, they call the former Process A, the latter Process B – is the weaving together of proximate cities of more equal size, á la the Randstad in the Netherlands or Germany's Rhine-Ruhr region. In their own words, 'large proximate cities become linked but there is no enveloping and upgrading of existing cities from a single centre' (Taylor and Pain, 2007, p. 65).

Most importantly, Taylor and Pain do not see these processes – which function in many ways as ideal types – as mutually exclusive. In the eastern United States they argue, we see a hybrid, with New York acting as a Process A 'primate' amidst a much larger Process B 'megaregion', which is being formed along the lines of an American Randstad (at a very American scale). They go so far as to argue that this theoretical contribution is more important to the megaregional conversation than the empirical work which dominates the paper (and their previous work as part of the European POLYNET project, see Hall and Pain, 2006). It is the differences between these two processes and the forms of hybridity evident virtually everywhere which are critically misunderstood or ignored by policy. The agenda is thus: 'A deeper understanding of the processes – A and B – operating in different regions, and their process and material infrastructure requirements, is needed' (Taylor and Pain, 2007, p. 65).

Unfortunately, this theoretical framing seems to have been largely ignored by scholars, with the critical exception of Daryl Martin's (2010) work on Northern England (discussed below). Moreover, Taylor and Pain do not extrapolate on the variety of hybrid forms of A + B, on more specific examples of the historical formation of these different types of the megaregions, or more critically, that both Processes A and B were set underway in every contemporary case at the earliest stages of the industrial revolution, not in the post-industrial rush for tech companies, finance capital and law firms.[2] Examples of these processes abound, both in the globalized, wealthy megaregions which they have studied and in smaller, less powerful regions, where one sees that both processes are foundational to urbanization writ large.

Moreoever, they do not develop the theory in much depth, glossing over critical issues in understanding the specifics of megaregional formation – for instance how to separate suburbanization from megaregionality in Process A type cities, or how to separate relatively new megaregions from ones which are a century old. In this next section, I attempt to illustrate the utility of Taylor and Pain's theory, albeit in a language of power, history and urban development as opposed to economic hierarchy. I work to flesh out their simplified A/B framework through three examples of different forms of megaregional development: Greater Paris, which is a prototypical A process in a very old region but a very new megaregion; Northern England, which is a classic (albeit less wealthy) and very old B process, albeit with a form of hybridity based on its relationship with London; and Northern California, which is a B à A hybrid that is simultaneously new and old. In doing so I maintain the focus on what is (not) driven by globalization, attempting to build a more specific understanding about what is 'megaregionalization' and how it relates to suburbanization and other forms of regional change.

4.4 THREE MEGAREGIONS IN FORMATION

4.4.1 The Island of France

Paris is a prototypical primate city-region, but one where there is some debate as to whether it is a megaregion in the first place (Figure 4.1). Frederic Gilli (2002, 2005, 2009), for example, has strenuously argued that the formal region – the Île-de-France – has in fact jumped its borders to connect to surrounding small cities which were never part of the

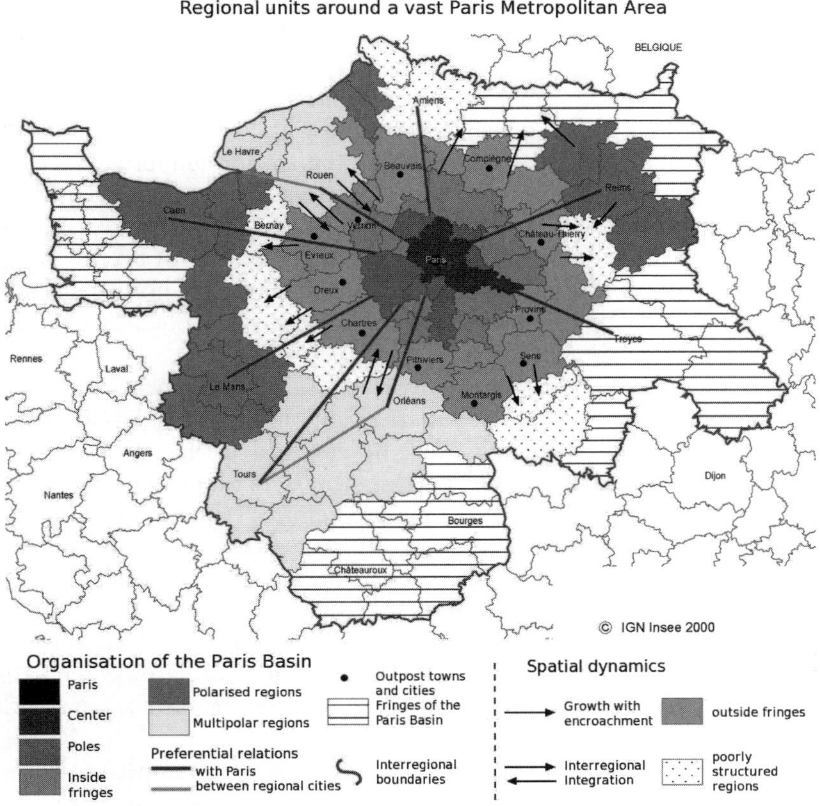

Figure 4.1   Greater Paris in flux

region historically. Ludovic Halbert (2006, 2008), writing as part of the POLYNET project, is more sceptical, in part because the APS firms that are the holy grail of globalization studies have remained firmly rooted in the traditional region. While Halbert's *economic* analysis is spot-on, it is Gilli (2005) who combines political-historical and economic analysis in a way that I believe can advance megaregional research.

When considered as the Île-de-France region, Paris has a population of almost 12 million people, or almost one in five residents of France. The region is both the administrative and financial and economic centre of France, with a regional GDP approaching 30 per cent of national GDP (Institut National de la Statistique et des Études Économiques, 2010).

Although much of its nineteenth-century industrial economic power
was built upon its central position in the French rail network – all roads
lead to Paris and all trains once terminated there – the core of the region
is some distance from other major cities. In an almost classic example
of the Jacobsian model which Taylor and Pain discuss, Paris quickly
absorbed most of its immediate neighbours either through formal annexation (Montmartre) or through suburbanization. Versailles, set up as an
almost rural counter-pole to Paris by Louis XIV, is now a large residential
bourgeois suburb; Saint Denis, the ancient burial ground of French kings,
is now the heart of the semi-post-industrial suburbs to the north – a centre
of ethnic diversity, long-time struggles with racialized inequality and new
white-collar office development.

Most of the history of 20th-century Parisian development is not one
of megaregionality, but one of suburbanization. State-led developments
such as La Défense – a major office development designed to compete
with Manhattan and the parallel development of London's Canary Wharf
for corporate headquarters and financial services (Chabard and Picon-
Lefebvre, 2012) – and the five primarily residential *ville nouvelles* (new
towns) in the outer suburbs (Deit, 1973) drove urban expansion within
the Île-de-France, but largely did not jump into neighbouring regions.
Illustrating this, a massive transportation system was built internal to the
Île-de-France region – the RER commuter network (Gaillard, 1991). Paris
expanded considerably during the 20th century, but it was not a network
of previously separate regions.

It is only since the late 1980s that Paris (tentatively) jumped scales – a
timeframe that would concur with Hall and Pain's argument that this is
the case in all megaregions. But I would argue this jumping had less to do
with globalization and information economies and more to do with old
fashioned urban development considerations – transportation, housing
costs and the need for a port – extending the region's reach outwards to
Bassin parisien (Paris Basin) and the ancient cathedral towns of Chartres,
Orléans, Rouen, Amiens and Reims. Indeed, no single factor is more
important to Paris's megaregionality than the development of the high-
speed rail system – the *Train à Grande Vitesse* (TGV).

After the success of the first line to Lyon, which largely bypassed neighbouring regions, lines were built to Tours and Le Mans (opened 1989),
Lille and Calais (opened 1993), which opened the Haute-Picardie commuter hub between Amiens and Saint-Quentin, and more recently the line
to Strasbourg connected small cities like Reims, Nancy and Metz. Cities
like Orléans (133 km) and Reims (144 km), fundamental parts of French
history which were near Paris but certainly not part of the region and not
part of the major commute shed, are now less than an hour away by train.[3]

This growth of TGV lines coincided with a steady increase in Parisian housing prices. Housing crises of one type or another have been a fact of life in Paris since before Haussmann and the creeping gentrification of the past 30 years has put pressure on middle and lower-income Parisians alike. The incomes provided by the uptick in APS jobs documented by Halbert (2006, 2008) may have been enough to mark Paris in the hierarchy of globality and pay for more expensive daily TGV transport, but not necessarily enough to get into the now globalized Parisian property market.[4] If you pay attention to the jobs, á la Halbert, Paris is less megaregional; if the focus is commuters or urban sprawl (Charmes, 2009), the borders have been breached.

A second form of megaregionality is driven by recent attempts by the city of Paris to connect to the Atlantic ocean (Ducruet et al., 2012). As an inland city in an age where container traffic is increasingly critical to global trade, the city of Paris – which has long dumped its garbage far downriver – has launched a complex set of interlinked projects aimed at turning the Le Havre–Paris corridor into a linear port. The goal is to create one of Western Europe's largest ports to compete with Rotterdam and the Randstad. This is clearly a globalization-driven part of the process, albeit one with very old economy roots – urban history could be written (and has by some) as a story of competition between cities for trade.

Both types of megaregionality – transport links with nearby cities which fuel commuting relationships and industrial infrastructure projects driven by the central city – are driven in this case by an über-powerful core city. While there have long been trade links, Le Havre and the Cathedral cities have fundamentally different regional identities. They are also sensitive to being swept up by a powerful and expanding central city, which like London is both the political and economic capital. There is a massive power imbalance in this type of monocentric Process A megaregionality, one that has little to do with 'globality' and everything to do with centuries of primate city development. Paris's relationship with the cities it is adding to its sphere is not just about APS firms, but about the very fact that this is not the Randstad, or the Rhine-Ruhr, or even the more in-between megaregions such as the Boston–Washington corridor or the Midwest in the United States. Equality amongst urban actors is not even remotely possible and has not been for centuries. Paris may be a megaregion but it is not truly polycentric and likely never will be. Indeed the political possibilities of intervention and planning will always be coloured by the stark power gaps produced by centuries of Parisian dominance in its eponymous basin. To be completely accurate this monocentric megaregionality should be known as *megaregional suburbanization* in recognition that this 'network of metropolitan centers' (Ross, 2009, p. 1) has not in any way altered fundamental core-periphery relations that have defined classic French patterns of urbanization for centuries.

4.4.2   England's 'Northern Way'

The urbanized area straddling the Pennine hills between Liverpool and Manchester in the west and Leeds, Bradford and Sheffield in the east is arguably the world's original industrial megaregion. A hyper-complex network of small and medium-sized cities originally centred around a canal and railroad system, the region does not have a single locality with a million people,[5] but it does boast five of the ten largest cities in the United Kingdom, all of similar size – Leeds (751 000), Sheffield (553 000), Bradford (522 000), Manchester (503 000) and Liverpool (466 000). Smaller areas such as Wigan, Wakefield and Kirklees are all in the top 25, with sizable communities in other older industrial cities (Warrington, St Helens, Bolton and Huddersfield).

Figure 4.2 shows a new census category of built-up areas which attempts to capture urbanization as opposed to purely political divisions or census geography. It gives a sense of the major conurbations, and of the series

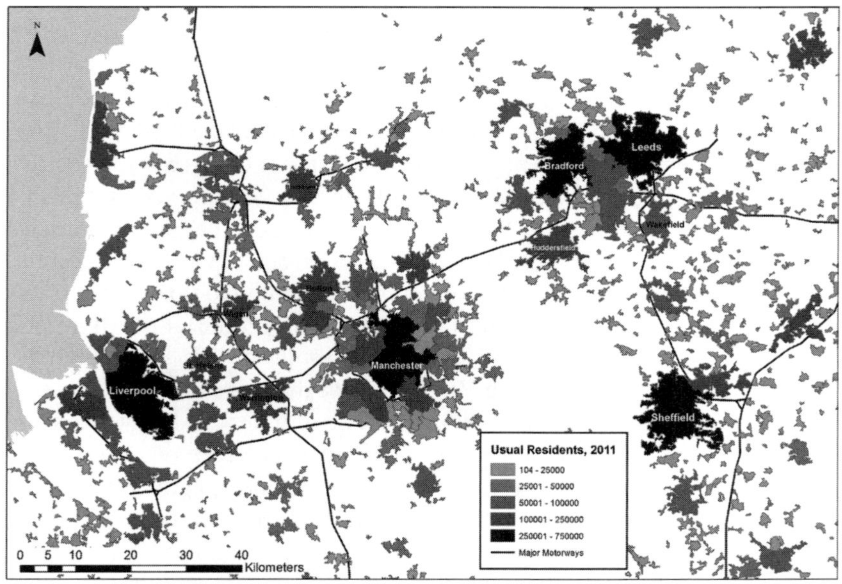

Source: Author, derived from UK Office of National Statistics.

Figure 4.2   The urbanized landscape of Northern England

of clustered cities which have interconnected commuting relations but are very different from the Process A cities of Paris or London (Taylor et al., 2009). This megaregion is home to very few 'new towns'[6] and the majority of suburban development has occurred in old industrial cities and agricultural villages. Bradford residents commute to Leeds; Leeds residents commute to Manchester or Sheffield; and the smaller industrial cities (Huddersfield, Halifax, Wigan, Warrington) which are 'proper' cities in their own right – each has an industrial heritage and your classic city centre – live in a complicated social and economic space, both separate and apart from the larger regions (Manchester City Region, Leeds City Region) of which they are technically a part. Every single one of the principal communities in the megaregion has preindustrial roots and they have been connected economically in urban ways since the advent of canal and rail traffic. With a population similar to the Netherlands and the lack of a truly dominant principal city, Northern England functions as an almost ideal-type for a Process B megaregion. It is not too dissimilar in industrial history or urban structure from the Rhine-Ruhr or Randstad (cf. Martin, 2010).[7]

The megaregionality of Northern England also has little or nothing to do with globalization – unless you define the early wool trade and textile manufacturing that built much of Northern England as the cornerstone of our current globalized system.[8] To argue even that contemporary globalization is now the driving force behind political action in this area is a controversial subject, for it remains a point of debate – at least in the north – whether efforts to plan and engage on the megaregional scale are a response to global economic pressures, to the political and economic weight of its national rival, London, or both.

It should not be a surprise, therefore, that much recent scholarly discussion of megaregionality in this area focuses on specific political attempts to weave together disparate sectoral and provincial actors to create a more unified planning and economic development apparatus in the North of England. The most prominent policy intervention was dubbed 'The Northern Way', a now abandoned policy scheme designed in 2004 as a response to the increasing economic dominance of the wealthy London megaregion (González, 2006; Goodchild and Hickman, 2006; Taylor et al., 2010).

The focus of the Northern Way on the economic divide (Morgan, 2002) between north and south (read London) is also a clue to the particular form of hybridity of this polycentric megaregion. For unlike its Dutch, German or US counterparts, it exists in a nation-state dominated by a Process A prototype in London. Whereas the Dutch and German cities never had to compete (directly) with London, Northern England did; more importantly, London was also making the decisions.

This is not to say that the struggles of the Liverpool–Manchester–Bradford–Leeds–Sheffield region are exclusively about the political power of the wealthier, more politically powerful – and yes, more global – London. For all the thinking which has been done about the future of the region, it seems to lack a name. The 'M62 corridor', the basis of another, more futuristic 21st-century plan for a linear megaregion by architect Will Alsop, excludes Sheffield (Alsop and Hulme, 2005; see Martin, 2010 for discussion). This namelessness is perhaps evidence of the incredible importance of micro-regional identities, intense rivalries between neighbouring cities and counties. Culturally, Liverpool versus Manchester is not simply a football match; Lancashire versus Yorkshire is not only the War of the Roses. With the racialization of Bradford and the ascendance of Leeds as a new back-office and financial centre, rivalries (based on class, race and ethnicity) exist even within formally recognized city-regions within the broader metropole.

Yet this lack of political or cultural unity is in part what makes this northern English agglomeration a true megaregion. As I will discuss more in the following section, megaregions should be defined in part by the fact that their urban networks exceed any attempts to unify them politically and likely always will.

4.4.3   Northern California

Northern California is an unusual megaregion, a case which illustrates the complex hybridity of megaregional processes. The economic core is the San Francisco Bay Area, an area identified by some European scholars as a mega-city region (Evers and de Vries, 2013), but which in the United States is generally considered simply as a region – albeit a polycentric one with three principal cities (San Francisco, Oakland, San Jose) and numerous smaller cities/suburbs (Scott, 1959). The Northern California megaregion is formed by combining the Bay Area with the Sacramento region to the northeast and the smaller Northern San Joaquin Valley regions to the east and southeast (principally Stockton and Modesto). While there are variations in the size and scope of the megaregion (Metcalf and Terplan, 2007) – some definitions extend the boundaries to include Reno, Nevada (350 km away) – this triangle is the heart of the megaregion (Figure 4.3).

The polycentricity of the region makes it appear to be a Process B megaregion. Most of the principal cities were founded at almost the exact same time, part of the telescoping of California history where in the immortal words of Carry McWilliams, 'the lights went on all at once' (McWilliams, 1949, p. 25). Northern California was in one sense born as a megaregion (Schafran, 2014), one of the first hyper-multipolar megaregions. There are

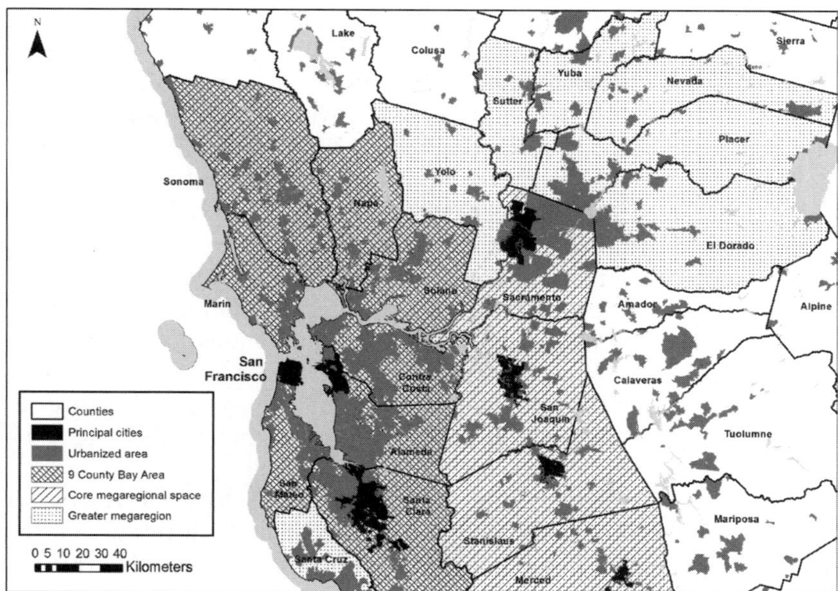

Source: Author

Figure 4.3   Spatialities within the Northern California megaregion

19 cities with more than 100 000 people, but none with a million. While San Francisco (800 000) and San Jose (945 000) are significantly bigger than Sacramento (466 000), Stockton (292 000) or Modesto (201 000), it is not by the orders of magnitude of either typical primate cities like Paris, or even American examples centred on New York, Chicago or Los Angeles.

Yet this deeply historic polycentricity masks a megaregionality which is more Process A in terms of power relations. Over the past four decades, unprecedented tech-fuelled economic growth, the lack of affordable housing development, the legacy of post-war racial discrimination and weak regional transportation investment spurred a massive wave of sub-urbanization into the neighbouring Sacramento and San Joaquin Valley regions. Subprime lending added fuel to the fire during the 2000s, leading to a megaregional structure marked by dramatic racialized inequality and major intra-megaregional differences in housing prices and foreclo-sure rates (Schafran, 2013; Schafran and Wegmann, 2012). The city of Stockton made international headlines when it briefly held the title as largest American city to declare bankruptcy – a title that now sadly rests with Detroit.

Put in European terms, the Bay Area has a Randstad core, a Parisian process of outward expansion from a powerful centre, but with a periphery that is more Northern English in nature. As with the other mega-regions, the focus on globalization as a driving force is misleading. At first glance, the Bay Area portion of the larger entity is exceptionally global. But the region's wealth is old-fashioned in nature – it is the centre of the right industry at the right time, an economic powerhouse virtually unprecedented in history. Like Northern England's former wealth, it is undoubtedly dependent on global trade, global branding and a brain drain machine that lures the best and brightest from every corner of the globe. But much of the capital is local and the foundations of the Bay Area tech engine go back to the gold rush when capital was pulled from the hills and invested in the military, industrial and agricultural industries which formed a foundation for the Silicon Valley miracle (Brechin, 2006; Walker, 2004).

More critically, whether or not the core of the Bay Area (the Randstad/ Process B portion) is global or not has little or nothing to do with the failures of this region to build housing and transportation networks that would have obviated the need for a megaregional suburbanization. Nor is globalization responsible for the long-term economic malaise and high inequality that plagued many of the Northern San Joaquin Valley com-munities; a weakness which tempted them into selling land for suburban tract development that are the urban tissue of Northern California's megaregionality. These decisions (or lack of decisions) like those in Paris to build high-speed trains and not build certain forms of housing in certain places, are fundamentally political decisions about space and place. It is these types of decisions, often made over centuries, which we need to understand if we are going to comprehend megaregional urbanization.

4.5 REDEFINING MEGAREGIONS BEYOND GLOBALIZATION

Table 4.1 summarizes some of the key differences discussed above. The goal of the three preceding examples was not to provide anything remotely like a comprehensive understanding of their development, but rather to illustrate the utility of the Taylor and Pain dichotomy for discussing the history and urban formation of megaregions, alongside the ways in which the two ideal-type processes can work in hybrid fashion. Clearly, much more sophisticated empirical work is needed to flesh these ideas out, work that may suggest expansion of this simplified dichotomy not considered to date, including a more satisfying taxonomy of hybridities.

Table 4.1 Three megaregions through the lens of historical urbanization and power politics

Megaregion	Type	Megaregional timeframe	Internal power dynamics	Source of challenges
Paris	Monocentric	Recent	Highly imbalanced	Primarily internal. Global power is only mildly threatened; holds political power over its own destiny. Major inequality issues are internal to old region, but megaregionality is putting pressures on infrastructure, and sprawl is now a concern.
Northern England	Polycentric	Deeply historic	Balanced, but with rivalries and emerging gaps	More external than internal. Functions as a hybrid with major economic pressures from monolithic London, limited control over political destiny. New high-speed rail could create new questions of suburban links with London. Deep internal rivalries and long struggles with post-industrial economics.
Northern California	Hybrid (polycentric core, but functionally monocentric)	Mixed	Imbalanced, hyper fragmented	Primarily internal, with key exceptions. Economic core is amongst the most powerful in history, but operates in a hyper-fragmented political landscape. Limited intervention from higher levels of government to encourage megaregional scale planning interventions.

Source: Author

Yet the purpose of these examples and the Taylor and Pain dichotomy is to illustrate the deep historical roots of megaregional urban form. While globalization is undoubtedly a powerful driver of certain forms of urban growth and development, scholarship needs to divorce itself from an overly economistic view of megaregionality as a product of globalization. Megaregionality is a fundamental urban form, a core aspect of both historical and contemporary urbanization, albeit one which has reached an unprecedented scale in the contemporary moment as urban populations grow throughout the world.

The time has come for a better definition of megaregions. This requires moving beyond size, questions of globality, or overly simplistic considerations which render them synonymous with polycentricity, to definitions which better understand urban process and power relations. To start this discussion, I would offer the following understanding:

> Megaregions are increasingly large, urbanized agglomerations formed through the complete or partial fusion of two or more previously separate or economically independent regions. This fusion is a fundamentally urban process, inseparable from processes of urbanization and its innumerable components: transportation linkages and commuting patterns, political and economic geographies, development and land use patterns, migration and demographic change, history and identity, power and inequality. Like all urbanization patterns, power differentials between spaces and places involved in this process determine and are determined by how, where, when and to what effect megaregionality occurs, and are critical factors in understanding the possibility of political intervention. One fundamental differentiation in the megaregional process is whether the fusion is a product of relatively equal cities, or is being driven by a fundamentally more powerful core.

This understanding of megaregions as a fusional urban process inseparable from historicized urbanization, is one of two key pieces to the broader puzzle of theorizing political intervention in megaregions (Wheeler, 2009, 2015; Innes et al., 2010; Benner and Pastor, 2011). The second is what I have previously discussed as the need to rethink the geography of megaregions (Schafran, 2014), pushing away from definitions which focus exclusively on their massive size and see them as a large envelope.[9] We need instead to consider a form of megaregional dialectic, where 'megaregional space' defines the total area under consideration and 'spaces of the megaregion' identifies the interstitial spaces where the process of megaregionality is being experienced most intensely.

Using the above examples, cities such as Amiens and Orleans are fundamental 'spaces of the megaregion'. They are areas where the megaregionality of Greater Paris is being experienced far more than in other areas where the outer expansion of the city is generally ignored. Likewise, the M62 motorway is itself the most fundamental space of the Northern England megaregion, a traffic-clogged artery which is a critical juncture for contemporary forms of fusion (Martin, 2008) – much like the river and canal cities were a generation ago. For Northern California, these spaces are mostly in the weaker regions of the Northern San Joaquin and Sacramento Valleys; places where this process is a major economic and political issue.

This more nuanced and dialectic conception of megaregional geography is critical, for in many ways one could add an addendum to the above definition: megaregions are defined by being larger and more complex than any form of comprehensive urban or regional governance structure possible. Megaregions force us to separate our scales of analysis from the scale of political intervention (Schafran, 2014). And intervening in this more human of scales – the 'spaces of the megaregion' as opposed to 'megaregional space' – is rendered more effective if we have a more historical and less econonomistic understanding of the megaregional processes and power dynamics which produced these spaces in the first place.

4.6   CODA: BEYOND THE SHADOW OF LOS ANGELES AND CHICAGO

On a final note, it is worth taking a step back and considering briefly how we arrived at this point. One of the most important aspects of the POLYNET work and related work earlier in Asia (McGee and Robinson, 1995; Xue-qiang and Si-ming, 1990) is that it is part of a wave in urban studies pushing away from American-based models of urban development. This is in much the same way that urbanists working in/on the Global South have been pushing away from models based on the Global North – including those developed by POLYNET participants (cf. Roy, 2009; Roy and Ong, 2011; Robinson, 2002). But what is often lost in debates about the Chicago and Los Angeles 'schools' of urban studies is that as cities they are actually quite similar – large, fundamentally monocentric metropoles, Process A cities in the Jacobsian way. Los Angeles School theorists may have been thinking polycentrically (Scott, 1982; Soja, 1989; Dear and Flusty, 1998; Scott and Soja, 1998), but their city was fundamentally a single messy core. Los Angeles may have swapped Chicago's dense core of industrial and financial production for one where numerous jobs were based in suburbs, but both existed far from any other sizable regions.

With the return to Christaller's (1933) ideas about central places – and thankfully not the featureless plains of location theory

(Lösch et al., 1954) – we should not focus on Europe or Asia or anywhere else for that matter as a model of a 'new' form of urban development. Rather, we should take a look backwards and recognize that in America a century ago there were two just as large and just as important metropoles – the San Francisco Bay Area and New York City – which are variations on Process B metropoles (or at least they were at the time) and which are just as important for understanding urbanization.

It was the power of newness, I would argue, which allowed some very smart urban theorists to convince the world that their strange new cities – one a nineteenth-century citadel built on new forms of industrial agriculture, immigration and the foundations of capitalist liquidity (Cronon, 1991); the other a 20th-century metroplex built on new forms of military industrialism, immigration, real estate development and the foundations of the capitalist culture industry (Scott, 2005; McWilliams, 1946) – were somehow models of anything. They were and are fascinating places, leading regions of one type, but our adherence to them as models blinded us to the importance of truly polycentric urban development. As monocentric and polycentric regions blend together to form megaregions the world over, urban theory must remember its historical errors and resist the urge to create new models. Instead we are better off learning to operate without them.

NOTES

1. This was part of the POLYNET project, a three-year project funded by European Regional Development Fund, INTERREG IIIB NWE, which examined changes in functional connections and information flows (physical/transportation and virtual/ICT) in major urban regions across North West Europe (for the main findings see Halbert et al. (2006), Hall and Pain (2006) and Hoyler et al. (2008)).
2. Part of the reason for this, I would argue, is this inability to break away from a narrow economic geography reading of megaregion formation. After a plea for the value of this theoretical innovation, Taylor and Pain (2007, p. 65) conclude their essay by stating that 'planning should not be carried out separate from the practice of current economic actors (firms) that use cities', once again erasing the majority of economic and political actors in cities.
3. It is worth noting that in medieval and Renaissance times Orléans was a rival to Paris for both wealth and political power, while Chartres was subservient to the Duchy of Orléans, not Paris.
4. This is one area where I would argue the attention to globalization is fully warranted. Super-wealthy foreign property investors are now major factors in Parisian property prices – as in London and New York – pushing Sassen's (1991) discussion of the human impacts of global citydom to new and some might say absurd heights.
5. In official data, English cities are historically underbounded. So, for example, the politically-bounded city of Manchester has its official population of 503 000. However, the continuous 'built up' or metropolitan/city-region of Manchester has a recorded population of 2.8 million. Likewise, Leeds and Bradford are politically

separate, but as an urban area they are considered together as Leeds-Bradford (population 2.2 million).
6. Skelmersdale (1961) and Runcorn (1964) being the two major ones.
7. It is this fact which led Martin (2010) to observe that the area followed Taylor and Pain's Process B definition.
8. Following Walker (1996) I would argue that industrial capitalism – as practied in Northern England – was an early form of globalization. As scholars and pundits alike discovered the growing interconnectedness of economies in the post-Cold War era, there was a tendency to forget centuries of growing international trade, economic dependency, satellite factories and shifting urban hierarchies – hence the title of Walker's (1996) piece: '*Another* round of globalization in San Francisco' (emphasis added).
9. This is by no means an exhaustive list: political intervention, or the possibility or impossibility of it, can be considered a third key thread, while transport and goods movement is likely the fourth.

REFERENCES

Alsop, W. and J. Hulme (2005), *Will Alsop's Supercity*, Manchester: Urbis.
America 2050 (2008), 'The emerging megaregions', available at http://www.america2050.org/images/2050_Map_Megaregions2008_150.png (accessed 27 September 2013).
Benner, C. and M. Pastor (2011), 'Moving on up? Regions, megaregions, and the changing geography of social equity organizing', *Urban Affairs Review*, **47** (3), 315–348.
Brechin, G. (2006), *Imperial San Francisco: Urban Power, Earthly Ruin*, Berkeley, CA: University of California Press.
Brunet, R. (1989), *Les Villes Européenes: Rapport pour la DATAR*, Paris: La Documentation Française.
Castells, M. (2000), *The Rise of the Network Society*, Malden, MA: Blackwell.
Chabard, P. and V. Picon-Lefebvre (eds) (2012), *La Défense: Dictionnaire et Atlas*, Marseille: Éditions Parenthèses.
Charmes, E. (2009), 'L'explosion périurbaine', *Etudes Foncières*, **138**, 25–36.
Christaller, W. (1933 [1966]), *Central Places in Southern Germany*, Jena: Fischer (translation into English by Carlisle W. Baskin), London: Prentice-Hall.
Cronon, W. (1991), *Nature's Metropolis: Chicago and the Great West*, New York: Norton & Co.
Dear, M. and S. Flusty (1998), 'Postmodern urbanism', *Annals of the Association of American Geographers*, **88** (1), 50–72.
Deit, P. (1973), 'Cinq villes nouvelles dans la région parisienne', *Economie et Statistique*, **50** (1), 61–66.
Ducruet, C., O. Joly and M. Le Cam (2012), 'The French port complex of the Seine Corridor', *Territorial Impact of Globalization for Europe and its Regions* – Working Paper, 16, available at http://www.espon.eu/export/sites/default/Documents/Projects/AppliedResearch/TIGER/DFR/TIGER_DFR_wp16_portlehavreCS.pdf (accessed 27 September 2013).
Evers, D. and J. de Vries (2013), 'Explaining governance in five mega-city regions: rethinking the role of hierarchy and government', *European Planning Studies*, **21** (4), 536–555.

Florida, R., T. Gulden and C. Mellander (2008), 'The rise of the mega-region', *Cambridge Journal of Regions, Economy and Society*, **1** (3), 459–476.

Gaillard, M. (1991), *Du Madeleine-Bastille à Météor: Histoire des Transports Parisiens*, Amiens: Martelle Éditions.

Gilli, F. (2002), 'Déplacements domicile-travail et organisation du Bassin Parisien', *L'Espace Géographique*, **31** (4), 289–305.

Gilli, F. (2005), 'Le Bassin parisien. Une région métropolitaine', *Cybergeo: European Journal of Geography* [online], **305**, available at http://cybergeo.revues. org/3257 (accessed 27 September 2013)

Gilli, F. (2009), 'Sprawl or reagglomeration? The dynamics of employment deconcentration and industrial transformation in Greater Paris', *Urban Studies*, **46** (7), 1385–1420.

Gilli, F. (2011), 'The "Paris Basin", a metropolitan region', *Cybergeo: European Journal of Geography* [online], **578**, available at http://cybergeo.revues.org/24913 (accessed 27 September 2013) [translation of Gilli (2005)].

González, S. (2006), 'The Northern Way: a celebration or a victim of the new city-regional government policy?' *ESRC/DCLG Postgraduate Research Programme Working Paper*, 28, Swindon: ESRC, available at http://www. esrc.ac.uk/my-esrc/grants/PTA-039-27-0030/outputs/read/51a51a2e-9145-438d-a04d-62634aba1e4c (accessed 23 September 2013).

Goodchild, B. and P. Hickman (2006), 'Towards a regional strategy for the North of England? An assessment of "The Northern Way"', *Regional Studies*, **40** (1), 121–133.

Gottmann, J. (1961), *Megalopolis: The Urbanized Northeastern Seaboard of the United States*, New York: Twentieth Century Fund.

Halbert, L. (2006), 'The Paris region: polycentric spatial planning in a monocentric metropolitan region', in P. Hall and K. Pain (eds), *The Polycentric Metropolis: Learning from Mega-City Regions in Europe*, London: Earthscan, pp. 180–186.

Halbert, L. (2008), 'Examining the mega-city-region hypothesis: evidence from the Paris city-region/Bassin Parisien', *Regional Studies*, **42** (8), 1147–1160.

Halbert, L., F.J. Convery and A. Thierstein (eds) (2006), 'Special issue: Reflections on the polycentric metropolis', *Built Environment*, **32** (2), 109–218.

Hall, P. and K. Pain (eds) (2006), *The Polycentric Metropolis: Learning from Mega-City Regions in Europe*, London Earthscan.

Hoyler, M., R.C. Kloosterman and M. Sokol (eds) (2008), 'Special issue: Globalization, city-regions and polycentricity in north-west Europe', *Regional Studies*, **42** (8), 1055–1217.

Innes, J.E., D.E. Booher and S. Di Vittorio (2010), 'Strategies for megaregion governance: collaborative dialogue, networks, and self-organization', *Journal of the American Planning Association*, **77** (1), 55–67.

Institut National de la Statistique et des Études Économiques (INSEE) (2010), *Produits Intérieurs Bruts Régionaux (PIBR) en Valeur en Millions d'Euros (XLS), 1990–2009*, available at http://www.insee.fr/en/ (last accessed 2 October 2013).

Jacobs, J. (1984), *Cities and the Wealth of Nations: Principles of Economic Life*, New York: Random House.

Lang, R.E. and D. Dhavale (2005), 'Beyond Megalopolis: exploring America's new megapolitan geography', *Metropolitan Institute Census Report Series*, 05:01, Alexandria, VA: The Metropolitan Institute at Virginia Tech.

Lösch, A., W.H. Woglom and W.F. Stolper (1954), *The Economics of Location*, New Haven, CT: Yale University Press.

Martin, D. (2008), 'The post-city being prepared on the site of the ex-city: re-aligning the provincial city along the M62 in the North of England', *City*, **12** (3), 372–382.

Martin, D. (2010), 'Mobilities-based urban planning in the North of England', *Mobilities*, **5** (1), 61–81.

McGee, T.G. and I.M. Robinson (eds) (1995), *The Mega-Urban Regions of Southeast Asia*, Vancouver: University of British Columbia Press.

McWilliams, C. (1946), *Southern California: An Island on the Land*, Layton, UT: Gibbs Smith.

McWilliams, C. (1949), *California: The Great Exception*, Berkeley and Los Angeles, CA: University of California Press.

Metcalf, G. and E. Terplan (2007), 'The northern California megaregion', *The Urbanist*, 446.

Morgan, K. (2002), 'English question: regional perspectives on a fractured nation', *Regional Studies*, **36** (7), 797–810.

Regional Plan Association and Lincoln Institute of Land Policy (2007), *The Healdsburg Research Seminar on Megaregions: Discussion Papers and Summary*, Cambridge, MA: Lincoln Institute of Land Policy.

Robinson, J. (2002), 'Global and world cities: a view from off the map', *International Journal of Urban and Regional Research*, **26** (3), 531–554.

Ross, C.L. (ed.) (2009), *Megaregions: Planning for Global Competitiveness*, Washington, DC: Island Press.

Roy, A. (2009), 'The 21st-century metropolis: new geographies of theory', *Regional Studies*, **43** (6), 819–830.

Roy, A. and A. Ong (eds) (2011), *Worlding Cities: Asian Experiments and the Art of Being Global*, Oxford: Wiley-Blackwell.

Sassen, S. (1991), *The Global City: New York, London, Tokyo*, Princeton, NJ: Princeton University Press.

Sassen, S. (ed.) (2001), *Global Networks, Linked Cities*, London: Routledge.

Schafran, A. (2013), 'Origins of an urban crisis: the restructuring of the San Francisco Bay area and the geography of foreclosure', *International Journal of Urban and Regional Research*, **37** (2), 663–688.

Schafran, A. (2014), 'Rethinking mega-regions: sub-regional politics in a fragmented metropolis', *Regional Studies*, **48** (4), 587–602.

Schafran, A. and J. Wegmann (2012), 'Restructuring, race, and real estate: changing home values and the new California metropolis, 1989–2010', *Urban Geography*, **33** (5), 630–654.

Scott, A.J. (1982), 'Locational patterns and dynamics of industrial activity in the modern metropolis', *Urban Studies*, **19** (2), 111–142.

Scott, A.J. (ed.) (2001), *Global City-Regions: Trends, Theory, Policy*, Oxford: Oxford University Press.

Scott, A.J. (2005), *On Hollywood: The Place, the Industry*, Princeton, NJ: Princeton University Press.

Scott, A.J. and E.W. Soja (1998), *The City: Los Angeles and Urban Theory at the End of the Twentieth Century*, Berkeley and Los Angeles, CA: University of California Press.

Scott, A.J. and M. Storper (2003), 'Regions, globalization, development', *Regional Studies*, **37** (6–7), 549–578.

Scott, M. (1959), *The San Francisco Bay Area: A Metropolis in Perspective*, Berkeley and Los Angeles, CA: University of California Press.

Soja, E.W. (1989), *Postmodern Geographies: The Reassertion of Space in Critical Social Theory*, London: Verso.

Taylor, P.J. and K. Pain (2007), 'Polycentric mega-city regions: exploratory research from Western Europe', in Regional Plan Association and Lincoln Institute of Land Policy (eds), *The Healdsburg Research Seminar on Megaregions: Discussion Papers and Summary*, Cambridge, MA: Lincoln Institute of Land Policy, pp. 59–66.

Taylor, P.J., D.M. Evans and K. Pain (2006), 'Organization of the polycentric metropolis: corporate structures and networks', in P. Hall and K. Pain (eds), *The Polycentric Metropolis: Learning from Mega-City Regions in Europe*, London: Earthscan, pp. 53–64.

Taylor, P.J., D.M. Evans, M. Hoyler, B. Derudder and K. Pain (2009), 'The UK space economy as practised by advanced producer service firms: identifying two distinctive polycentric city-regional processes in contemporary Britain', *International Journal of Urban and Regional Research*, **33** (3), 700–718.

Taylor, P.J., M. Hoyler, D.M. Evans and J. Harrison (2010), 'Balancing London? A preliminary investigation of the "Core Cities" and "Northern Way" spatial policy initiatives using multi-city corporate and commercial law firms', *European Planning Studies*, **18** (8), 1285–1299.

Walker, R. (1996), 'Another round of globalization in San Francisco', *Urban Geography*, **17** (1), 60–94.

Walker, R. (2004), *The Conquest of Bread: 150 Years of Agribusiness in California*, New York: The New Press.

Wheeler, S.M. (2009), 'Regions, megaregions, and sustainability', *Regional Studies*, **43** (6), 863–876.

Wheeler, S.M. (2015), 'Five reasons why megaregional planning works against sustainability', in J. Harrison and M. Hoyler (eds), *Megaregions: Globalization's New Urban Form?* Cheltenham, UK and Northampton, MA, USA: Edward Elgar, pp. 97–118.

Xue-qiang, X. and Si-ming, L. (1990), 'China's open door policy and urbanization in the Pearl River Delta region', *International Journal of Urban and Regional Research*, **14** (1), 49–69.

5. Five reasons why megaregional planning works against sustainability

Stephen M. Wheeler

5.1 INTRODUCTION

For the past decade 'megaregions' – very large-scale constellations of urban regions – have been a popular focus of attention at academic conferences. They have also attracted the attention of non-governmental organizations (NGOs) specializing in urban and regional planning as well as governmental agencies at multiple levels. It is easy to see why. Thinking at a (relatively) new scale generates intellectual excitement as well as new research and funding opportunities. Researchers have been able to create intriguing maps showing the new urban geographies. This larger scale of planning brings into play attractive technologies such as high-speed rail. Equally importantly, it provides a respite from the challenge of dealing with the gridlocked politics and often ineffective institutions at other levels. As a result of such factors, efforts at megaregional planning and infrastructure development are gaining speed, with few voices raised in opposition.

However, rather than helping bring about more sustainable societies this new scale of planning is likely to accelerate what some climate change scientists have labeled BAU ('business-as-usual') forms of development. If conducted primarily to coordinate new infrastructure or to promote globalized forms of economic development, the consequences of megaregional planning are likely to be disastrous. The result may well be to facilitate the physical sprawl of urban development between cities, to increase the amount that people travel and associated greenhouse gas emissions, to worsen disparities between different populations and communities, and to strengthen economic globalization trends that undermine local place and global sustainability. In this chapter I will develop the case that megaregional planning and research should thus be undertaken with a very cautious eye, within the larger umbrella of a move towards more local and sustainable communities.

Let me dispense with one likely objection to start with. I know that many planners and scholars will argue that trends are moving inexorably toward development of megaregions already, and that therefore the best approach is to work with existing forces to ensure that the best possible forms come about. This objection is similar to those that have been raised about other dimensions of progressive planning and activism historically. For example, many have thought it necessary to work with suburban sprawl developers so as to improve project design rather than opposing development on unbuilt land in the first place and supporting infill development instead. Thus in the US we see many sprawling subdivisions featuring cosmetic improvements such as landscaped medians on access roads and sidewalks in front of houses, without changing the underlying single-use, low-density, motor-vehicle-dependent nature of the development. Other local officials have supported the development of big box retail in their communities on the grounds that such stores will be built nearby anyway and if located in their jurisdiction will provide tax revenues that can be used for beneficial purposes. Thus countless US towns feature large stand-alone chain stores, malls and commercial strips on the outskirts of town which have helped in turn kill Main Street businesses, ironically necessitating further public expenditures to attempt to redevelop the historic core. There are always rationalizations for collaborating with the status quo. But on a planet whose climate is now radically changing due in part to past urban planning decisions, stronger backbones are needed.

The development of megaregions is not a fait accompli. Planners can do a great deal to work together at the megaregional scale on those issues that merit it – for example to protect large-scale ecosystems – while resisting the temptation to plan large-scale infrastructure that will only facilitate exurban development, promote extreme commuting, raise greenhouse gas emissions and deepen inequities. Megaregional projects should only be undertaken if they clearly contribute to sustainability goals and if other more sustainable alternatives do not exist. To give just one example, my home state of California is currently considering spending at least $68 billion to build a high-speed rail system of dubious value when local transit systems, renewable energy initiatives and public education are languishing. If such money is to be spent on transportation, a case can be made that far greater sustainability benefits would arise from strengthening local bus and rail systems serving far larger numbers of less affluent people while promoting revitalization of existing urban areas.

With that prologue, let me now move on to some specific arguments for more cautious exploration of the megaregional concept. The following points are by no means the only ones possible, but are particularly important at this time given the current need to move rapidly toward sustainability planning. I will briefly illustrate each point with discussion of dynamics within my home megaregion of Northern California.

5.2 WHY MEGAREGIONAL PLANNING WORKS AGAINST SUSTAINABILITY

5.2.1 We Can Hardly Plan at the Regional Scale, Let Alone for Megaregions

The region – whether defined as a metropolitan area or a watershed, airshed, bioregion or cultural region – is generally seen as the weakest scale of planning. Institutions are less strong at this level than at local, state, provincial or national scales and face many well-known challenges. Local governments are notoriously fragmented within regions, creating many opposing interests that work against regional coordination (Danielson and Doig, 1982; Self, 1982; Dear, 2000). Consolidating local governments can help (Rusk, 1999), but is difficult politically. The voluntary nature of many regional agencies works against their success. Councils of Governments (COGs) in the US are for the most part voluntary associations of local officials with little statutory authority; each COG representative has primary responsibility to the local voters who elected him or her, not to the overall region. Cities, towns and counties are free to ignore regional agreements or withdraw from regional consensus-building exercises. In the UK, metropolitan agencies have at times been stronger, but suffer from inconsistent political support, having been abolished by Conservative governments in 1979 and 2010. Regional planning is little covered in the media and the public is not used to thinking regionally. Although some scholars (for example Innes et al., 2010) argue that regional and megaregional governance strategies based on collaborative dialogue, networks and self-organization hold great promise, in practice these processes are difficult, time-consuming and vulnerable to sabotage by powerful special interests. They are likely to produce lowest-common-denominator solutions or to work only with the additional incentive of higher-level governmental action to motivate change.

Although there have been some regional successes in terms of environmental planning (for example air quality in many US metro regions), growth management (for example spatial planning within regions such as Stockholm, Copenhagen, London, the Dutch Randstad and Portland, OR) and transportation planning (for example the Parisian web of public transit systems) the track record of regional planning for sustainability is not great (Wheeler, 2009). Metropolitan regions worldwide have had difficulty managing their growth, ensuring social equity, protecting local environments and significantly reducing their energy consumption and greenhouse gas emissions. Rural regions have often had similar difficulties in protecting environmental quality and ensuring adequate employment and quality of life for residents.

Yet if regional planning is challenging, the megaregional level would be even harder. In the US this scale typically crosses state boundaries, and so not just multiple municipalities but multiple states (and at times governments within Canada and Mexico) would be required to work with one another. The number of jurisdictions involved becomes exponentially greater (see Glass, 2015). There is some precedent for action at this scale – for example with regard to environmental protection in the Great Lakes area (Mazmanian and Kraft, 2009) and the Regional Greenhouse Gas Initiative (RGGI) consortium establishing a market in greenhouse gas emissions in the northeastern US and adjoining Canadian provinces. But these processes have focused on single-issue planning rather than broad-based visions for the future and have suffered from inconsistent political commitment from their many stakeholders. Broad-based megaregional planning to coordinate urbanization in North America is still nonexistent, with the exception of some initial studies carried out by universities and the nonprofit America 2050 organization. In the European Union many mechanisms for large-scale cooperation have been set up, but Faludi (2009, p. 32) argues that few people are interested in planning for spatial development at a megaregional scale, and that 'there is no clearly defined policy other than encouraging seed money for research, networking, and initiatives from below'.

Developing institutions at the megaregional scale will be difficult simply because it is often hard to define these areas. In the US researchers disagree on many megaregional boundaries. For example, Ross (2011) proposes one combined California megaregion, while America 2050, affiliated with the venerable New York-based Regional Plan Association, identifies two separate Northern and Southern California megaregions (America 2050, 2013a). Ross also proposes a Central Plains megaregion that does not exist in the America 2050 typology, while the latter shows Front Range and Gulf Coast megaregions not found by Ross. The two teams have sharply different boundaries for Piedmont and Midwestern megaregions. Nelson and Lang (2011) present a version of the America 2050 map with most of the megaregions divided into sub-regions, for example 'Twin Cities', 'Chicago', 'Michigan Corridor', 'Steel Corridor' and 'Ohio Valley' portions of the Great Lakes Megaregion. Their map shows clear areas of daylight between these sub-regions, raising the question of how integrated these megaregions really are. This team also uses the term 'megapolitan' rather than 'megaregion' (see Fleming, 2015). Another group led by economic theorist Richard Florida proposes yet another set of borders and names for North American megaregions (Creative Class Group, 2008). Instead of 'megaregions', some European scholars talk about 'mega-city regions' that are larger than metropolitan areas and yet smaller than megaregions (for example Hall, 2011). With such disagreement about the territories involved, how can authorities be expected to develop effective institutions and governance strategies for these areas?

Spatial planning for the megaregion will also be difficult because its on-the-ground development forms undermine widely held physical planning objectives for compact cities, infill development, transit-oriented development, neighbourhood centres and balanced land use mix. Like metropolitan regions, megaregions tend to be characterized by what Lang (2003) has called 'edgeless city' development – a sprawling and decentralized form of growth that contains a larger proportion of the region's employment and population than the 'edge cities' identified by Garreau (1991). These 'edgeless city' areas are characterized by a profusion of poorly connected, inwardly focused forms such as suburban tracts, office parks, shopping malls and upscale enclaves, in addition to some relatively new physical types such as 'rural sprawl' (Wheeler, 2008; Wheeler and Beebe, 2011). It is much more difficult to provide public transit and services to such spatial forms than it is for denser, more centralized, more mixed-use communities. These newer built landscapes are also strongly motor vehicle-dependent and partly as a result tend to have high levels of greenhouse gas emissions. Political cohesion is difficult, and their politics tend to be more conservative (for example Beebe and Wheeler, 2012). Asia, interestingly, may be less susceptible to some of these problems than North America, due to its higher population densities and tendencies toward top-down planning (Yang, 2009). However, Xu and Yeh (2011) caution that in China there are still many obstacles to coordination of large city-regions including administrative fragmentation, changing institutional frameworks, dispersed governance and laissez-faire culture.

Benner and Pastor (2008) point out that the megaregion is a particularly difficult scale for public interest organizing. Advocacy groups have made progress at the regional scale in recent decades, developing coalitions in many North American metro regions around smart growth, social equity, regional greenspaces planning and public transportation. But the megaregional scale is vastly harder for nonprofit organizations to work at. Distances are greater, relationships do not exist between constituencies to the same extent, and institutional targets for organizing are lacking. Work at this scale could also take away energy from local and regional organizing efforts.

All of these challenges to megaregional planning can be seen within Northern California. The definition of the Northern California Megaregion, first of all, is open to question, with maps by America 2050 and the San Francisco Planning and Urban Research Association (SPUR) showing many possible ways that this area could be defined (America 2050, 2013b; SPUR, 2007). No statistical information is currently available for this megaregion; rather, the US Bureau of the Census recognizes four different metropolitan statistical areas that cover only a limited part of the territory. Depending on definition, this megaregion includes at least three existing regional councils of governments, approximately 24 counties and several hundred incorporated cities and towns within two states. There are dozens of other units of government as well, including air districts, water districts, park districts, public transit agencies and school districts. The Bay Area alone already has five regional agencies; getting these and other institutions to coordinate on a regional smart growth plan ('Plan Bay Area') was an organizing task that occupied many individuals and organizations for at least 20 years. Efforts at regionalism in the Bay Area date back nearly a century (Orman, 1976), with major failures in the early 1960s – when efforts collapsed in the state legislature to produce a strong regional government – and the early 1990s – when a 'Bay Vision 2020' process sponsored by the nonprofit Greenbelt Alliance and the business-oriented Bay Area Council failed to produce agreement on anything but generalities. Arguably the only reason that a (voluntary) regional growth plan finally emerged in 2013 was passage of state legislation in 2008, S.B. 375, that requires the state's regions to adopt a Sustainable Communities Strategy reducing greenhouse gas emissions (it remains to be seen whether the targets and mechanisms for such reductions are sufficient).

Needless to say there are no existing megaregional agencies for Northern California. Several large-scale consensus-building efforts have been attempted, primarily around water and air quality issues, but with limited success. Enormous political obstacles exist to megaregional coordination. Cities such as San Francisco, Berkeley, Oakland and Santa Cruz are among the most liberal in the US, while many suburban Bay Area jurisdictions are moderately conservative and communities within the Central Valley and Sierra Nevada Foothills are far on the right of the American political spectrum. The eight counties of the San Joaquin Valley have been unable to cooperate even among themselves on regional planning, let alone San Francisco, and so consequently each of these counties is recognized as a stand-alone Metropolitan Planning Organization by the federal government. Throughout the megaregion literally hundreds of different cultural groups exist, speaking different languages, with tens of

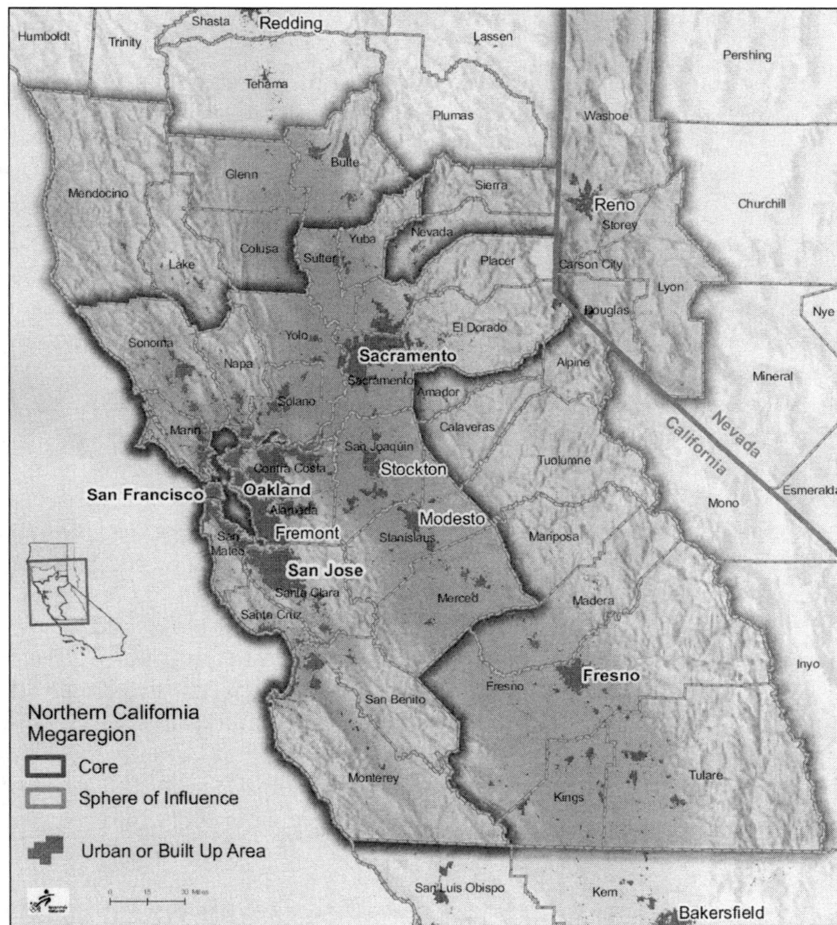

Source: San Francisco Planning and Urban Research Association (SPUR). Reproduced by permission.

Figure 5.1   The geography of the Northern California megaregion

thousands of residents in the country illegally and unable to speak English. Perhaps someday all of these fragmented communities and jurisdictions will come together into a megaregional whole. But at least for the foreseeable future the physical, political, cultural and jurisdictional challenges of megaregional planning in Northern California are staggering (see Schafran, 2015).

5.2.2   Infrastructure Alone Does Not Make Good Planning

At many times throughout history infrastructure has been built at a mega-regional scale. Ancient Greek colonial towns, Roman roads and aqueducts, Indian ceremonial centres, Chinese city regions and Mesoamerican religious and cultural facilities were all built across very large distances (Sutcliffe, 1993). But beginning in the 1800s new forms of infrastructure and technology have played a crucial role in bringing about larger and more permanent forms of megaregional development. Railroad networks combined with steam power and the rise of factory production to create new urban constellations such as the British Midlands and the German Ruhr Valley, and to facilitate early forms of suburban sprawl around many cities. Large-scale water systems enabled regional and more recently megaregional development on the East and West Coasts of the US. The New Deal's Tennessee Valley Authority constructed dams, power plants and industrial facilities across portions of seven US states in a vast economic development initiative. Most powerfully, 20th-century freeway networks enabled the vast expansion of metropolitan areas in North America and elsewhere, and continue to tie metro regions ever more closely together. In fact, the Interstate Highway System can be viewed as the dominant form of megaregional planning in the US to date (Yaro, 2011).

Continuing this infrastructure-oriented tradition, recent megaregional enthusiasts have focused primarily on high-speed rail (HSR) as their initiative of choice, perhaps because such infrastructure is virtually the only planning 'handle' that exists for most megaregions. Ross (2011, p. 341) argues for investment in high-speed rail as a means for 'providing greater connectivity between and within megaregions'. Yaro (2011, p. 246) argues that HSR is essential to 'create the foundation for new economic synergies between metropolitan areas and among metropolitan centers and second-tier cities, in the process enabling them all to reach their full economic, social, and environmental potential'. But how exactly HSR would do these things is usually left unsaid. In the low-density US context it is not at all clear that such systems would achieve significant ridership or yield economic synergies not already provided by air and motor vehicle travel. It is likely that equal investment within existing metropolitan areas would yield better results. As a result Seltzer (2011, p. 355) comments that 'we have work to do before we can even explain why we are pursuing mega-region-scale strategies, particularly infrastructure-based strategies, first and ahead of all others'.

Emphasizing infrastructure favours some goals such as increased mobility and rapid economic development over other objectives such as environmental protection and social equity. Transportation infrastructure of course undercuts environmental goals if it leads to suburban sprawl and increased greenhouse gas emissions or local air pollution. It also undercuts equity goals if it facilitates spatial segregation of different socioeconomic populations. Conversely, improving equity requires very little infrastructure, but rather policy revisions to share resources more equally between jurisdictions, to improve public education and services for disadvantaged communities, and to introduce more progressive taxation, higher minimum wages and other policy changes.

Advocates of technologies such as high-speed rail try to argue that their approach has environmental and equity advantages, but these are debatable. In locations such as Europe and the northeastern US, high-speed rail may make environmental sense if it accommodates passengers who would otherwise have flown or driven. However, even for the Northeastern Corridor in the US, Amtrak's own estimates are that 20 to 30 per cent of the 2040 ridership would be new 'induced demand' (Amtrak 2012, p. 29) – that is, building high-speed rail would lead to substantially more trips and greenhouse gas emissions than otherwise. In China likewise, which has recently built a very extensive high-speed rail system, there is evidence that many of the trips being taken are new ones that would not have been taken otherwise (Bradsher, 2013). In low-density areas such as California where driving is an easy option, the proportion of induced demand is likely to be even higher. Suburban and exurban sprawl around high-speed rail nodes – leading to secondary motor vehicle trips to and from stations and within low-density communities – is an additional concern.

In the Northern California Megaregion, those few megaregional planning exercises taken to date have focused primarily on infrastructure for HSR or on modest changes to existing land use. The only public sector planning effort to date at this scale, the *Planning for the Northern California Megaregion* vision document developed in 2009 by the Bay Area's Metropolitan Transportation Commission in conjunction with other regional agencies, focused primarily on land use and transportation options in the Interstate 80 corridor (MTC, 2009). The agencies developed three scenarios, but either because these alternatives were quite similar or because the models were unable to incorporate other policy variables related to road pricing, housing affordability, or economic development, their sustainability impacts were not significantly different. Carbon dioxide emissions, for example, differed by only 4 per cent from the baseline for all scenarios, with all three alternative scenarios producing higher emissions than the baseline. Thus by focusing on a narrow range of policy alternatives for a single corridor, this exercise clearly failed to address megaregional sustainability needs. Several reports by SPUR – the main Northern California non-governmental organization interested in megaregional planning – have focused almost exclusively on high-speed rail (SPUR, 2007, 2011). SPUR admits that few tools exist to limit sprawl in conjunction with a high-speed rail system, and that one of the lessons of the earlier Bay Area Regional Transit (BART) system was the importance of having land use controls in place before new transportation infrastructure is built (SPUR, 2011). However, perhaps entranced by the lure of megaregional infrastructure, this group, along with the TransForm regional smart growth coalition and other environmental organizations, have supported HSR anyway.

5.2.3 Promoting Megaregions Will Further Fuel Growthmania

A basic theme of the sustainability discourse from the beginning has been that the growth of human societies has limits – in terms of population, resource consumption, pollution, physical expansion and mobility (Wheeler, 2013). Not for nothing were two of the most influential early texts entitled *Limits to Growth* and *Small is Beautiful* (Meadows et al., 1972; Schumacher, 1975). Working within limits does not of course mean accepting a static or declining society; many types of qualitative improvement in human and ecological welfare would be possible even while reducing quantitative consumption, pollution and spatial expansion. Rather, it means looking for 'appropriate' levels of growth, technology and population.

From the start this 'limits' theme has been vigorously fought by opponents who argue that human ingenuity and the supposedly self-correcting nature of markets will be able to address environmental problems (for example Simon, 1981). In some areas these arguments have merit. Industries, for example, are often good at substituting certain materials for others that may be in short supply, and in recent years the fossil fuel industry has also proven remarkably adept at maintaining production through increasingly creative extraction processes. But in other areas such as global climate change, the 'limits' perspective must be taken very seriously.

Campbell (2009) argues that urban planning has been characterized by similarly contradictory impulses for rapid growth and 'small is beautiful' thinking. However, megaregional planning in particular seems guided by a logic of rapid growth of physical, economic and social systems, likely fueling economic globalization and the sort of consumption-oriented society that Daly (1973) labeled 'growthmania'. The point of most megaregional advocacy to date seems to be to knit urban areas together into larger and more cohesive units, and to have these units compete successfully within an increasingly global economy. Ross, for example, entitles her 2009 book *Megaregions: Planning for Global Competitiveness*, and argues elsewhere that megaregions provide a framework 'to direct infrastructure investment and enhance competitiveness' aimed at 'economic growth' (Ross, 2011, p. 343). Although she mentions 'sustainability' as a goal as well, there is little indication of how this is to be achieved, in contrast to the strong expectation that megaregional infrastructure will enable some parts of the world to position themselves better within a globalizing economy.

Advocates tend to assume that megaregions are the world's main engines of economic activity, and presumably would generate more economic development if better planned. But economic development of what sort? It is likely that these large urban constellations will be most suited to multinational businesses that will benefit from the global linkages, concentrations of capital and well-developed supply chains present in these areas. Thus enhancing the primacy of megaregions is likely to promote economic globalization at the expense of smaller-scale, more locally oriented communities and economies. Such economic globalization has been strongly critiqued by many sustainability advocates who see it as promoting highly consumptive lifestyles, potentially damaging forms of financial speculation, and excessive pollution, resource consumption and exploitation (for example Korten, 1995; Shuman, 1998).

Spatial growth is almost certain within a megaregional planning framework as jobs and housing spread outward from core urban areas and new edge cities emerge within the megaregion. Gottmann (1961) and others first identified megaregions precisely because of suburban sprawl's role in tying together clusters of cities. Glaeser (2007) sees megaregions as characterized by increasing decentralization, and finds that less dense regions grow faster in economic, population and spatial terms than denser ones. Unless strong steps are taken to manage spatial expansion (which is unlikely given political realities in many countries), this physical growth seems set to continue. Construction of megaregional infrastructure such as high-speed rail is likely to speed spatial expansion, since the experience of past transportation infrastructure has been that in the absence of strong growth management policies land development follows the new facilities outward. The result will be the opposite of the compact urban growth model usually preferred by sustainability advocates.

Growing mobility is yet another concern. Researchers have often assumed that this is desirable and should characterize megaregions. In fact the Regional Plan Association has used growing business travel between cities as an indicator of emerging megaregions (Goldfeld, 2007, p. 8). However, increased mobility works strongly against sustainability in a number of ways. No mode of transportation is carbon-neutral except for biking and walking (very local-scale modes), or is likely to be so anytime soon. So growing mobility means increased greenhouse gas emissions. Indeed, for decades increases in per-capita vehicle miles travel have been offsetting improvements in vehicle fuel efficiency. Moreover, even completely carbon-neutral vehicles would still damage natural and human environments in many ways, for example through the detrimental effects of traffic on communities, embodied energy in the production of the vehicles, and runoff from roads and parking lots. The more sustainable alternative is for planners to prioritize 'access' instead of 'mobility' – seeking to reduce people's travel needs through design of more compact, well-balanced communities and transportation demand management programs, rather than encouraging more travel by constructing new long-distance systems. But instead of doing this, even environmental organizations tend to assume that growth in motor vehicle and air travel is inevitable, and then rationalize high-speed rail as a less-damaging alternative mode (for example SPUR, 2011; Cohen, 2012).

Within California, an extreme example of the pro-growth approach to megaregional analysis is Landis and Reilly's study *How We Will Grow* (2003), whose title gives away the assumption that growth is inevitable. These authors map an expanding urban footprint in California from 33 million residents in 1997 to 92 million in 2100, and provide detailed maps showing much of the state eventually covered with new urban development. Predictably, urban areas merge along existing highway corridors to form one massive megaregion. The study never asks whether such growth is desirable or sustainable, or considers the possibility that state jurisdictions might seek to aggressively limit their urban footprint (for example by establishing greenbelts or urban growth boundaries) or that the state might stabilize its population at lower levels through better family planning, reductions in poverty and improvements in the status of women (three leading mechanisms for population stabilization globally). Rather, the authors take into account only relatively minor variations in land use regulation. Such a growth-oriented BAU orientation is a major problem with much megaregional analysis.

Similarly, one of the arguments that SPUR uses to support high-speed rail in California is the threat of falling behind other global competitors, pointing out that 'Far smaller economies and regions have built or are building high-speed rail' (Terplan and Gao, 2012, p. 2). The group also backs HSR on the grounds that it 'provides armature for the state's growth' (ibid., p. 4). Although it provides some good suggestions for how land use could be improved in conjunction with HSR, the organization fails to condition its support on adoption of such land use planning, and like Landis and Reilly fails to express concern that California is expected to add 20 million people by 2050. Rather, this population growth is taken for granted. While the City of San Francisco, whose development SPUR has historically advocated, is likely to benefit by being an HSR terminus and a main node in the development of a California megaregion, the organization fails to consider the overall sustainability of the growth-oriented trajectory it is recommending.

On the ground it is far from clear that rapid economic development, integration into the global economy and spatial expansion have been good for the Northern California Megaregion in the past. Certainly many jobs have been created and tax dollars generated by the expansion of industries related to computers, bio-technology, finance and other fields. But growth has created large and often unappreciated costs as well. Large amounts of farmland and open space have been lost to sprawl, large quantities of greenhouse gases have been generated, and many low-income residents have been burdened with pollution, expensive housing, poor schools and long commutes. Silicon Valley, long seen as a global model of economic development, is in fact a highly congested, extremely expensive locale with great social inequities, substantial pollution, bad traffic and a sprawling, poorly designed public realm. Rather than producing new centres of civilization such as London, Paris or Rome, past regional growth has created an amorphous sprawl of unattractive office buildings, freeways and subdivisions. San Jose, California's third largest city which often bills itself as the capital of Silicon Valley, is considering cutting pensions and health care for existing workers in an effort to avoid bankruptcy (Lyman and Walsh, 2013). Clearly the region's growth has had very mixed results and expanded megaregional development should be viewed with caution.

5.2.4   Local Solutions Will Be De-emphasized

Funding, institutional attention and advocates' energy can only be focused on so many places at once. An emphasis on megaregional planning and infrastructure is likely to decrease chances that more locally oriented development strategies are undertaken. Constructing high-speed rail, for example, may well tie up funding that could instead be spent on central city transit or less glamorous track and equipment upgrades within existing metropolitan areas. Developers and homebuyers may turn their attention to new outlying subdivisions near high-speed rail stops rather than inner-city infill. Large-scale energy and water infrastructure may distract from local conservation efforts. Political efforts to develop megaregional institutions and governance may sap energy from local and regional campaigns.

Large-scale systems, fast speeds and high technology are often sexy in ways that simpler, lower-consumption, more local lifestyles are not. But while they may attract the attention of planning experts as well as large economic interests who stand to benefit, these larger-scale strategies are not necessarily the most sustainable or desirable in terms of quality of life. Several times before societies have turned away from the path of assuming that bigger, faster and high-tech is better. In the 1970s a concerted environmental organizing campaign as well as engineering and economic challenges limited production of supersonic transport (SST) planes to a small number serving only trans-Atlantic routes. Although this technology like HSR offered the potential of significantly reducing air travel times and knitting the world more closely together, policymakers deemed costs such as sonic booms and potential damage to the ozone layer not worth the benefits. Also, most societies chose not to pursue nuclear power beyond those facilities built during the 1960s and 1970s, often emphasizing the vastly more sustainable strategy of energy conservation instead. Again, large-scale, high-tech systems were found to have significant downsides. There is precedent, in other words, to the idea that planning for a megaregional future is not necessary and that smaller-scale solutions may be preferable.

Within Northern California, grass-roots movements for localism are relatively strong, shown for example by local foodshed planning (for example Thompson et al., 2008) and buy-local campaigns (for example Sustainable Business Alliance, 2013). However, these movements still operate on a niche scale, and larger organizations representing mainstream businesses such as the Bay Area Council are pushing strongly for megaregional-scale initiatives such as high-speed rail (for example Bay Area Council, 2012). Economic and lifestyle trends have also undercut a focus on local communities. Over the past 60 years or more the decentralization of retail and employment – abetted by suburban land use planning – has meant the abandonment of many downtowns and central city areas, a condition which cities such as Oakland, San Jose, Richmond and Stockton are still seeking to recover from. High housing prices have meant that many workers in core cities such as San Francisco, Oakland, San Jose and Sacramento have had to commute from great distances, and that large new 'bedroom suburbs' have sprung up in places like Tracy, Stockton and Elk Grove. Freeway expansions, commuter rail extensions and NIMBY ('not-in-my-backyard') opposition to affordable housing in infill locations have facilitated such dispersal away from existing communities. The most powerful forces at work in the megaregion, in short, are still strongly against localism. Although many nonprofit organizations and some local governments are promoting place-based lifestyles, they face an uphill battle.

5.2.5   Equity Loses Again

As others have noted (for example Benner and Pastor, 2011), whenever equity advocates make progress at a given scale of planning the emphasis has often shifted to a larger scale. When progressive political constituencies gained control of many North American cities in the mid-20th century, suburban growth moved the effective scale of development to the metropolitan level. Now, after a wave of 'new regionalism' in the 1990s and 2000s (Wheeler, 2002; Pastor et al., 2009a) that made modest progress toward some regional equity-related goals (growth management; balanced distribution of affordable housing; environmental justice organizing), the megaregion threatens that gain and may be a particularly difficult scale at which to address equity issues (Dewar and Epstein, 2007). Fainstein and Fainstein (2009, p. 192) argue that state governments in the US already have the capacity to address large-scale equity issues, if these can be made more prominent policy objectives, and that large-scale consolidation of planning institutions 'holds little promise for erasing disadvantage'.

If increased wealth and opportunity can be distributed fairly within megaregions, then conceivably the old adage that 'a rising tide lifts all boats' will apply. Benner and Pastor (2012) argue that regional structural factors such as educational systems, governmental consolidation, more diverse economies and a common vision can potentially promote both equity and growth, and conversely that more equitable regions have higher chances for economic growth. However, ensuring equity in practice has been extraordinarily difficult at the regional scale let alone the megaregional level. Moreover, a focus on megaregions might well create additional disparities and poses four main equity threats.

The first of these equity challenges is continued spatial segregation of socioeconomic groups within the expanding geographical area. The sprawling metropolitan region of the 20th century allowed wealthier, predominantly white residents to leave the central city, decentralizing into gated enclaves and upscale suburbs typically with a conservative political character. People of different types had less need to see each other on a daily basis let alone share facilities such as parks and schools. Job and educational opportunities declined for less-advantaged populations; Hall (2009, p. 811) notes an increased 'educational apartheid' in British city-regions. Financial disparities between jurisdictions increased, resulting for example in the 2013 bankruptcy of the City of Detroit within a metropolitan region characterized by a reasonably healthy economy overall and many wealthy suburbs (Reich, 2013; Stiglitz, 2013). With the exception of the Minneapolis-St. Paul region, which adopted a partial tax-base sharing program in 1982 (Orfield, 1997), regional governments have had little success in stemming these growing spatial inequities. Across megaregions, segregation would be of an even larger scale and mechanisms for sharing resources and promoting equity even weaker. The poorest communities would be literally hundreds of miles away from the wealthiest, and the latter would likely feel even less responsibility towards the former. The possibilities for resource distribution would be slight indeed.

A second, related equity threat is that gentrification of urban cores and other desirable locations within the megaregion may displace less affluent populations to far-flung fringes, burdening them with long commutes to work, lower levels of services and loss of their existing neighbourhoods. Within metropolitan regions such displacement has had a long history, but within the new megaregional form it may take place over much vaster distances, as discussed further in the Northern California discussion below.

A third main threat is that through a focus on megaregional planning, public and private institutions will neglect the 'white areas' between megaregions on maps. Investment in potentially catalytic facilities may go disproportionately to these favored areas, which after all account for a large share of the population and economy. Well-educated, creative people may also disproportionately flock to these megaregions, since those places have the social tolerance, quality of life, job opportunities and amenities they desire (Florida, 2008). Within the US, Appalachia, the Plains States, the Mississippi Delta, much of the Deep South and the Northern Rockies would be left behind as the coasts and a few other megaregions take off. Thus large-scale spatial inequities would increase. Yaro (2009) has proposed strategies to reduce such disparities, including a US Regional Development Fund and reforms to agricultural subsidies, but the prospects of these steps being enacted are slight. On a global scale, Roy (2009, p. 824) worries that emphasizing certain cities and regions then 'drops all other cities from the map'. This framework might recapitulate past 'core–periphery' dichotomies of global development, resulting in great injury to much of the developing world.

A final equity threat has to do with the extent to which megaregional planning promotes economic globalization and undercuts local businesses and progressive governance. Increased mobility within and between megaregions can potentially allow capital to play off different locations against one another to seek the lowest level of regulation and obligation. The Tieboutian world of public choice might come to its logical conclusion: extreme mobility of capital and elites would weaken local initiative and leave communities and the environment at the mercy of the private sector. The rich would locate in well-serviced locations within favoured megaregions, while the environment and less advantaged populations suffer.

Within the Northern California megaregion, many of these dynamics can already be seen at play. Spatial segregation is increasing at the megaregional scale for a number of reasons. As housing prices have risen, new residents moving into core areas such as San Francisco are increasingly wealthy (Pastor et al., 2009b). Meanwhile, low-income, predominantly ethnic populations have moved increasingly from the core to older inner ring suburbs or to Central Valley locations such as Fresno, Modesto and Sacramento. Many newer immigrants bypass the central Bay Area entirely for these cheaper locales. Also, soaring housing prices during the 1990s and 2000s displaced many middle-income Silicon Valley workers to the Central Valley cities of Stockton and Tracy, where 2–3-hour commutes to high-tech jobs became common. Wages for low-income Bay Area workers have fallen in the past decade, while salaries for the upper end have risen particularly rapidly (Avalos, 2012), further aggravating disparities. Analysis by the USC Program for Environmental and Regional Equity shows that blacks and Latinos in the Bay Area increasingly lack the educational background required for the new jobs being created there, a trend that promises increasing racial inequality in the future (Pastor et al., 2009b, p. 8). Although the State of California has sought to require jurisdictions in regions such as the Bay Area to build their fair share of affordable housing, such requirements have few teeth and have failed to stem the tide of spatial inequity.

5.3   CONCLUSION

Sustainability, of course, requires action at every scale of planning and government and development of mutually reinforcing initiatives across different levels. So some attention to the megaregional scale is desirable. But the above discussion should lead to great caution. Uncritical development of infrastructure, institutions and programs at the megaregional level could accelerate BAU trends that are leading to disastrous climate change, growing social inequity and other sustainability problems. It is imperative to avoid this future.

To the extent that megaregional planning is pursued, it will be important to rethink its goals. Environmental sustainability, quality of life and social equity should be leading objectives, rather than rapid economic expansion, increased mobility, or further integration of megaregions into the global economy. More specifically, policymakers might pursue the following strategies:

- Preserve open land between metropolitan regions through the creation of greenbelts, urban growth boundaries, or regional preserves, and through lower tax levels for agricultural land;
- Reduce commuting between metropolitan regions through appropriate road, rail and air transport pricing, and through restraint in building transportation infrastructure that encourages such commuting;
- Prioritize slower-speed, more local pedestrian, bike and public transit facilities instead of freeways, high-speed rail, airport expansions and other facilities for long-distance travel;
- Develop compact, well-balanced cities and towns whose residents do not need to commute elsewhere for jobs, housing, schools, or recreation;
- Adopt strong regulation to protect ecosystems on a bioregional scale;
- Support locally owned, small- or medium-scale businesses serving local and regional markets, rather than economic development strategies aimed at multinational corporations and export-oriented growth; and
- Reduce megaregional inequities through state, provincial, or national efforts aimed at tax base equalization as well as fair distribution of affordable housing, livable minimum wages, and adequate schools, transit and other services.

Undoubtedly other strategies could be added to this list. The end result would be more balanced, locally oriented communities where most of life is lived on a scale of a few miles rather than many hundreds. Such an alternative has many benefits in terms of quality of life, reduced environmental impact, improved social equity and enhanced social capital. Ideally a greater commitment to stewardship of particular places would go along with this change and an ethic of interdependence between socioeconomic groups.

Rather than being seduced by megaregional analysis and technologies such as high-speed rail, the need is for policymakers to develop visions of a sustainable society at all scales of planning. The megaregional scale may be a useful one in some cases. But it should probably remain a relatively small player in the planning universe, with much emphasis placed locally and regionally instead, or else at higher levels of government where mechanisms already exist to adopt strong sustainability initiatives.

REFERENCES

America 2050 (2013a), 'U.S. Megaregions', available at http://www.america2050.
org/maps/ (accessed 26 July 2013).

America 2050 (2013b), 'Northern California', available at http://www.america2050.
org/northern_california.html (accessed 13 August 2013).

Amtrak (2012), *The Amtrak Vision for the Northeast Corridor: 2012 Update Report*,
Washington, DC: Amtrak, available at http://www.amtrak.com/ccurl/453/325/
Amtrak-Vision-for-the-Northeast-Corridor.pdf (accessed 26 September 2013).

Avalos, G. (2012), 'Wage disparity: Bay Area's lower-paid workers fail to keep up
with inflation, while top earners see bigger checks', *Contra Costa Times*, 5 July
2012.

Bay Area Council (2012), 'High speed rail decision a big win for California, the Bay
Area and the Bay Area Council', news release, 10 July 2012, available at http://
www.bayareacouncil.org/news/2012/07/10/high-speed-rail-decision-a-big-win-
for-california-the-bay-area-and-the-bay-area-council/ (accessed 26 September
2013).

Beebe, C. and S.M. Wheeler (2012), 'Gold Country: the politics of landscape in
exurban El Dorado County, California', *Journal of Political Ecology*, **19**, 1–16.

Benner, C. and M. Pastor (2008), 'Fractures and fault lines: growth and equity
in California's megaregions', report presented to the America 2050 Research
Seminar on Megaregions, available at http://www.america2050.org/2009/03/
fractures-and-faultlines-growth-and-equity-in-californias-megaregions.html
(accessed 26 September 2013).

Benner, C. and M. Pastor (2011), 'Moving on up? Regions, megaregions, and the
changing geography of social equity organizing', *Urban Affairs Review*, **47** (3),
315–348.

Benner, C. and M. Pastor (2012), *Just Growth: Inclusion and Prosperity in
America's Metropolitan Regions*, New York: Routledge.

Bradsher, K. (2013), 'Speed trains transform China', *The New York Times*,
24 September 2013, 1.

Campbell, S. (2009), 'The imperative of growth, the rhetoric of sustainability:
the divergence of the ecoregion and the global megaregion', in C.L. Ross (ed.),
Megaregions: Planning for Global Competitiveness, Washington, DC: Island
Press, pp. 127–139.

Cohen, S. (2012), *Moving Ahead with High-Speed Rail*, Oakland, CA: TransForm.

Creative Class Group (2008), 'Mega-regions of North America', available at
http://www.creativeclass.com/_v3/whos_your_city/maps/#Mega-Regions_of_
North_America (accessed 26 July 2013).

Daly, H.E. (ed.) (1973), *Toward a Steady-State Economy*, San Francisco, CA:
W.H. Freeman.

Danielson, M.N. and J.W. Doig (1982), *New York: The Politics of Urban Regional
Development*, Berkeley, CA: University of California Press.

Dear, M.J. (2000), *The Postmodern Urban Condition*, Malden, MA: Blackwell.

Dewar, M. and D. Epstein (2007), 'Planning for "megaregions" in the United
States', *Journal of Planning Literature*, **22** (2), 108–124.

Fainstein, N. and S.S. Fainstein (2009), 'Social equity and the challenge of
distressed places', in C.L. Ross (ed.), *Megaregions: Planning for Global
Competitiveness*, Washington, DC: Island Press, pp. 191–215.

Faludi, A. (2009), 'The megalopolis, the Blue Banana, and global economic integration zones in European planning thought', in C.L. Ross (ed.), *Megaregions: Planning for Global Competitiveness*, Washington, DC: Island Press, pp. 18–34.

Fleming, B. (2015), 'Towards a megaregional future: analysing progress, assessing priorities in the US megaregion project', in J. Harrison and M. Hoyler (eds), *Megaregions: Globalization's New Urban Form?* Cheltenham, UK and Northampton, MA, USA: Edward Elgar, pp. 200–229.

Florida, R. (2008), 'Megaregions: the importance of place', *Harvard Business Review*, March, 18–19.

Garreau, J. (1991), *Edge City: Life on the New Frontier*, New York: Doubleday.

Glaeser, E. (2007), 'Do regional economies need regional coordination?', in K.S. Goldfield (ed.), *The Economic Geography of Megaregions*, Princeton, NJ: The Policy Research Institute for the Region, pp. 11–57.

Glass, M.R. (2015), 'Conflicting spaces of governance in the imagined Great Lakes megaregion', in J. Harrison and M. Hoyler (eds), *Megaregions: Globalization's New Urban Form?* Cheltenham, UK and Northampton, MA, USA: Edward Elgar, pp. 119–145.

Goldfield K.S. (ed.) (2007), *The Economic Geography of Megaregions*, Princeton, NJ: The Policy Research Institute for the Region, pp. 11–57.

Gottmann, J. (1961), *Megalopolis: The Urbanized Northeastern Seaboard of the United States*, New York: Twentieth Century Fund.

Hall, P. (2009), 'Looking backward, looking forward: the city region of the mid-21st century', *Regional Studies*, **43** (6), 803–817.

Hall, P. (2011), 'The polycentric metropolis: a Western European perspective on mega-city regions', in J. Xu and A.G.O. Yeh (eds), *Governance and Planning of Mega-City Regions: An International Comparative Perspective*, London: Routledge, pp. 29–50.

Innes, J.E., D.E. Booher and S. Di Vittorio (2010), 'Strategies for megaregion governance: collaborative dialogue, networks, and self-organization', *Journal of the American Planning Association*, **77** (1), 55–67.

Korten, D. (1995), *When Corporations Rule the World*, San Francisco: Berrett-Koehler Publishers.

Landis, J.D. and M. Reilly (2003), 'How we will grow: baseline projections of the growth of California's urban footprint through the year 2100', IURD Working Paper, 2003-04, Berkeley, CA: Institute of Urban and Regional Development, available at http://www.escholarship.org/uc/item/8ff3q0ns (accessed 26 September 2013).

Lang, R.E. (2003), *Edgeless Cities: Exploring the Elusive Metropolis*, Washington, DC: Brookings Institution Press.

Lyman, R. and M.W. Walsh (2013), 'Struggling San Jose plans to cut worker benefits', *The New York Times*, 24 September 2013, 1.

Mazmanian, D.A. and M.E. Kraft (eds) (2009), *Toward Sustainable Communities: Transition and Transformations in Environmental Policy*, 2nd edition, Cambridge, MA: MIT Press.

Meadows, D., D.L. Meadows, J. Randers and W.W. Behrens III (1972), *The Limits to Growth*, New York: Universe Books.

MTC (Metropolitan Transportation Commission) (2009), *Planning for the Northern California Megaregion*, Oakland: MTC, available at http://www.

mtc.ca.gov/planning/smart_growth/I-80/I-80_Land_Use_Tranport_Study.pdf (accessed 26 July 2013).

Nelson, A.C. and R.E. Lang (2011), *Megapolitan America: A New Vision for Understanding America's Metropolitan Geography*, Chicago, IL: APA Planners Press.

Orfield, M. (1997), *Metropolitics: A Regional Agenda for Community and Stability*, Washington, DC and Cambridge, MA: Brookings Institution Press and Lincoln Institute of Land Policy.

Orman, L.A. (1976), *Planning the Metropolis: Regional Planning in the San Francisco Bay Area*, Masters Thesis, University of California at Berkeley.

Pastor, M., C. Benner and M. Matsuoka (2009a), *This Could Be the Start of Something Big: How Social Movements for Regional Equity are Reshaping Metropolitan America*, Ithaca, NY: Cornell University Press.

Pastor, M., R. Ortiz, J. Tran, J. Scoggins and V. Carter (2009b), *State of the Region: Growth, Equity, and Inclusion in the Bay Area*, Los Angeles, CA: USC Program for Environmental and Regional Equity (PERE).

Reich, R. (2013), 'Detroit, and the bankruptcy of America's social contract', blog posting, 20 July 2013, available at http://robertreich.org/ (accessed 26 September 2013).

Ross, C.L. (ed.) (2009), *Megaregions: Planning for Global Competitiveness*, Washington, DC: Island Press.

Ross, C.L. (2011), 'Transport and megaregions: high-speed rail in the United States', *Town Planning Review*, **82** (3), 341–353.

Roy, A. (2009), 'The 21st-century metropolis: new geographies of theory', *Regional Studies*, **43** (6), 819–830.

Rusk, D. (1999), *Inside Game/Outside Game: Winning Strategies for Saving Urban America*, Washington, DC: Brookings Institution Press.

Schafran, A. (2015), 'Beyond globalization: a historical urban development approach to understanding megaregions', in J. Harrison and M. Hoyler (eds), *Megaregions: Globalization's New Urban Form?* Cheltenham, UK and Northampton, MA, USA: Edward Elgar, pp. 75–96.

Schumacher, E.F. (1975), *Small is Beautiful: Economics as if People Mattered*, New York: Harper & Row.

Self, P. (1982), *Planning the Urban Region: A Comparative Study of Policies and Organizations*, Tuscaloosa, AL: University of Alabama Press.

Seltzer, E. (2011), 'Comment: megaregions and nations', *Town Planning Review*, **82** (3), 354–356.

Shuman, M. (1998), *Going Local: Creating Self-Reliant Communities in a Global Age*, New York: Simon & Schuster.

Simon, J.L. (1981), *The Ultimate Resource*, Princeton, NJ: Princeton University Press.

SPUR (San Francisco Planning and Urban Research Association) (2007), 'The Northern California Megaregion', *The Urbanist*, November/December.

SPUR (San Francisco Planning and Urban Research Association) (2011), *Beyond the Tracks: The Potential of High-Speed Rail to Shape California's Growth*, San Francisco: SPUR.

Stiglitz, J.E. (2013), 'The wrong lesson from Detroit's bankruptcy', *The New York Times*, 11 August 2013, Opinionator column.

Sustainable Business Alliance (2013), 'Think local', available at http://www.sustainablebusinessalliance.org/ (accessed 14 August 2013).

Sutcliffe, A. (1993), 'The giant city as a historical phenomenon', in T. Barker and A. Sutcliffe (eds), *Megalopolis: The Giant City in History*, New York: St. Martin's Press, pp. 1–13.

Terplan, E. and H. Gao (2012), 'Getting high-speed rail on track', *The Urbanist*, July, 2–4.

Thompson, E. Jr., A.M. Harper and S. Kraus (2008), *Think Globally, Eat Locally: San Francisco Foodshed Assessment*, American Farmland Trust, available at http://www.farmland.org/programs/states/ca/Feature%20Stories/documents/ThinkGloballyEatLocally-FinalReport8-23-08.pdf (accessed 26 September 2013).

Wheeler, S.M. (2002), 'The new regionalism: key characteristics of an emerging movement', *Journal of the American Planning Association*, **68** (3), 267–278.

Wheeler, S.M. (2008), 'The evolution of built landscapes in metropolitan regions', *Journal of Planning Education and Research*, **27** (4), 400–416.

Wheeler, S.M. (2009), 'Regions, megaregions, and sustainability', *Regional Studies*, **43** (6), 863–876.

Wheeler, S.M. (2013), *Planning for Sustainability: Toward Livable, Equitable, and Ecological Communities*, 2nd edition, New York: Routledge.

Wheeler, S.M. and C.W. Beebe (2011), 'The rise of the postmodern metropolis: spatial evolution of the Sacramento metropolitan region', *Journal of Urban Design*, **16** (3), 307–332.

Xu, J. and A.G.O. Yeh (2011), 'Coordinating the fragmented mega-city regions in China: state reconstruction and regional strategic planning', in J. Xu and A.G.O. Yeh (eds), *Governance and Planning of Mega-City Regions: An International Comparative Perspective*, London: Routledge, pp. 213–235.

Yang, J. (2009), 'Spatial planning in Asia: planning and developing megacities and megaregions', in C.L. Ross (ed.), *Megaregions: Planning for Global Competitiveness*, Washington, DC: Island Press, pp. 35–52.

Yaro, R.D. (2009), 'Toward a national reinvestment strategy for underperforming regions', in P. Todorovich and Y. Hagler (eds), *New Strategies for Regional Economic Development*, Cambridge, MA: Lincoln Institute of Land Policy, pp. 13–19.

Yaro, R.D. (2011), 'Moving forward: the promise of megaregions and high-speed rail', in E. Seltzer and A. Carbonell (eds), *Regional Planning in America: Practice and Prospect*, Cambridge, MA: Lincoln Institute of Land Policy, pp. 243–268.

6. Conflicting spaces of governance in the imagined Great Lakes megaregion

Michael R. Glass

6.1 INTRODUCTION

> Almost no one favors metropolitan area government except a few political scientists and intellectuals. Proposals to replace suburban governments completely are therefore doomed. That is why fewer than a dozen or so metropolitan areas have regional governments. (Downs, 1994, p. 170)

The megaregion concept provides a compelling vision for the way that spatial relations in the US are structured, with advocates proposing that they could form the basis for cooperative integrated planning (Hagler, 2009). Interest in megaregions has grown in recent years and not only in the US, as the other contributions to this volume make clear. The megaregion is thus deserving of considerable scrutiny: especially if proponents like Sudjic (1992), Ross (2009), Lang and Knox (2009) are correct in suggesting that the era of the 100 mile metroplex is close at hand. Characterized by polycentricity, interconnectivity and other tangible and intangible forms of cohesion, the megaregion is considered as a planning framework and as a conceptual device to understand the reassertion of a new type of modernity (Lang and Knox, 2009). Despite the growing interest in categorizing the megaregion concept, the notion of the megaregion as a space for coordinated planning shares much in common with other utopic planning visions like Howard's Garden City model, or the 1927 Regional Plan for a metropolitan 'greater' New York – both of which proposed broader spatial units for urban management under the premise that modern urbanism involves problems which are resistant to management at more fragmented scales. Certainly, the recent evidence put forth by the Regional Plan Association (RPA) in support of America's new megaregional geography has an apparently unimpeachable logic: the extent of the proposed megaregions account for approximately three-quarters of the US population and Gross Domestic Product. In addition, cycles of investment and disinvestment mean that the urban places in these broad catchments face problems to do with infrastructural redevelopment, environmental protection, and economic vitality that preclude localized solutions.

However, as alluring as the prospect for rescaling the framework of regional planning initiatives seems, I argue that there is no capacity to enact a new regional governance framework – at any scale – detached from the inherited and often overlapping political, social, and economic geographies of those spaces. In this chapter, I use a poststructural political economy (PSPE) perspective to explain that we should consider the megaregion concept to be a geographic imaginary that is neither natural nor neutral, but that is instead conceived, performed and enacted by specific stakeholders to bring about particular spatial effects. A specific political project is attempted here through the repetitive discursive proclamation of the megaregion (through invocation of classic models, through maps, terminology, institutional symbols and invocations of the authority of researchers and institutions), and yet the ability for this space to gain legitimacy – defined here as political sovereignty – is challenged by the fact that there is no stable, prediscursive geography predating the geographical imaginary being put forth by the RPA and others: in other words, there is no *tabula rasa*, but rather a confusion of administrative and economic spaces, as well as other regional visions which make implementation of the megaregion much more problematic than its proponents presume.

In this chapter I describe the components of regional government and governance in the US which make the policy implementation of the megaregion concept difficult in practice. Focusing on the Great Lakes megaregion – a space which spans from Pennsylvania westwards to Minnesota – we find hundreds of competing governance spaces, all with different legacies, authorities and sociospatial constituencies. This leads to three propositions. First, the inherited legacy of governance spaces complicates the capacity for proposed governance spaces to easily provide a new or coherent space for formalized regional planning. Second, the real and preexisting political geographies which exist within the space of the Great Lakes megaregion are themselves examples of successful geographical imaginaries. This creates friction which works against the implementation of new geographic projects, as proponents of new governance spaces come into conflict with defenders of established spaces. Third, existing political geographies matter, and cannot be an afterthought when creating new geographic projects. The political units constituting America's urban system may well be outdated, but still contain significant meaning for their residents, as suggested by the opening quote from regional economist

Anthony Downs. When tied to general suspicion about the motives and merit for non-local government which exists across the US, promotion of new governance frameworks at such extensive spatial scales seems a quixotic proposition.

In the following section, I provide a brief overview of the US megaregion concept, introducing the proponents of this geographical imaginary, and their purpose for promoting the megaregion as a new space for regional governance and analysis. Next, I explain how an approach based in poststructural political economy treats imaginaries such as the megaregion. Focusing on Western Pennsylvania, I provide examples of former successful and proposed geographical imaginaries which share similarities with the megaregion, although at smaller spatial scales. I then introduce the Great Lakes megaregion, explaining how the seemingly stable megaregion space is fraught with complications based on the underlying political geographies which pre-exist the megaregion concept. The layering of different governance spaces indicates both the complexity of enacting the megaregion concept, as well as the underlying challenges facing this Midwestern region. Finally, I argue that although the megaregion concept is unlikely to be implemented as a space for planning, some value exists to regarding this spatial project. First, the megaregion discourse reveals the prevailing narratives and theories which compel stakeholders to act, allowing us to look for the hidden architectures and scaffolds that underpin the seemingly neutral maps of the planner. Second, they can denote shifting practices in how we conceive urban and regional geographies, especially when we pay attention to the way that the now classic analyses of geographers including Jean Gottmann and Jim Vance are used over time. Third, by tackling critically the megaregion and similar geographical imaginaries, we engage with what Gibson-Graham (2004) called fields of encounter: prompting us to greater reflexivity over our own research practices, and how we develop our own imaginative projects.

6.2   THE US MEGAREGION CONCEPT

6.2.1   From Gottmann to the RPA

Despite the recent revival of interest in the megaregion concept, the American megaregion has a lengthy lineage. Accounts of its provenance regularly touch upon the work of the mid-20th century geographer Jean Gottmann, who used the term 'megalopolis' to define the economic integration of the northeastern US (Gottmann, 1961). Gottmann's highly detailed study emblematizes the best of mid-20th century geography, as it constructs a unified accounting of the history, physical environment, economy, and politics of the northeastern seaboard which he claims constitutes an interdependent space of economic and social flows which is hindered to some extent by the region's political fragmentation. Beyond Gottmann, modelers such as J.E. Vance also noted the increasing polycentrism of US urbanization. Vance, who was an urban geographer with a deep interest in transportation systems and urban growth (Godfrey, 1999), developed the 'urban realms' idea which claimed cities within a metropolitan region were less dependent on a monocentric Central Business District, and that the 20th century American metropolis was integrated at a larger scale than was usually presumed (Vance, 1977).

These classic accounts have become necessary referents for scholars and practitioners working to rethink America's regional geographies, although it is less certain that close attention is paid to the arguments of these works; for instance, whereas Gottmann's title is frequently cited, there is less engagement with the content of his arguments, including his abiding sense that whereas economic integration in the US was occurring at increasing spatial scales, the country's federal system and local parochialism would preclude effective coordinated governance at similarly broad geographic extents. Gottmann's realism concerning the barriers to intergovernmental cooperation appears clearly in *Megalopolis: The Urbanized Northeastern Seaboard of the United States*, and many of the barriers he outlined remain vexing issues for contemporary governance reformers. While Gottmann was optimistic that politics could change to reflect the new megalopolis, his rationale appears rooted in the modernist ethos of centrally planned urban redevelopment projects and low citizen participation. For instance, he argued '[t]o get people to behave like good neighbors despite local antagonisms and rivalries requires ethical and moral teaching and the invoking of high principles' which would involve the leadership of political and religious communities (Gottmann, 1961, p. 740). Basing plans for governance reform on a premise such as this seems unreasonable in the 21st century and yet his thesis is treated uncritically, with the presumption that it can be used to substantiate current policy proposals such as the megaregion. Hence, the persisting reference to Gottmann is motivated less by his original analysis, and more by the purpose of contemporary regionalists. As Allen et al. (1998) described in their book *Rethinking the Region*,

> [Regional] studies are always done for a purpose, with a specific aim in view. Whether theoretical, political, cultural or whatever, there is always a specific

focus. One cannot study everything, and there are always multiple ways of seeing a place: there is no complete 'portrait of a region'. Moreover . . . 'regions' only exist in relation to particular criteria. They are not 'out there' waiting to be discovered; they are our (and others') constructions. (Allen et al., 1998, p. 2)

This critique, while originally targeted at research in the United Kingdom context, is also applicable to work on the megaregion in the US. For proponents of the megaregion concept, classic studies which indicate the large-scale regionalization of America's urban geographies become evidence for naturalizing the sense that there is, in fact, a megaregional geography 'out there', waiting to be revealed. This certainly seems to be the goal of the RPA's America 2050 platform, which hypothesizes the existence of 11 US megaregions.

6.2.2 Recent Initiatives – RPA Megaregions

In the introduction to an RPA position paper defining the megaregion as a new spatial reality for the US, the following claim is being made:

> As metropolitan regions continued to expand throughout the second half of the 20th century their boundaries began to blur, *creating a new scale of geography* now known as the megaregion. Interlocking economic systems, shared natural resources and ecosystems, and common transportation systems *link these population centers together*. As continued population growth and low density settlement patterns place increasing pressure on these systems, *there is greater impetus to coordinate policy at this expanded scale*. (Hagler, 2009, p. 1; emphasis added)

This statement positions the megaregion as a reality, creating the impression that growth and increasing interdependence are inevitable aspects of urbanism in the US. Following this proposition, the document invokes notions of connectivity and linkage to claim that there is a 'greater impetus' for coordination at broader scales, which can 'incorporate population centers as well as natural landscapes' (Hagler, 2009, p. 1). Unspoken in this argument is any information on who is creating the greater impetus for coordination – simply that it occurs. Based on the underlying premise that these megaregions exist and only needed to be discovered and 'revealed', the RPA and partner organizations developed a methodology to codify these new scales of geography.[1]

The RPA methodology to identify the megaregional geography of the US included five questions to determine whether a location was part of a megaregion (Hagler, 2009, p. 2):

1. Is a county part of a Core Based Statistical Area?
2. Does the population density of the county exceed 200 people per square mile in the 2000 Census?
3. Is population growth of over 15 per cent (and which exceeds 1000 people) expected by 2025?
4. Will population density increase by 50 people per square mile between 2000 and 2025?
5. Will employment growth exceed 15 per cent (and by total growth of at least 20 000 jobs) by 2025?

Working with American county units, these five criteria were used to devise scores for each US county. While this is not the venue to critique the full methodology, it should be noted that there is room for interpretation on each of these vectors, and for the selection of counties, rather than other geographic units, as the base units of analysis. The RPA criteria were used to create an aggregate score for all 3140 US counties, and these were then used to identify the megaregions of the US. In all, 988 of 3140 counties were considered as part of a megaregion – or 31 per cent of all counties. The resulting megaregion map is by now familiar: centred on the key urban areas of the US, the eleven megaregions include large amounts of territory across the country (see Harrison and Hoyler, 2015, Figure 1.1).

6.2.3   Goals of Megaregion Proponents

Proponents of the megaregion at institutions including the RPA and Washington, DC-based think-tank the Brookings Institution are explicit about their goals for these conceptual spaces: they intend megaregions to be the spatial containers for a new or renewed regional planning which transcends the problems of the contemporary city by creating new geographic scales to meet new challenges. After the 11 US megaregions were defined, policy analysis began focusing on the challenges and opportunities of specific megaregions. In an early evaluation of the Great Lakes megaregion, the language used by Brookings researchers is strongly constructionist – they 'articulate', 'enhance', 'expand' and 'create' when describing the need to enact a megaregional approach to the Great Lakes area (Austin and Affolter-Caine, 2006). In the introduction to the report, the authors explain that whereas the 12 states of the region contain a large population, important cities and valuable resources, the vitality of the region is threatened through globalization and economic change. Accordingly, 'the time is now for Great Lakes leaders to articulate a meaningful agenda for what the states of the region and the federal government can do together to ensure that this economic giant steps in the right direction' (Austin and Affolter-Caine, 2006, p. 4). The policy prescription for these perceived challenges is for federal and state agencies to create a collaborative platform to enhance region-wide competitiveness. Indeed, economic justifications for action are frequently cited as the fundamental concern driving the megaregion discourse – for instance, an influential volume edited by planner Catherine Ross promoting the megaregion concept is subtitled 'Planning for Global Competitiveness' (Ross, 2009). Although there is certainly nothing intrinsically flawed with policies for economic development, this does bring to mind Doreen Massey's critique of addressing 'regional problems' through territorially circumscribed approaches that overlook the structural and often exogenous influences affecting the region (Massey, 1979). Furthermore, the emphasis placed on economic imperatives indicates that efforts to 'reveal' and empower the megaregion are less neutral or technocentric than might first be anticipated, and such proposals are instead aligned with neoliberal discourses of economic competition based on rescaled governance and interregional competition (Storper, 1997; Brenner, 2004).

6.3 IMAGINATIVE GEOGRAPHIES

To engage with proposed geopolitical entities such as the megaregion is to engage with the geographic imaginaries of those proposing the new political spaces. This is to say that despite the appearance of naturalness, neutrality or inevitability presented in maps of American megaregions published by the Regional Plan Association's America 2050 programme or in studies by advocates of the megaregion, such spaces are anything but neutral. Rather, they are the consequence of intentional designs and practices by planners and other interested actors seeking to institute the megaregion – first as a cartographic reality, and consequently as fully instituted spaces for political governance and power. Such imaginative geographies therefore carry significant implications for planning, and should be subject to critical scrutiny before imagination succumbs to inevitability. If this observation in and of itself seems self-evident, it is only because of the work on the discursive production of space which strips the veneer of neutrality and permanence from political maps and planning documents. For instance, critical cartographer Mark Monmonier describes how maps are implemented as symbols of the state, with authoritative declarations of sovereignty made through cartographic practices in atlases, maps, coinage and stamps (Monmonier, 1996). In a related vein, critical theorist Henri Lefebvre's *Production of Space* notes that the final products of spatial practices only seem neutral and permanent, once the scaffolding of conflict, construction, and debate is removed (Lefebvre, 1991). More recently, poststructuralist perspectives have engaged with imaginative geographies to understand how they arise and why they are not always successfully implemented. My reading of the megaregion concept is strongly influenced by these perspectives, and in particular the work that political geographers have developed to examine the performative enactment of scale, identity and the nation-state (Weber, 1998; Kuus, 2007; Kaiser and Nikiforova, 2008). Put simply, performative perspectives argue that subjects come into being through the articulation and rearticulation of discursively mediated and embodied practices (Glass and Rose-Redwood, 2014). Within geography, social theorist Judith Butler's early work on gender norms has played a key role in shaping geographical theorizations of performativity as 'the power of discourse to produce effects through reiteration' (Butler, 1993, p. 20). Her work makes the influential claim that there is no such thing as a (gendered) subject prior to its constitution and reiteration through discourse, hence enabling subjects (such as political regions) to form through practices that challenge hegemonic norms.

6.3.1 Poststructural Political Economy and Political Performativity

The US is a comparatively young country, yet its territory has already been the canvas for considerable experimentation in the political geographies used to guide policy and define community boundaries. Looked at from abroad, the dominant characteristics of the US political system would seem to be the federal government and the state system – a framework which intends to provide policy flexibility at the regional scale while providing for more cohesive strategies and programmes for issues of national significance. When considered from this perspective the US system seems robust – even when allowing for inevitable political disagreements over the shape or character of federal mandates, and the calibration between federal policy and state rights. However, the US has obviously changed since being founded, with the 13 original colonies expanding over time to the present 50 states through a process of territorial expansion and population growth. Some intended colonies – such as Benjamin Franklin's proposed trans-Appalachian state – never eventuated, while the boundaries of the modern states developed at different times through different methods of surveying, with boundaries which were often subject to amendment and active contestation. 'Below' the state scale, considerable dynamism exists regarding minor civil divisions (MCDs – counties, townships, municipalities and cities) because each state is responsible for allocating specific powers to the MCDs, including the ability for MCDs to change their geographic extent through the annexation of adjacent territory. Whereas county divisions are now generally considered stable, there was considerable change in the number and shape of counties during the 19th century. Townships, municipalities and cities are subject to more dynamism, and terminology for these political units varies by jurisdiction (Kinda, 2001). For example, in the Commonwealth of Virginia townships or counties can be redefined as cities once a population threshold is reached, while in Pennsylvania there was considerable fluidity in the number of MCDs during the mid-19th century due to a laissez-faire attitude on the part of the Commonwealth toward community rights to self-organize.

Despite the comparative stability of modern American MCDs, broader patterns of metropolitan change continue to challenge the political boundaries inherited from earlier centuries. Patterns of employment, financial distress and success, commuting patterns and urban development all change with a speed that outpaces the capacity for static political boundaries to contain these changes or for local politicians and planners to control them. Consequently, metropolitan planners and other urban leaders have on occasion recommended reconstituting the political boundaries of urban regions through structural or functional boundary reforms (Rusk, 1995; Orfield, 2002). Structural reforms involve the eradication or adjustment of existing political geographies through annexation. Such strategies are slow, politically charged, and incapable of preventing future changes which might render the new political map obsolete. Functional reforms involve the erection of new special districts by local, state or federal authorities – essentially overlaying a new layer of governance upon the existing political map for a specific purpose (Miller, 2002). These strategies avoid some of the political problems created by structural reform efforts, but are problematic given the additional bureaucracy they entail (Glass, forthcoming 2015). In either instance, these strategies entail the articulation of new geographical imaginings for how city-regions should best be structured.

Whether through functional or structural reform, the new political projects that re-imagine the spatialities of urban and metropolitan life are social constructions rather than natural spaces which merely awaited discovery. Beginning with that premise, examining the efforts to create new spaces can reveal significant details about the subjects engaged in those efforts, and the ontological perspectives guiding their actions. It is apparent that the megaregion concept presented in the last section is an example of what can be termed an imaginative geography – a notion which has gained interest as a way to indicate an emergent project, space or policy (Le Heron, 2009; Bialasiewicz et al., 2007). Bialasiewicz et al. use this term to explain US foreign policy in the early 21st century. This policy was enacted and remains evident through the official documents, academic rhetoric and media representations of the period. Using a perspective rooted in PSPE and performativity, they argue that the recitation and reiteration of practices through such materialities reveals the discursively constructed and subjective nature of policy – in other words, refuting notions that new geographical projects (such as new planning spaces) are neutral or natural.

For political geographers and other researchers, the antifoundationalist claims provoked by Judith Butler's early work are particularly valuable to understanding the constitution and reconstitution of territorial units such as new spaces for planning, and for questioning the normativity and neutrality which are often assigned to sovereignty and the state. As political scientist Cynthia Weber (1998, p. 78) explains, 'I suggest, as have so many others, that sovereign nation-states are not pre-given subjects but subjects in process and that all subjects in process (be they individual or collective) are the ontological effects of practices which are performatively enacted'. Weber calls for international relations research to move beyond treating sovereignty as an object that is possessed by those who rule. Instead, she urges political theorists to focus their attention on sovereignty as a material-discursive effect of practices including speeches, cables, press conferences, and other performative enactments used by subjects to legitimize an authority which can never be absolute, and which must instead be continually rearticulated. Less work using a PSPE approach exists 'below' the level of the nation-state, although the same practices, performative acts and issues of subjectification and sovereignty occur in cases such as the megaregion.

Kaiser and Nikiforova indicate how PSPE can enliven discursive analysis of how new geographical scales materialize in their examination on Estonian identity. They argue new geographic scales arise 'through the repetition of sets of citational practices that stabilize as well as challenge the boundary, fixity, and surface effects that materialize' (Kaiser and Nikiforova, 2008, p. 542), noting that the performativity of scale is seen most easily through the discursive construction of 'the global scale', which has gained rapid currency as a 'representational trope' (p. 543) to explain processes occurring in the contemporary era. The naturalization of 'the global scale' has consequences, as the globalization discourse is subsequently used by other actors to legitimize their strategies in different political arenas. The scale effects that they cite include monument erection and removal, education textbooks, tourist guides and passports, but they are careful to note that these enactments are not guaranteed to succeed. Those actors who exist outside the particular scalar discourse that 'official' practices are attempting to construct can partake in counter-performances which 'produce the gaps and fissures which destabilize the new scalar discourses' (p. 552).

I argue that the megaregion concept is another materialization of geographical scale which becomes naturalized by proponents using specific performative enactments to create a new subjectified space. There are three components to the subjectification of the megaregion. First, subjectification of the megaregion is best considered a process. Through the design, dissemination and discussion of discursive materialities such as planning maps, planning guidelines, logos and research using the megaregion as the given geographic scale of reference, proponents of the concept actively create the notion that the concept is 'real'. This occurs gradually, as support for the new geographic imaginary is gathered, tenets are decided upon, research is conducted, and the findings are published and discussed. Second, expressions of regional identity are reiterated – performatively – constantly by the proponents of the megaregion. From a performative perspective it is the practices which matter to the process of identity construction rather than the actors who conduct them. This is because there is, to use Kuus's terminology (Kuus, 2007), no stable pre-discursive subject which pre-exists the creation of the geographic imaginary which is proposed. Third, the political sovereignty of proposed spaces such as the megaregion can never be completed – the authority of the megaregion as a viable political space, including its value to continue through time – must be continually reasserted, or else new geographical projects and imaginaries will co-opt the semblance of legitimacy which the megaregion as geographical imaginary has constructed. Taken together, these three components provide a framework for analysing the creation of political spaces. The next section draws on examples from Western Pennsylvania to illustrate the approach.

6.3.2   Brief History of Imaginative Spaces – Western Pennsylvania

The City of Pittsburgh and Allegheny County have lengthy experiences with boundary reform proposals, and hence the persistent nature of performances intended to create new geographical projects. During the 20th century, periods of urban growth, decline and resurgence caused the region's political boundaries to be reassessed, since replication of services by small municipalities seemed to create a potent drag on the overall competitiveness and efficiency of the county. Consequently, stakeholders enacted a sequence of representational tropes and attempts at redefining the nature of the city-region, all with a goal of bolstering the economic competitiveness of the region. The county's first significant effort at boundary reform occurred during the 1920s, when local civic reformers sought to join a (still thriving) City of Pittsburgh to the broader region, creating a Greater Pittsburgh. There were two key reasons for this early attempt at structural governance reform. First, the City of Pittsburgh was losing population to the surrounding municipalities. This concerned local boosters, as the population loss would lower Pittsburgh's comparative population ranking among cities in the 1930 Census. Second, metropolitan reform plans were popular nationally during the Progressive era. Civic reformers advocated structural reforms, arguing that fragmentation reflected outdated needs which did not match 20th century urbanism (Fishman, 1992).

Pittsburgh's political, civic and business leaders heeded calls for merging city and county services, yet the compromises of the political process only added confusion to the municipal structure of the county (Glass, 2011). Allegheny County next attempted structural reforms in the 1950s. By this stage, suburbanization had further weakened the City of Pittsburgh.[2] Local and national reformers again called for a new metropolitan government to enhance good regional governance by bolstering the role performed by Allegheny County's government (Jensen, 2004). These plans were again stymied, as municipal leaders feared regionalism as a socialist plot against local control and freedom (ibid.). Until the late 1970s and 1980s, the question of regional reform for Pittsburgh was posed in terms of how to manage economic decline. The closure of steel mills greatly affected the communities of Allegheny County which were faced with significant legacy costs in the form of pension obligations and civic infrastructure, while tax revenues collapsed with the loss of businesses and residents. This created a challenging environment for regional politicians who, for the first time, had to consider urban governance in the face of economic stagnation and decline.[3]

By the 1980s the Pittsburgh region's governance framework still reflected its early 20th century roots, in spite of several attempts to modernize government through a Home Rule charter (Lonich, 1991). While local communities continued to resist functional reforms of the region's governance, Councils of Government (COGs) provided a framework for localized cooperation.[4] Eight COGs operated in Allegheny County, enabling contiguous municipalities to share services and work toward common goals, such as responding to the challenges of de-industrialization. As this system developed, the City of Pittsburgh was facing significant population decline – based on US Census statistics, Pittsburgh's population had fallen from 604 332 in 1960 to 423 959 in 1980. The 'hollowing out' of the city-region's core would continue to prompt several calls for boundary reform between 1980 and 2000.

Attempts at structural consolidation were floated periodically, as the situation was considered untenable – a common complaint levied was with 130 minor civil divisions, eight COGs, numerous school districts and other administrative units, the county was a national 'poster child for fragmentation', and that something needed to be done for the reputation and competitiveness of the Pittsburgh city-region. Consequently, by the early 2000s, new studies were commissioned to reconsider the century-old notion of city-county merger. By the mid-2000s, elected officials were again interested in exploring the prospects for enhancing city-county consolidation. Pittsburgh Mayor Luke Ravenstahl and Allegheny County Executive Dan Onorato empanelled the Citizens Advisory Committee on the Efficiency and Effectiveness of City-County Government (CAG) in October 2006. The CAG was tasked with refreshing the debate on city-county governance by constructing a profile on the history of regional reform attempts, and considering the county's options in the wake of prominent examples of successful reform – with the Louisville–Jefferson County case cited as a best-practice model. Chaired by University of Pittsburgh Chancellor Mark Nordenberg, the CAG's name shows the dual emphasis for their work – the evaluation of regional government efficacy and efficiency. The project findings (released in April 2008) defined these terms by focusing on economic imperatives for the city-region in the context of increasing global inter-urban competition (Archibald and Sleeper, 2008; Citizens Advisory Committee, 2008).

The CAG report focused solely upon the city and county – none of the other 129 local governmental units, or any of the special districts (specifically, schools) were to be considered as part of the committee's work. The final report took a favourable perspective toward consolidation for the benefits it could provide for economic development goals – benefits such as unity of leadership, increased planning capabilities, and a reduction of intergovernmental competition (Citizens Advisory Committee, 2008). The CAG was also wary that such reforms could be enacted in the city-region, given the numerous historic failures of reform efforts. Drawing upon the rhetoric of economic competitiveness and the logic of governmental efficiency, the findings of the CAG report echo the suggestions of successive generations of municipal scholars. The CAG report therefore represents the next iteration in a long series of reports which considered structural city-region consolidation to be the next phase for regional governance.

As Pittsburgh's leaders continue to plan new reforms for the city-region, different proponents are interested in creating new geographic scales of governance that encompass a much broader area. The Power of 32 (P32) is an imaginative geography promoted by specific stakeholders to construct a new regional space over which some degree of political sovereignty could be asserted. The nature of the stakeholders matters greatly for the shape of the imagined geography of the region, and for the discursive boundaries of the P32 regional agenda. The initial leader of P32 was Allen Kukovich, who was a Pennsylvania state senator and then served as the Pennsylvania Democratic State Chairman. His Executive Director was Selena Schmidt, who joined the P32 after serving as the Chief of Staff for the Council President of the City of Pittsburgh. The P32 was sponsored by 12 institutional partners, nine of whom are charitable foundations headquartered in Pittsburgh with organizational missions to serve Pittsburgh and Southwest Pennsylvania. Of the other three sponsors, one (Comcast) is the dominant television cable provider in the region, one (Highmark) is a non-profit health insurance company with operations in Pennsylvania and West Virginia, and the other (Chesapeake Energy) is a for-profit natural gas company with significant interests in the Marcellus Shale gas field which is centred on the western Pennsylvania region.

The P32 imaginary was promoted as a regional visioning exercise in an area spanning 32 counties and four states. Although nominally community-based, the visioning exercise was based on goals created by the proponents of the plan which largely focused upon economic competitiveness – collaborative agenda setting, shared identity formation, public–private partnering and connectivity across communities which are nominally linked, but significantly different in terms of lifestyle, assets, urbanity and politics. The P32s leaders established specific benchmarks for success – namely, an improved quality of life, opportunity and 'success' for the entire region – 'rural, exurban, suburban, urban'. Based on data collected during the visioning sessions, P32 staff aggregated the results into action items which were disseminated to project committees (Glass, 2014a). While as yet unproven, the P32 shows not only that multiple geographical projects can occur concurrently, but that they can conflict with one another – whereas the communities of Pittsburgh and Allegheny County have particular goals for their city-region, these are not aligned with what a different plan at a different scale envisions.

6.3.3   Stakeholders and Practices: Who Calls For the Megaregion?

The value of a PSPE approach is the capacity to interrogate the rationales for action created by its proponents through an emphasis on practices – as Kuus (2007) states, to focus on the deeds, rather than the doers. This is important because there is no stable, preexisting spatial identity which awaits discovery by the proponents of new geographic imaginaries. Instead, this section shows that the success of new spatial projects is the consequence of active practices which are manifested through specific material and discursive formations. Such practices can be and are contested, especially when different stakeholders approach regional problems from different perspectives and geographic scales. In the next section, I show how the Great Lakes megaregion is problematized by the existence of these conflicting regional visions.

6.4 PLANNING SPACES IN THE GREAT LAKES MEGAREGION

6.4.1 Specifics of the Great Lakes Megaregion

The megaregion project conceived by America 2050 and associated advocates has constructed a new geography for the governance of American city-regions: RPA's 2008 map of posited megaregions shows the boundary of the spaces along with major highways and American metropolitan areas (see Harrison and Hoyler, 2015, Figure 1.1). Such a map will seem familiar from a European perspective, as similar visions have developed through the European Spatial Development Perspective's demarcation of transnational regions (Faludi and Waterhout, 2002; Zonneveld, 2005; Smas and Schmitt, 2015). Collectively, the American megaregions are undoubtedly significant from an economic and social perspective, accounting collectively for over 75 per cent of the US's population and gross domestic product, and as they also include many (but by no means all) of the country's major urban areas. The smoothed borderlines of the megaregion map suggest the extent of supra-metropolitan interconnectivity, and the superimposition of national and state boundaries implies how traditional political boundaries cannot control the geographic connections of contemporary society. However, inasmuch as this representation of the megaregion intends to make a policy point, there is a broader purpose for this particular map. Smoothed maps of the megaregion are used by proponents to create support for a new imagined geography by implying that this cartographic representation reveals a planning reality that awaited discovery and codification. Conflict, dissent and contradiction are erased, and an implication of organic realism is presented. The purpose for conceptual and highly polished maps such as the RPA's 'Emerging megaregions' map or similar products created in the European context around the European Spatial Development Perspective (Committee on Spatial Development, 1999) is unmistakable, and such unambiguous representations are often necessary to make policy recommendations. However, I argue that the apparent homogeneity of this map and the underlying presumption that megaregions can be delineated belies the confusion of socially and politically heterogeneous spaces which are elided by the maps (and slogans, such as Europe's 'Blue Banana') used to promote such interregional planning spaces (Fedeli, 2006; Evers, 2008). Focusing on the Great Lakes megaregion (GLM), this section categorizes the governance spaces that the GLM is superimposed upon: states, counties, urbanized areas, non-urbanized spaces and minor civil divisions – because of the RPA's interest in promoting a vision of unity, the megaregion project does not emphasize these political spaces or the other functional governance spaces that also complicate the political map for this (and other) regions. This project, therefore, follows the practice of other geographical imaginaries by presuming a fallaciously stable pre-existing (regional) subject; the presumption that the megaregion may be seamlessly and smoothly embedded as a new space for regional planning complicates attempts to enact the megaregion as a catchment for spatial planning, and diverts attention away from the material conditions and lived experiences of local communities both inside and outside these bounded spaces.

6.4.2   Governance Structures

Beyond the smoothed maps of the megaregion as proposed by the RPA is a complicated layering of governance structures – not only the nested hierarchy of political units including states, counties and MCDs, but also special districts deriving their powers from different sources, including education and resource protection districts. Furthermore, the imagined planning space of the GLM intrudes upon different geographical imaginaries, including plans for expanded city-region coordination around cities within the megaregion catchment. Drawing on the data provided by the RPA, this section explains the competing spaces for government and governance which are obscured by the planned megaregion.

States

The smoothed GLM map, indicated by the dashed line in Figure 6.1, intersects with 11 US states with a combined 2010 population of 93 729 688 (see Harrison and Hoyler, 2015, Figure 1.1). However, this number varies depending on the projection used to define the megaregion. The base map used by the RPA to designate the boundaries of the megaregion differs from the smoothed map: Minnesota (and hence the Minneapolis–St. Paul conurbation) is excluded, while New York (and hence the cities of Buffalo and Syracuse) is included. Therefore, depending on the map used to define the GLM, the population varies: compared to the smoothed map, the base map population was significantly lower: 79 655 511 residents. Beyond

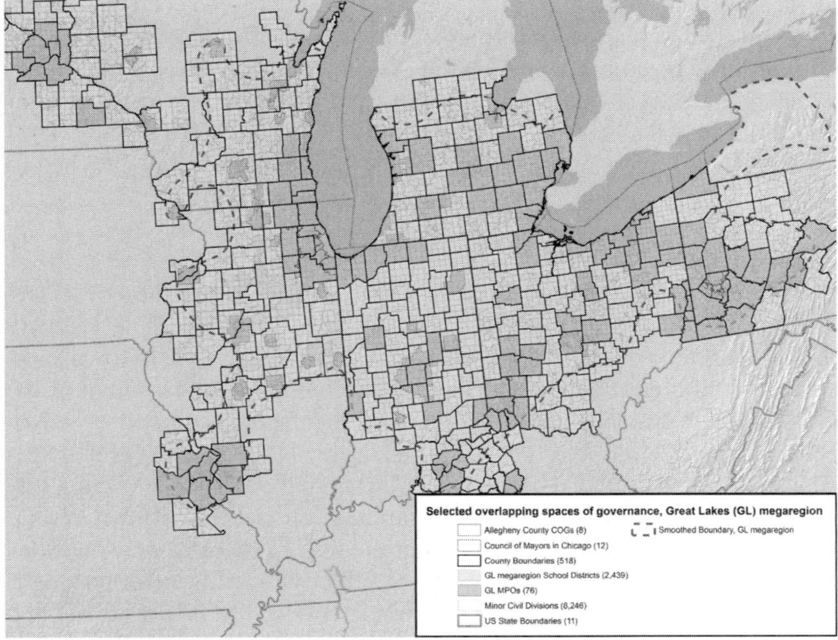

Source: Author

Figure 6.1   *Conflicting spaces of governance in the Great Lakes megaregion*

these numerical variations, the inclusion of multiple states in the mega-region certainly creates base challenges for interregional governance, as explained in the previous section. Not only do state constitutions problematize the capacity for seamless governance, but the inclusion of specific areas of given states within the megaregion's borders poses potential legal challenges, should excluded urban areas within the state feel that resources and legislation are being apportioned unevenly.

Counties

At the county scale, either 388 (base map) counties with a total population of 39 958 934 or 369 (smoothed map) counties with a total population of 53 252 325 are included in the GLM. This number of counties includes significant variation – not only in geographic location and land use, but also regarding regulation, population density and social characteristics. Most significantly, in the US political system counties are treated as 'creatures of the state', meaning that states – and states alone – can establish or dissolve counties, and are also responsible for setting all powers which can be administered by counties and MCDs. This means that governance bodies which operate across state lines must mediate between different state constitutions as well as powers granted to counties which are frequently legal artifacts with significant histories of contestation and identity attached to them.

Municipalities

If the aggregation of states and counties included within the borders of the megaregion are not sufficient argument for the hidden heterogeneity of this geographical imaginary, the 8246 minor civil divisions (townships, cities and different municipal categories) included in the base map of the GLM should provide further evidence of the challenges faced by advocates of megaregions. Each MCD is the legacy of local histories and specific geographical imaginaries in their own right. MCDs were frequently founded to identify with a particular land use or speculative form of land use planning – associated with different phases of urbanization or notions of morality. For instance, in the Pittsburgh city-region several boroughs were created – and frequently gerrymandered – by industrialists seeking control over the areas in which they had built factories (Muller, 2001), while the borough of Temperanceville was erected during the 19th century through a moral imperative, with the sale of liquor prohibited in the MCD's boundaries (Glass, 2014b). Even though the original intent for the MCD may have passed, the legacy of historic boundaries proves hard to shift. This is a variable phenomenon, as local power and resources mean that specific (often wealthy) MCDs have greater capacity to avoid annexation events than other MCDs. However, as explained in the previous section, despite the variation in local power, there is usually a great amount of antagonism on the part of local communities when suggestions of extra-local administration are made. Such concerns may be raised through fears of a loss of local identity, or through fears about the type of obligations which might arise if adjacent MCDs with different socioeconomic profiles and debt loads are consolidated.

Special districts and regional councils

In addition to the ten states, 388 counties and 8246 MCDs in the GLM, governance of the region is further complicated by the operation of numerous special districts. These districts were created over time through functional governance reforms and legislative fiat of federal and state governments to focus on specific issues or projects. Perhaps the most prominent form of special district from a community perspective are school districts, since these resources serve as points of local identity and social capital (Allen et al., 2011), and are of great importance to families with school-aged children. There are 2439 public school districts in the GLM with facilities catering for the public education of students aged 6–18 (Figure 6.1). The funding sources for public education in the US include a mixture of federal, state and local funds, although nationally nearly half of district funding comes from local property taxes. For instance, in Pennsylvania approximately 76 per cent of district revenue is sourced from taxes based on property assessments, creating significant differences in the funding levels of high versus low socioeconomic status districts. This situation creates problematic inequalities, as poor districts become increasingly disadvantaged by the inability of residents to adequately fund schools (Martin, 2006; Flaherty, 2013).

Whereas the megaregion concept is intended to enhance regional collaboration and coordination, this goal is already enacted by two other types of Regional Council: Councils of Government and Metropolitan Planning Organizations across the US. Federal policies have encouraged or required inter-jurisdictional cooperation since the 1960s, with COGs used to provide voluntary platforms for interjurisdictional cooperation between MCDs. The use of COGs has grown over time and there are currently over 500 nationally (Wolf and Bryan, 2009) and 73 in the GLM. The National Association of Regional Councils defines COGs as 'a multi-service entity with state and locally-defined boundaries that deliver a variety of federal, state, and local programs while continuing its function as a planning organization, technical assistance provider and "visionary" to its member local governments' (NARC, 2010). In practice, this means that the function of COGs depends on the needs of the local communities they serve: depending on the context, COGs could be responsible for implementing programmes related to transportation or the environment, or other issues with interjurisdictional interest (Wolf and Bryan, 2009).

More recently, the Intermodal Surface Transportation Efficiency Act of 1991 (ISTEA) mandated the creation of new regional councils for the coordination of transportation planning in metropolitan areas with a population of 50000 or more. Termed Metropolitan Planning Organizations (MPOs), these organizations could be created according to local circumstance: in areas where COGs already existed, these could take on the role of the local MPO; in other cases, entirely new organizations were formed as freestanding MPOs, county-level MPOs, or as state-run entities. In either case, MPOs function as the intermediaries for federal transportation funding, whereby funds are allocated to the MPO which consequently determines the best local allocation for those funds. Therefore, depending on the constitution of the MPO board and the character of local politics, transportation funding could be allocated toward road construction and maintenance, public transit, sidewalks and so forth. There are currently 76 MPOs within the proposed GLM. Some, such as the East–West Gateway Council of Governments in St. Louis, the Louisville Area MPO, the La Crosse Area Planning Commission and the Cincinnati–Northern Kentucky MPO coordinate functions across state lines, while most have a more limited jurisdiction, usually based on the county scale. Despite the federal mandate for MPOs, there remain concerns over the differences between MPOs, especially with regard to urban-suburban representation and ethnic diversity. Writing in 2006, Sanchez found that most MPO boards were weighted toward suburban constituencies, despite the generally urban population of MPOs. Similarly, MPO boards were composed of 88 per cent white members, with black and Hispanic members being underrepresented compared to the population of the corresponding metropolitan areas (Sanchez, 2006).

Summary

This section has provided an overview of the existing spaces of governance in the area defined by proponents as the Great Lakes Megaregion. Beyond the structural elements of the region's political system – 10 states, 388 counties, 91 congressional districts and 8246 minor civil divisions – there are many special districts including school districts, COGs and MPOs. Moreover, while there are 660 urbanized areas within the Great Lakes catchment, there are also many nonurban spaces which separate the region's cities – this is highly dissimilar to Gottmann's Megalopolis, which although similarly fragmented from the perspective of metropolitan governance was defined by the contiguous population density and urbanism of the northeastern seaboard.

What this array of governance spaces across the notional Great Lakes megaregion should indicate is the significant state-, county- and community-level differences in capacity, resources, obligations, stakeholders, regulations, visions and ideologies. Whereas the proponents for megaregions would consider this difference to be the grounds for a new space for planning and coordination, this would require an unrealistic ideological shift amongst the citizens and stakeholders of the region, all of whom function in the American political context which favours localism above regionalism (Bogart, 2006; Weir, 1995). The federal system of the US provides states with the power to create and destroy MCDs, yet local political spaces have some legal protection against forcible annexation. Furthermore, as federal and state grants are disbursed to localities, there is little incentive for MCDs – and particularly wealthy localities – to cede control over their territory or assets. This situation has become complicated by the current political climate in the US, where a vocal segment of the electorate is raising concern over what they consider threats to national sovereignty arising from non-local sources (Johnson, 2006; Saltzstein et al., 2008).

6.5   WHITHER THE MEGAREGION?

Despite the best efforts of advocates for regionalism at scales from the mega to the meso, conditions within the US preclude enactment of grand visions such as the megaregion. There are two key exigencies preventing the megaregion becoming reality. First are the political exigencies of American life. The underlying political geography of the US – federalism and legally protected minor civil divisions – includes an unevenness in terms of leadership capacity, available resources, problems such as under-funded public obligations, differences in legal governance, competing and conflicting stakeholders, and multiple visions for the region which make the abstracted cohesiveness of the megaregion unlikely, to say the least. Furthermore, electoral politics still matters; defensive localism still matters; and in the modern American electorate there is a deeply held suspicion about the utopian intentions of regional planners calling for 'solutions' like the megaregion. Finally, the federal government, which has a vested interest in its own conceptions of space, either legislatively through ISTEA or politically through calls for infrastructure reinvestment in items like high-speed rail, means that the megaregion of the RPA might well be coopted by other narratives and alternative visions. This means that proponents of the megaregion must be capable of continually reasserting the value and need for this geography over the likely long time it will take for the megaregion notion to be enacted and granted political legitimacy.

Added to those challenges are geographic exigencies. Despite the best efforts of generations of reformers, there is a general inability to reshape the political geographies of any scale of government at the same pace as geographic patterns change – spatial dynamism combined with legal ossification means that even if a megaregion was to be successfully implemented as a recognized planning space, it is a near certainty that geographic change would render such a region obsolete from the outset. Meanwhile, the scale of lived experience for local communities in no way reflects the grand scales of theory proposed by planners. The quotidian demands of American families – for jobs, healthcare and quality schools – makes the megaregion much more abstract than in international comparative cases where megaregion planning is centralized, as in China, or is politically legitimized through international spatial planning, as in the

European Union (Xu and Yeh, 2011). In addition, the delineation of the US into megaregions creates a division which leaves many communities detached from the attention that the megaregions would receive if they gained legal recognition as planning spaces. Because of the likely disconnect between the mega and the quotidian experience of a single citizen the mega is unlikely to either be supported or acknowledged by communities and is likely unable to solve issues of regional inequality (Benner and Pastor, 2011).

To summarize, I have argued that the megaregion is just the latest geographical imaginary to presume the presence of a stable, pre-discursive subject – in other words, that the megaregion is an actual space which simply awaited discovery by researchers interested in such a vision. However, the US megaregion imaginary is not a coherent space for formalized regional planning. Geographical politics such as those described above still matter and cannot be an afterthought when considering new spatial projects. The focus on geographical imaginaries like the megaregion detracts from, and ignores the complexity of, the many material and political processes which make me highly cynical that the megaregion can be actuated as a space for interregional cooperation and integrated capacity. So, whither the megaregion? I have said that the megaregion imaginary is not a coherent space for formalized planning, and that it is based in a flawed ontology which presupposes a stable, pre-discursive subject. Given these problems, and the fact that material conditions fight against such utopic visions, what are megaregions good for? I think three things.

First, by regarding geographical imaginaries such as the megaregion, we can reveal and understand the prevailing discourses and political projects which compel stakeholders such as the advocates of the megaregion at the RPA and elsewhere. Through the rhetoric depicted in pro-megaregion accounts, we find a perspective which remains strongly rooted in the neoliberalization of political life, as the American megaregion seems predicated on the presumption of interregional global competitiveness. Second, the rhetoric of new projects like the megaregion can assist researchers to understand the evolving practices which connote urban and regional geographies. The early work of Gottmann, Hall and Vance, as well as the modern work of Ross, Sudjic and Lang is of value for comprehending how socio-spatial relations change over time, and how they remain constant. For instance, Gottmann's work raises significant concerns about the capacity for metropolitan populations to live in politically fragmented regions. Given these concerns continue to be raised by the modern generation of researchers, how might we tackle such a seemingly intractable aspect of urban geographic life as political fragmentation? This is obviously a large question, but recent debates regarding the relationality and 'fuzziness' of regions offer one promising option (Harrison, 2013; Heley, 2013). In these debates – to date largely centred on the United Kingdom – researchers are interested in understanding how the networked character of people and places can transcend territorially based conceptions of space, enabling theory – and ideally policy – to comprehend the mobilities and modalities of contemporary society (Agnew, 2013; Varró and Lagendijk, 2013).

Thirdly, although I am strongly sceptical of the value of the megaregion concept to spur interregional cooperation, I am more confident in the merits of the increasingly reflexive approach to regional discourse. There is more sensitivity to the methodologies and consequences of conceptualizing regions, as a recent special issue of the journal *Regional Studies* (Jones and Paasi, 2013) indicates. The editors of that issue called on their readers to 'reflect on the perpetual significance of regional concepts and how they are mobilized by various actors to maintain or transform the contested spatialities of societal power relations' (Jones and Paasi, 2013, p. 4). A reflexive approach by planners and researchers about how they mobilize discourses such as 'megaregion' can lead to a stronger understanding of how our research practices are performative (Law and Urry, 2004), and can in certain instances lead to new social realities.

NOTES

1. For a perspective on the methodology underlying the identification of European megaregions, see Hall (2011).
2. According to US Census statistics, between 1920 and 1960 the City of Pittsburgh's population increased from nearly 534 000 to 604 000 – a growth rate of 13 per cent. However, in the same period, the rest of Allegheny County increased by 111 per cent to slightly over one million residents, or nearly two-thirds of the entire county population.
3. Pittsburgh's de-industrialization during the period is well recorded, and sits as part of the broader de-industrialization events which created America's 'Rust-Belt' cities (Bluestone and Harrison, 1982; Lubove, 1994). Disinvestment, declining profits, economic globalization and mismanagement are all cited as partial causes of the collapse of Pittsburgh's steel industry, but regardless of the culprit, the cumulative effect was severe for the city-region's economy and psyche.
4. These were enabled by Pennsylvania's Intergovernmental Cooperation Act (1972).

REFERENCES

Agnew, J. (2013), 'Arguing with regions', *Regional Studies*, **47** (1), 6–17.
Allen, A., M. Glassman, L. Riegel and H. Dawson (2011), 'Investigating constituent values and school policy', *Education and Urban Society*, **45** (3), 340–361.

Allen, J., D. Massey and A. Cochrane (1998), *Rethinking the Region*, New York: Routledge.

Archibald, R. and S. Sleeper (2008), *Government Consolidation and Economic Development in Allegheny County and the City of Pittsburgh*, Pittsburgh, PA: RAND Corporation.

Austin, J. and B. Affolter-Caine (2006), *The Vital Center: A Federal-State Compact to Renew the Great Lakes Region*, Washington, DC: Brookings Institution, Metropolitan Policy Program.

Benner, C. and M. Pastor (2011), 'Moving on up? Regions, megaregions, and the changing geography of social equity organizing', *Urban Affairs Review*, **47** (3), 315–348.

Bialasiewicz, L., D. Campbell, S. Elden, S. Graham, A. Jeffrey and A.J. Williams (2007), 'Performing security: the imaginative geographies of current US strategy', *Political Geography*, **26** (4), 405–422.

Bluestone, B. and B. Harrison (1982), *The Deindustrialization of America*, New York: Basic Books.

Bogart, W. (2006), *Don't Call it Sprawl*, Cambridge: Cambridge University Press.

Brenner, N. (2004), *New State Spaces: Urban Governance and the Rescaling of Statehood*, Oxford: Oxford University Press.

Butler, J. (1993), *Bodies that Matter*, New York: Routledge.

Citizen's Advisory Committee (2008), *Government for Growth: Forging a Bright Future*, Pittsburgh, PA: University of Pittsburgh.

Committee on Spatial Development (1999), *European Spatial Development Perspective*, Luxembourg: European Commission.

Downs, A. (1994), *New Visions for Metropolitan America*, Washington, DC: Brookings Institution.

Evers, D. (2008), 'Reflections on territorial cohesion and European spatial planning', *Tijdschrift voor Economische en Social Geografie*, **99** (3), 303–315.

Faludi, A. and B. Waterhout (2002), *The Making of the European Spatial Development Perspective: No Masterplan*, London: Routledge.

Fedeli, V. (2006), 'The difficult construction of the European Union: a field of institutional imagination for the problems of (local) public?', in L. Doria, V. Fedeli and C. Tedesco (eds), *Rethinking European Spatial Policy as a Hologram*, Aldershot: Ashgate, pp. 191–208.

Fishman, R. (1992), 'The regional plan and the transformation of the industrial metropolis', in D. Ward and O. Zunz (eds), *The Landscape of Modernity: Essays on New York City, 1900–1940*, New York: Russell Sage, pp. 106–125.

Flaherty, S. (2013), 'Does money matter in Pennsylvania? School district spending and student proficiency since No Child Left Behind', *Eastern Economic Journal*, **39** (2), 145–171.

Gibson-Graham, J.-K. (2004), 'Area studies after poststructuralism', *Environment and Planning A*, **36** (3), 405–419.

Glass, M.R. (2011), 'Metropolitan reform in Allegheny County: the local failure of national reform advocacy, 1920–1929', *Journal of Urban History*, **37** (1), 90–116.

Glass, M.R. (2014a), '"Becoming a thriving region": performative visions, imaginative geographies, and the Power of 32', in M.R. Glass and R. Rose-Redwood (eds), *Performativity, Politics, and the Production of Social Space*, New York: Routledge, pp. 202–225.

Glass, M.R. (2014b), 'Performing the geographical imaginary in 19th-century

Pittsburgh', in K. Gulliver and H. Tóth (eds), *Cityscapes in History: Creating the Urban Experience*, Farnham: Ashgate, pp. 13–34.

Glass, M.R. (forthcoming, 2015), 'New city-region partnerships for economic competitiveness: Pittsburgh's CONNECT initiative', in K. Jones, A. Lord and R. Shields (eds), *The City Region in Prospect: Exploring the Meeting Points between Place and Practice*, Montreal: McGill-Queens University Press.

Glass, M.R. and R. Rose-Redwood (eds) (2014), *Performativity, Politics, and the Production of Social Space*, New York: Routledge.

Godfrey, B.J. (1999), 'The geography of James E. Vance Jr. (1925–1999)', *Geographical Review*, **89** (4), 580–589.

Gottmann, J. (1961), *Megalopolis: The Urbanized Northeastern Seaboard of the United States*, New York: Twentieth Century Fund.

Hagler, Y. (2009), 'Defining U.S. megaregions', America 2050, New York: Regional Plan Association, available at http://www.america2050.org/2009/11/defining-us-megaregions.html (accessed 10 April 2013).

Hall, P. (2011), 'The polycentric metropolis: a Western European perspective on mega-city regions', In J. Xu and A.G.O. Yeh (eds.), *Governance and Planning of Mega-City Regions: An International Comparative Perspective*, London: Routledge, pp. 29–50.

Harrison, J. (2013), 'Configuring the new regional world: on being caught between territory and networks', *Regional Studies*, **47** (1), 55–74.

Harrison, J. and M. Hoyler (2015), 'Megaregions: foundations, frailties, futures', in J. Harrison and M. Hoyler (eds), *Megaregions: Globalization's New Urban Form?* Cheltenham, UK and Northampton, MA, USA: Edward Elgar, pp. 1–28.

Heley, J. (2013), 'Soft spaces, fuzzy boundaries and spatial governance in post-devolution Wales', *International Journal of Urban and Regional Research*, **37** (4), 1325–1348.

Jensen, B.K. (2004), *Masters of Their Own Destiny: Allegheny County Government Reform Efforts, 1929–1998*, unpublished PhD thesis, Pittsburgh, PA: Carnegie Mellon University.

Johnson, K.M. (2006), 'Sovereigns and subjects: a geopolitical history of metropolitan reform in the USA', *Environment and Planning A*, **38** (1), 149–168.

Jones, M. and A. Paasi (2013), 'Regional world(s): advancing the geography of regions', *Regional Studies*, **47** (1), 1–5.

Kaiser, R. and E. Nikiforova (2008), 'The performativity of scale: the social construction of scale effects in Narva, Estonia', *Environment and Planning D*, **26** (3), 537–562.

Kinda, A. (2001), 'The concept of "townships" in Britain and the British colonies in the seventeenth and eighteenth centuries', *Journal of Historical Geography*, **27** (2), 137–152.

Kuus, M. (2007), 'Ubiquitous identities and elusive subjects: puzzles from Central Europe', *Transactions of the Institute of British Geographers*, **32** (1), 90–101.

Lang, R.E. and P.L. Knox (2009), 'The new metropolis: rethinking megalopolis', *Regional Studies*, **43** (6), 789–802.

Law, J. and J. Urry (2004), 'Enacting the social', *Economy and Society*, **33** (3), 390–410.

Le Heron, R. (2009), '"Rooms and moments" in neoliberalizing policy trajectories of metropolitan Auckland, New Zealand: towards constituting progressive spaces through post-structural political economy', *Asia Pacific Viewpoint*, **50** (2), 135–153.

Lefebvre, H. (1991), *The Production of Space*, London: Blackwell Publishers.

Lonich, D. (1991), *Metropolitics in Allegheny County*, unpublished PhD thesis, Pittsburgh, PA: Carnegie Mellon University.

Lubove, R. (1994), *Twentieth-Century Pittsburgh*, Pittsburgh, PA: University of Pittsburgh Press.

Martin, A.L. (2006), 'Been there, done that: what next? Looking back and ahead at litigation prospects for school funding reform in Pennsylvania', *Widener Law Journal*, **15** (3), 815–866.

Massey, D. (1979), 'In what sense a regional problem?', *Regional Studies*, **13** (2), 233–243.

Miller, D.Y. (2002), *The Regional Governing of Metropolitan America*, Cambridge, MA: Westview Press.

Monmonier, M. (1996), *How to Lie with Maps*, Chicago, IL: University of Chicago Press.

Muller, E.K. (2001), 'Industrial suburbs and the growth of metropolitan Pittsburgh, 1870–1920', *Journal of Historical Geography*, **27** (1), 58–73.

NARC (National Association of Regional Councils) (2010), 'What is a Regional Council?', August, available at http://narc.org/resource-center/cogs-mpos/what-is-a-council-of-government/ (accessed 15 June 2013).

Orfield, M. (2002), *American Metropolitics: The New Suburban Reality*, Washington, DC: Brookings Institution Press.

Ross, C.L. (ed.) (2009), *Megaregions: Planning for Global Competitiveness*, Washington, DC: Island Press.

Rusk, D. (1995), *Cities without Suburbs*, Washington, DC: Woodrow Wilson Center Press.

Saltzstein, A.L., C. Copus, R.J. Sonenshein and C. Skelcher (2008), 'Visions of urban reform comparing English and U.S. strategies for improving city government', *Urban Affairs Review*, **44** (2), 155–181.

Sanchez, T. (2006), *An Inherent Bias? Geographic and Racial-Ethnic Patterns of Metropolitan Planning Organization Boards*, Washington, DC: Brookings Institution.

Smas, L. and P. Schmitt (2015), 'Brave new "megaregional worlds"? Reflections from a North European perspective', in J. Harrison and M. Hoyler (eds), *Megaregions: Globalization's New Urban Form?* Cheltenham, UK and Northampton, MA, USA: Edward Elgar, pp. 146–174.

Storper, M. (1997), *The Regional World: Territorial Development in a Global Economy*, New York: Guilford Press.

Sudjic, D. (1992), *The 100-Mile City*, San Diego, CA: Harcourt Brace.

Vance, J.E. (1977), *This Scene of Man: The Role and Structure of the City in the Geography of Western Civilization*, New York: Harper's College Press.

Varró, K. and A. Lagendijk (2013), 'Conceptualizing the region: in what sense relational?', *Regional Studies*, **47** (1), 18–28.

Weber, C. (1998), 'Performative states', *Millennium: Journal of International Studies*, **27** (1), 77–95.

Weir, M. (1995), 'Poverty, social rights, and the politics of place in the United States', in S. Leibfried and P. Pierson (eds), *European Social Policy: Between Fragmentation and Integration*, Washington, DC: Brookings Institution, pp. 329–354.

Wolf, J.F. and T.K. Bryan (2009), 'Identifying the capacities of Regional Councils of Government', *State and Local Government Review*, **41** (1), 61–68.
Xu, J. and A.G.O. Yeh (eds) (2011), *Governance and Planning of Mega-City Regions: An International Comparative Perspective*, London: Routledge.
Zonneveld, W. (2005), 'Expansive spatial planning: the new European transnational spatial visions', *European Planning Studies*, **13** (1), 137–155.

7. Brave new 'megaregional worlds'? Reflections from a North European perspective

Lukas Smas and Peter Schmitt

7.1 INTRODUCTION

How can the established concept of 'Norden' – which covers the Northern European countries of Denmark, Finland, Iceland, Norway and Sweden – be understood in a brave new world of megaregions? The significance of Norden, which literary means 'the North', is often acknowledged to be a 'stabilised' transnational (mega)region (Gustafsson, 2006). This is due, in part, to the Nordic countries sharing a number of cultural and historical commonalities, somewhat similar political trajectories through the 20th century and a well-known welfare state tradition. Yet, on closer inspection, we have seen in recent years various diverging development paths in territorial policy and politics in general, and urban and regional planning in particular. Furthermore, when adopting a relational perspective, we can detect how a number of Nordic city-regions are being formed and transformed – through transnational (business) networks and various related state spatial strategies – with the aim being to strategically place them as nodes within the global space of flows. What this amounts to is a more fluid geographical image of Norden.

Against this backdrop the concept of Norden is an interesting example of how (mega)regions are being constructed through particular sets of relations, processes and mechanisms, while at the same time being challenged and deconstructed by other sets of relations, processes and mechanisms. In this chapter, we seek to problematize these happenings, providing critical reflections from a North European perspective. The research presented derives from a range of studies and observations produced by Nordregio – The Nordic Centre for Spatial Development. Following this introduction, we first discuss different avenues for interpreting the construction of megaregions from both academic and policy perspectives. We then proceed to question the conceptualization of Norden. We do this by placing contemporary urban planning and regional development approaches within the context of the convergent and divergent policy trajectories in the Nordic states, alongside the continuous redevelopment of the so-called Nordic model. This is important because until recently, regions – as subnational spatial entities – have had a limited administrative role within Nordic spatial planning systems and welfare models (which have largely focused on state re-distribution). However, Nordic regional development policies have changed significantly since the mid-1990s, in the light of the increased importance of European territorial polices and what can be termed 'new Nordic regionalism' (Dosenrode and Halkier, 2004; Bukve et al., 2008). Following this, we empirically deconstruct (and inevitably re-construct) Norden as a megaregion by investigating emerging Nordic city-regions. In particular we aim to demonstrate how their external relations and choices of transnational governance arrangements have helped to establish a nearby, and to some extent competing, megaregion around the Baltic Sea. Finally, we discuss what conclusions can be distilled from our analysis in relation to the scope and limitations of megaregions and the megaregion concept in general, and as objects for policymaking in particular.

7.2   WAYS OF (DE)CONSTRUCTING MEGAREGIONS

We concur with Dubois et al. (2009), who argue that the conceptual understanding of a macro- (or mega) region is related to the exercise of how to define a region regardless of the prefixes – mega, macro, meso, micro – used. Numerous authors have highlighted the increasing role of 'regions' and ways to capture the regional concept from a more scientific and/or more policy oriented perspective (for example Storper, 1997; Keating, 1997). Alongside this, since the fall of the Iron Curtain, a 'Europe of regions' has become an omnipresent label describing not only the existence of various, and for the most part very different, arrangements of territorial jurisdictions within nation states, but also for the emergence of numerous kinds of cross-border and/or transnational spatial settings (Deas and Lord, 2006; Medeiros, 2013). Jones and Paasi (2013) note that similar developments can also be observed beyond Europe.

Although 50 years old, the quotation below demonstrates a typical and to some extent still common way of identifying regions by emphasizing three important elements: (1) a defined territorial unit, which is either based on (2) territorial commonalities (for example distribution of population) or (3) a more strategic reasoning (for example territorial scope of business):

> The term 'region' is undoubtedly one of the catchwords of our day among both popular and scientific writers. To the practical man of affairs a region is simply an area with certain characteristics (often mere size), in virtue of which it is a suitable unit for some particular purpose of business or administration. To the scientist, and above all the geographer, a region is an area which is homogeneous in respect of some particular set of associated conditions, whether of the land or of the people, such as industry, farming, the distribution of population, commerce, or the general sphere of influence of a city. (Dickinson, 1964, p. 3)

Nonetheless, what a 'suitable unit' is for business or administration has radically changed with globalization. Also one needs to emphasize that these three elements are grounded on rather analytical rationales, but do not necessarily match those that are inherent in respect of region-building within politics where mechanisms such as control and power are the driving forces.

In recent years, academic literature has provided a number of rationales for the establishment of regions. Some emphasize the formation of politically motivated regions as a more or less logical reflex caused by changing conditions such as accelerating globalization, the emergence of the network society or the new geopolitical landscape (for example Keating, 1997; Jessop, 2012; Jonas, 2012). The basic argument is that the formation of 'new *regional* state spaces' (followed by specific governance arrangements) should help to better organize or even control these new framework conditions (Brenner, 2004). Other scholars explain the strategic and interest-led 'production' of regions particularly as a search for a 'better' spatial arrangement in order to respond to issues such as territorial competitiveness, the need for new modes of governance and policy integration and the re-framing of 'regional identities' (Paasi, 2013; Zimmerbauer, 2013). As a consequence we can observe that traditional 'state spaces', particularly between the national state level and the local or municipal level, in the form of clearly defined political jurisdictions, are becoming more porous and are complemented by additional layers of territorial governance (cf. Brenner, 2004; Lidström, 2007).

Indeed a region is still, more often than not, recognized as a subnational spatial unit. However, of late there has been a resurgent interest in other regional formations such as transnational cross-border regions (Deas and Lord, 2006; Löfgren, 2008; Garcia-Alvarez and Trillo-Santamaria, 2013), mega-city regions (Hall and Pain, 2006; Evers and De Vries, 2013), Euro- or meso-regions (Medeiros, 2011, 2013) and megaregions (Florida, 2008; Ross, 2009). These regions tend to transcend political jurisdictions internal to the nation state, but many of them also extend beyond the nation state. Some authors also make efforts to distinguish between these increasingly frequent pre-fixes in terms of their size (Medeiros, 2013), or in a partly arbitrary way by using a rather dogmatic tone (Lindeborg, 2011).

Nonetheless, to understand the formation of (mega)regions we argue that it is essential to bridge the gap between analytical considerations about emerging relational geographies and the formation of regions for policy negotiation and delivery. To start with, it is important to note that regions are not pre-given as physical objects; they are social constructs being formed and framed through specific practices and representations. There are no pre-given conditions or criteria for what constitutes a (mega) region, even though certain coherent structures and characteristics – be they cultural, social, economic, political and/or geographical – can help to mobilize and thus construct a (mega)region. Those structures and characteristics are often revealed through spatial research, particularly in human geography and regional studies. In some instances a number of criteria and thresholds have been identified to demarcate, then define, regions. In a European context, the work undertaken within the European Observation Network for Territorial Development and Cohesion (ESPON) provides numerous examples of exactly this. Representations of the region captured by such exercises are often taken up by policy elites to construct and advance particular political discourses, thus connecting analytical and empirical research with normative connotations or concepts. Illustrative examples in the European spatial planning discourse are the famous 'Blue Banana' and 'Global Economic Integration Zone' (also labelled the 'Pentagon'). Both are transnational configurations which are supposed to demarcate the geoeconomic core of Europe, backed up by some analytical investigations (Jensen and Richardson, 2004a; Faludi, 2009). Unsurprisingly, both have been contested and their metaphorical and symbolic power has led to vibrant discussions about the definition and implications of 'core' and 'periphery' in Europe, and on normative concepts ('polycentricity', 'territorial cohesion') invoked to respond to this challenge (Faludi, 2005, 2013; Van Well, 2012). In this vein, defining a (mega)region also means to outline what is considered to be a 'spatial entity' and thus to distinguish between who, what and where is included and excluded. It should not be overlooked how private actors (for example transnational corporations, regional businesses) might (also) have an interest in drawing the new geographies, for instance, to pinpoint their main markets or catchment areas for their labour supply (cf. Harrison, 2014).

In general terms (mega)regions can be considered as (temporary) products of various types of stakeholder strategies – be they private actors, policy and decision-makers, and to some extent even researchers – in search of providing knowledge on the coherence/non-coherence of various spatialities. However, such strategies can change over time if, for example, competing images become hegemonic in societal discourses. In this light, Paasi (1986, 2001, 2011, 2013) has persistently argued that regions should be analysed as temporarily congealed products of processes of regionalization and understood as 'collective institutional structures' (Paasi, 2001, p. 25). When reflecting on the related concept of territory, Painter (2010, p. 1094) similarly notes that regions (and other spatial entities) can be seen as 'porous, historical, mutable, uneven and perishable . . . a laborious work in progress, prone to failure and permeated by tension and contradiction . . . never complete, always becoming'. This may also be an underlying rationale for adding various prefixes to the word region to generate discussions about the emergence of 'new' types of regions and at the same time questioning the existence of established notions.

Within the institutionalization of regions, the formation of regional identity plays a critical role (Paasi, 1986, 2013). It can either bring forward or restrain the process of institutionalization of regions depending on the legitimizing power of such discourses, which are in turn bounded to specific cultural, political and societal circumstances. This raises an important question: how can a megaregional identity be developed? In the case of less extensive polycentric urban regions (such as the Ruhr or the Basque Country), Van Houtum and Lagendijk (2001) distinguish between cultural, functional and strategic identities. The latter is most interesting for the discursive production of megaregions. This is because if we assume that megaregions are more than an analytical phenomenon stretching beyond the debates within the academic community, then we need to investigate any intended identification with a megaregion where this serves specific normative interests.

In addition to the discursive production of megaregions as (new) objects of spatial policy, another item is the claim that (as subjects) 'they' may unfold capacities to shape and negotiate 'their futures'. A crucial question is to what extent coordinative and regulative institutional arrangements are in place, since the production of megaregions offers a new scale for territorial governance. The discursive production of megaregions as new objects for policy attention challenges the installation of new modes of territorial governance to literally fill up the organizational and institutional vacuum that is occurring when the formation of megaregions is at stake. As noted by Dubois et al. (2009) in view of the emerging macro-regional strategies across Europe, megaregions can also be considered as a specific interface between different established scales due to their multi-scalar relations which stretch from the local up to the global. As a result, political and organizational capacities are supposed to be activated to install a new mode of governance for negotiating, directing, implementing and developing policies which do not harm the existing modes of governance and government. Since the development of new forms of territorial governance tended, until recently, to ignore the 'scale' of the megaregion there is clearly potential for a power struggle to ensue. This does not necessarily revolve solely around this new scale but on its relation to existing scales (local, regional, national, international) and the articulation between such scales (Dubois et al., 2009).

Establishing a specific mode (or modes) of territorial governance for the scale of the megaregion is made more difficult because the rationale for defining megaregions usually follows a functional logic (economic integration, business networks, commuting patterns, transport systems and so on) (cf. Harrison and Hoyler, 2014, 2015a). The relevant political stakeholders are, however, constrained by territorial politics (that is the politico-administrative scope of municipalities, provinces, counties, countries and so on) and the inherent institutional restrictions. This means a powerful discourse is required to overcome these territorial and institutional limitations by promoting some convincing rationales to motivate stakeholders to invest their resources and capacities to negotiate a new or (as they might feel) better mode of governance for the scale of this particular megaregion.

Considering the critical body of literature which now exists about the concept of (mega)regions, alongside other terms relating to regions, regionalism and regionalization, the reflections above have to be considered as being sketchy due to the rather cursory assemblage of only some of the key arguments. Yet what is clear is that the prefix 'mega' (and maybe others) adds to the inherent complexity within this literature, in particular due to its seemingly arbitrary application to various sorts of positive ascriptions of larger or (as some might feel) superior types of regions (Hesse, 2015). Nonetheless, we argue that the (de)construction of (mega) regions should be followed by an in-depth analysis of the various, and what we assume to be competing, discourses to uncover the different rationales, interests and reasons therein. Some attempts in this direction are made in the following sections.

7.3 THE CONCEPT OF NORDEN: COHERENCY AND DIFFERENCES IN POLITICS AND PLANNING

From a European perspective, the geographical image of Norden is characterized by large areas with low population densities, a number of small and medium-sized cities and towns scattered throughout the countryside and growing city-regions around the capital cities – Copenhagen, Helsinki, Oslo and Stockholm. The geographic image of Norden is associated with notions of 'rurality', or even 'remoteness', with many places facing severe demographic challenges (aging, shrinking labour force, out-migration of female population and so on). Nonetheless, here we want to focus on the main metropolitan areas of Norden which have been high on the political agenda in recent years. An important issue is how to adapt urban planning and regional development to globalization processes, a changing relational network economy and increased competitiveness between different places (Baeten, 2012; Galland, 2012). Particularly significant is how the development of two regional urban formations is currently being emphasized simultaneously. These are the construction of sub-national city-regions, primarily around the capital regions, and regional network formations at the transnational megaregional scales. To understand these seemingly paradoxical spatial processes it is vital to first recognize the historical similarities and differences between them, the convergent and divergent policy trajectories in Norden, and the continuous redevelopment of the 'Nordic model' in light of processes of neoliberalization.

Scandinavia and Norden are often used interchangeably but they do not refer to exactly the same area (Jones and Olwig, 2008). The Scandinavian Peninsula includes the states of Norway and Sweden and the northern parts of Finland. But Scandinavia is also a linguistic region of North Germanic languages that include Swedish, Danish and Norwegian. Finnish is a non-Indo-European Uralic language, but Swedish is spoken in parts of Finland, where it has equal legal standing with Finnish. Norden usually refers to a larger geographical area of the five states of Denmark, Finland, Iceland, Norway and Sweden plus the three autonomous territories of the Faroe Islands, Greenland and the Åland Islands (Figure 7.1). These are also the eight territorial units of the formal political Nordic co-operation and the Nordic Council. In total, the territorial area of Norden has a population of approximately 26 million people (for illustrative purposes, the EU-28 includes approximately 508 million people), which is extremely unevenly dispersed across a vast area of 3.5 million km^2 (the EU-28 covers 'just' 4.38 million km^2). Thus Scandinavia is perhaps a geographical and partly cultural megaregion but Norden seems to be a more relevant political and socioeconomic transnational megaregion.

The Nordic states have a long history of rivalry and war, collaborations and unions (Boje and Olsson Hort, 1993; Dosenrode and Halkier, 2004; Jones and Olwig, 2008). After the Second World War the Nordic Council, an inter-parliamentary body, was established and the cooperation remains one of the oldest and most comprehensive multilateral political partnerships in the world. The cooperation is based on the historical

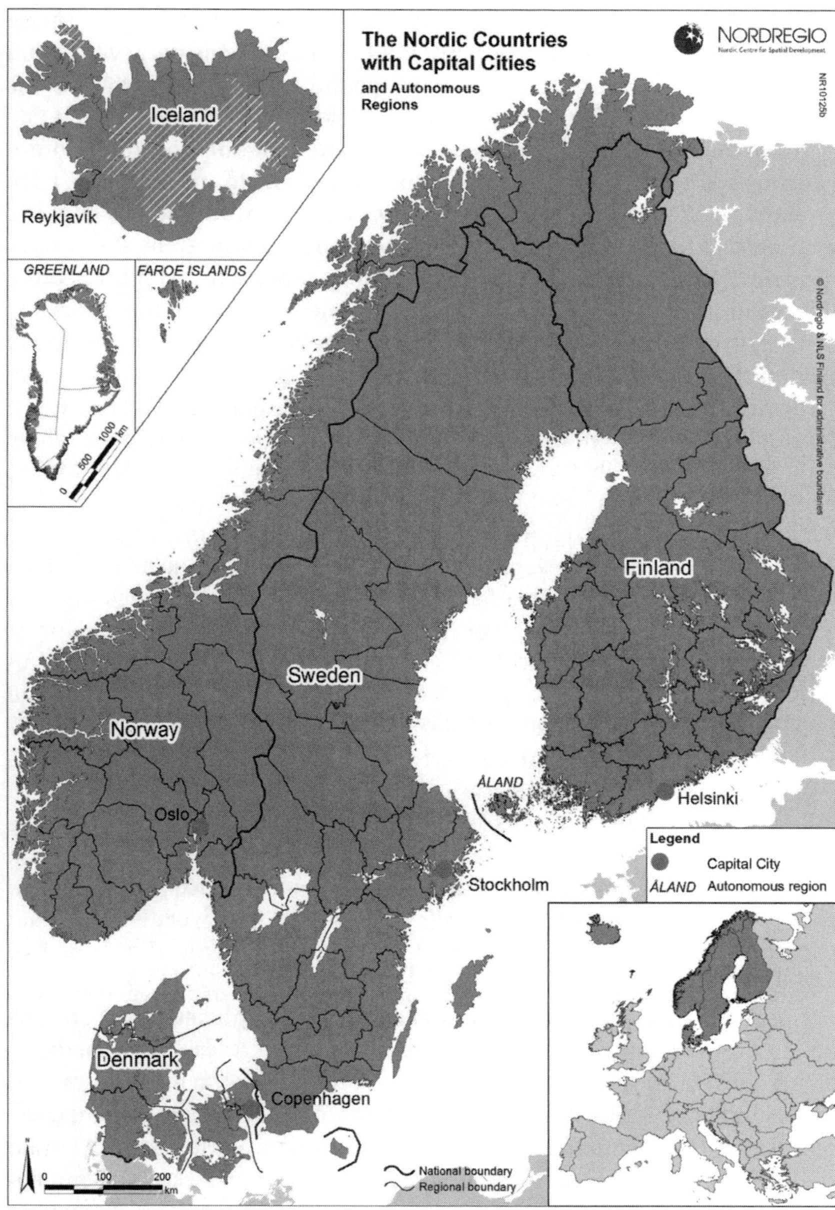

Source: Nordregio

*Figure 7.1   The Nordic countries with capital cities and autonomous
regions*

and cultural affinity of the states and has evolved and developed during the 20th century. In the early 1970s, the Council of Ministers, which can be considered as the official intergovernmental body for cooperation, was established (Nordic Council of Ministers, 2011).

From an outside perspective, Norden might seem to be a rather homogeneous region. In international comparisons, the Nordic countries have a relatively high degree of integration, with a passport union (1952) and a common labour market (since 1954) – even if the different states have historically pursued rather divergent policies (Jones and Hansen, 2008). For example, with regards to the involvement in other supranational cooperation: Denmark, Iceland and Norway are NATO members; Denmark, Finland and Sweden are members of the European Union, but only Finland is part of the Eurozone. Although, in this light, the Nordic states are pursuing partly different political trajectories, there also seems to be some convergence and transformation towards more neoliberal policies in combination with a still extensive welfare system, which has received significant international attention (Wooldridge, 2013). There has been a large degree of political consensus around these transformations, with both left- and right-wing political parties more or less in agreement. Jessop (2010), for example, has described the Nordic transformations as 'neoliberal policy adjustments' in a pragmatic tradition. This is contrasted with the neoliberal system transformation (evident in Russia and Eastern Europe), neoliberal regime shifts (experienced in the US and UK) and neoliberal structural adjustment programs (implemented in the Global South) (Jessop, 2010). To continue developing the Nordic welfare model is also at the heart of the agenda for the Nordic Council: 'The Nordic welfare model and the cultural affinity in the Region are both unique. Further developing the welfare model to cope with global competition, while maintaining that very affinity and cohesion, is an important aspect of co-operation' (Nordic Council of Ministers, 2011, p. 12).

Despite such general similarities between the Nordic states, there are, on closer inspection, significant differences within, for example, the fields of urban and regional planning and housing policies, which are related to the diverging transformation processes of the welfare state across Norden (Lujanen, 2001; Bengtsson and Ruonavaara, 2010; Alestalo et al., 2009). For example, housing policies in Norway and Iceland emphasized ownership while rental apartments used to be a central focus in Sweden and Denmark. However, housing regimes in the Nordic welfare states have changed dramatically in the last two to three decades or so. For example, since the 1990s, Swedish housing policies and the housing market have been transformed from being extensively regulated to one of the most liberal markets in Europe (the rental market is still substantially regulated). A neoliberal policy shift which has had far-reaching consequences, the result is a socially and economically polarized and geographically uneven housing market, most clearly manifested in a housing shortage, growing gaps between different forms of tenure, increasing super-gentrification and low-income filtering (Hedin et al., 2012). This is indicative of the transformations of the political and socioeconomic landscape in the Swedish welfare state since the mid-1980s.

In Sweden (as well as in the other Nordic countries) the political, economic and social landscape changed markedly after the economic crisis in the 1970s. During the following decades, the changes have been institutionalized in various forms through financial (credit and currency market) deregulation in the 1980s and the deregulation of infrastructure (telecommunication, electricity market, railroads, domestic airways), and tax and pension reforms in the 1990s (Bergh and Erlingsson, 2009). During the 2000s development has continued with privatization and reforms in service provisioning. How public services are being provided has shifted significantly: 'The previous system of public provision of uniform services, allocated through bureaucratic planning, has been profoundly transformed, replaced with a system where the choices of service users play a much bigger role, where private providers have re-established themselves (especially in the bigger cities) and where relations between actors within the system are conducted in an increasing market-like environment' (Blomqvist, 2004, pp. 140–141). The political re-orientation and policy reforms are ongoing and to a large degree a response to external and internal economic and demographic changes, but also of cultural and political shifts following globalization and increased urbanization. As Wooldridge (2013, p. 5) explains:

> The Nordic model is still a work in progress. The three forces that have obliged the Nordic countries to revamp it – limited resources, rampant globalisation and growing diversity – are gathering momentum. The Nordics will have to continue to upgrade their model, but they will also have to fight to retain what makes it distinctive.

The tensions between market-oriented transformations and continuous reformation of Nordic welfare, which Harvey (2005) described as circumscribed neoliberalization, is clearly evident within the field of urban and regional planning. During the last decades there has been a re-orientation towards more neoliberal urban planning policies in many parts of Europe and beyond (Sager, 2011). A general shift away from land use oriented planning towards more strategic forms of planning has resulted in a transition from planning by rules to planning by goals (Castells, 2002). In the

Nordic states this tendency is also evident with increased focus on strategic spatial planning, which, for example, in Denmark clashes with more traditional regulatory frameworks (Olesen and Richardson, 2012). There seem to be increased tensions between transparent, inclusive and democratic planning processes and new forms of market oriented management – between input legitimacy and output efficiency (Mäntysalo et al., 2011).

These tensions are clearly evident in the Öresund region, a cross-border region encompassing the larger city-region of Copenhagen on the Danish side and Malmö on the Swedish side. The planning practices and projects there illustrate what Baeten (2012) calls the normalization of neoliberal planning since, for instance, urban planning projects in both Denmark and Sweden are heavily focused on specific prestigious places, for example redevelopment of harbour areas close to the inner city, and at the same time bypass larger territories and thus neglect other places. In this light, the urban development around Öresund has been described as a 'space war' on two fronts: between cities and places, and between global capital and local citizens (Lund Hansen, 2006). This episode of place-based entrepreneurial oriented urban and regional governance in the Öresund region is in opposition to the common understanding of planning in Norden, but it is in line with the ongoing transformation of the Nordic welfare model with regard to neoliberal urban and regional planning and the formation of new 'mega-city' and/or cross-border regions.

7.4 CITY-REGIONAL NETWORKS AND (DIS) CONNECTIONS ACROSS NORDEN

> The Nordic capitals may compete between themselves on a regional level but they will need to collaborate to be successful on a global level against other cities and regions to gain businesses, investments and tourists. (PricewaterhouseCoopers [PwC], 2012, p. 4)

Collaborate to compete is another way to formulate the above conclusion and policy recommendation from a benchmarking study of the Nordic capitals. The report produced by PwC also emphasizes Norden as a competitive 'global region' in some areas, such as intellectual capital and innovation, but identifies a vital need for increased strategic and visionary cooperation, and new infrastructure connecting the region through efficient transport systems to become a 'globally relevant cluster' (PwC, 2012, p. 59). However, there is no lack of visionary new infrastructure projects and new regional formations in line with these recommendations. For example, Scandinavia's '8 million city' project envisions connecting Copenhagen, Malmö, Gothenburg and Oslo through 'a high speed rail link that will physically connect these 8 million inhabitants and contribute to making this region one of the world's most competitive' (8 Million City, 2013).

Although a megaregion connecting Oslo and Copenhagen might seem to be utopian at first glance, there are underlying, observable empirical changes both confirming increased relational interconnectivity and re-establishing urban territorial hierarchies of the Nordic city-regions. A recent study on the intercity connectivity networks of financial and other business service firms and ICT service firms based in the Nordic capital regions shows that there still is a rather hierarchal urban system within the Nordic states, but that the capital regions are also horizontally inter-connected through transnational business networks (Schmitt and Smas, 2012a, 2012b). These networks and flows are creating new challenges for planning in the growing and expanding Nordic capital regions, which in an increasingly urbanized world form the core of the Nordic megaregion. But the economic flows and business networks are intensely connected with other places and regions around the world, across nation states and governance territories.

Stockholm, followed by Copenhagen, Oslo and Helsinki are confirmed in relational terms as the major Nordic nodes in the global network economy (Hall and Pain, 2006; Taylor et al., 2011). This can partly be explained by the integrated Nordic history with dense social, economic and cultural networks (Hermelin, 2011). In the abovementioned study by Schmitt and Smas (2012a, 2012b), Stockholm stands out at the Nordic scale in terms of relatively high intercity connectivity through financial and other business service firms. Compared to this, considerably more variations exist in respect of the ICT service sector, where a rather uneven geographical pattern emerges. At the national scale there is a significant gap between the capital regions and other national cities which indicates monocentric urban systems within the Nordic states. As larger cities stand out a plausible explanation is that market size still matters. Nonetheless, there are also indications that Norden can be considered as one, increas-ingly coherent, market, which is not surprising since businesses are not as bounded to territories as most policymakers.

The Nordic capitals have a strong role in linking Norden to the global economic network. How the city-regions are interconnected differs slightly between the four Nordic capital regions. There are also differ-ences between the business sectors, which indicates regional specialization and the different functions the Nordic capitals have within the global economy. For example, at the European scale Paris appears to be the most interconnected city with the Nordic capital regions through ICT service firms, while Singapore is the most interconnected city worldwide. Through the financial and business service sector, the Nordic capital regions are closely connected to London and New York, but also to cities in Eastern Europe. The Nordic capital regions seem to be well interconnected with cities around the world and in particular with the BRIC states through the networks of both financial and market services and ICT service firms.

It is, however, evident that the Nordic capital city-regions are more intensively connected with each other than with other Nordic cities (through financial and market services and ICT service networks). The four subnational (and partly cross-border) capital city-regions of Oslo, Copenhagen, Stockholm and Helsinki are beginning to form the core of a potential Nordic transnational megaregion. Other studies have also identified different economic clusters centred on the interconnections of capital regions; for example ICT in Helsinki–Stockholm–Copenhagen (PwC, 2012). There is thus an evident need of a relational perspective to grasp the transnational connections but also to combine this with territorial perspectives and the 'realpolitik' of policymaking. In policy terms it could be argued that the studies above highlight the need to think much more in terms of complementarities rather than focusing primarily on competitiveness between the Nordic capital regions. Such policy options were even acknowledged and agreed upon as meaningful by a number of policymakers from the Nordic capital city-regions when the results were first presented. In practice there are, however, significant challenges of implementing complementary policies and approaching urban and regional development in relational terms. It is not only a problem with doing things outside political and jurisdictional territories, it is also about the thorny issue of how to align political rhetoric and policymaking to both people's everyday needs and practices and to the requirements of transnational business networks.

The Öresund region is often portrayed as a model of cross-border collaboration in policy terms and a flagship region within the EU (OECD, 2003). The top down political project centred around a physical bridge connecting the city of Malmö in the Swedish province of Skåne with Copenhagen and Danish Zealand has been thoroughly researched from various perspectives (for example Berg et al., 2000; Jensen and Richardson, 2004b; Hospers, 2006; Hall, 2008). This illustrates the difficulty of delineating regions, the unevenness of regionalization projects, the asymmetries of naturalizing borders and the complex cultural dynamics within Norden (Löfgren, 2008).

In 2000 the Öresund bridge was inaugurated and after a decade the development of the region is still a work in progress. Today Malmö has a clear focus on the Danish capital Copenhagen. The cooperative atmosphere is exemplified by the fact that both cities use exactly the same

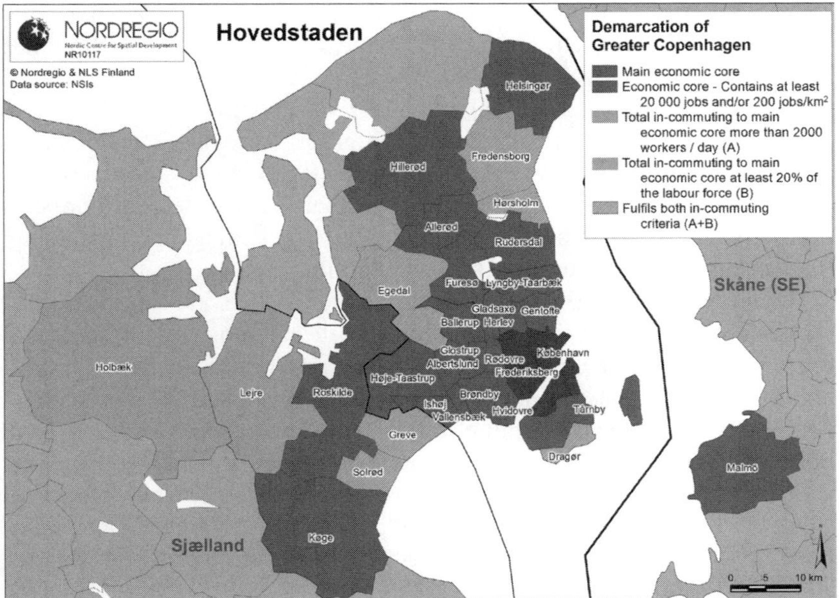

Source: Schmitt and Smas (2012b, p. 19). Reproduced by permission.

Figure 7.2   The Greater Copenhagen capital region

illustration and the spatial representations of the Öresund region are identical in their comprehensive plans, and thus invokes the image of being parts of the same region. This is supported by cross-border governance structures and strategic projects as well as significant commuting across the bridge. In the aforementioned study of Nordic intercity connectivities (conducted between 2010 and 2012) Malmö was thus included in the Greater Copenhagen functional urban area (Figure 7.2) – something which proved to be a rather controversial issue when discussing the results with state representatives from Denmark. Regional development strategies and policy discussions on both sides of Öresund are progressing even further south towards Hamburg, Germany. A new strategic megaregion is emerging, spurred partially by the construction of a bridge across the Fehmarnbelt between Denmark and Germany. The Fehmarnbelt region is envisioned to span across three countries, from southern Sweden in the north to Germany in the south, including a population of approximately 9 million inhabitants with Hamburg and Copenhagen as the two major urban nodes (Femern, 2013).

Similarly, another megaregional arrangement is the STRING region.

Since 1999, the counties of Storstrøm and West Zealand in Denmark, the Land Schleswig-Holstein and the Free and Hanseatic City of Hamburg in Germany, together with the Swedish-Danish partners of the Öresund region, have cooperated within the STRING (Southwestern Baltic Sea TransRegional Area – Inventing New Geography) project. The aim of this long-term cooperation is to develop joint strategies in view of the region's economic potentials. To that end, the partners have entered a cooperation agreement that is based on three pillars for strategic policymaking: innovation, entrepreneurship and sustainability.

However, despite the bridge over the Öresund, there are significant discontinuities within the city-region (and to a megaregion of Nordic capital regions). This is not only in terms of everyday practices, but also with regard to functional business networks, strategic planning and policymaking. The strategic planning and urban development projects have been criticized for being overly focused on certain places and people, while neglecting, but also separating 'economic development from social concern' (Baeten, 2012, p. 40). This could result in a fragmented and splintered urban region with 'premium network spaces' (Graham and Marvin, 2002, p. 257) connecting targeted nodes while effectively bypassing other places, which risks creating an inside and outside both in relational and territorial terms. As pointed out by the OECD in their territorial reviews of Copenhagen (OECD, 2009) and Skåne (OECD, 2012), alongside governance issues, segregation is one of the key challenges facing policymakers. In addition, there is also a gap between the strategic representations – such as 'The Fehmarnbelt Region' or 'The 8 Million City' – and the everyday life of people living and working in the regions. Moreover, there is a mismatch between the relational networks of transnational businesses operating both at a megaregional scale and a city-regional scale, and the organization of territorial government in administrative regions. Seen in this light, it appears that the Öresund region provides a specific 'transnational laboratory' for new forms of territorial governance (Jensen and Richardson, 2004b) where new public–private collaborations are being tested. Alongside this, what Allmendinger and Haughton (2009, 2010) might regard as 'soft spaces' within and beyond Norden are also being explored.

To sum up, the capital cities of Stockholm, Copenhagen, Oslo and Helsinki are undeniably the urban nodes of the monocentric urban systems in the Nordic states. Each capital region is growing and increasing its relative economic position within Norden while also expanding functionally beyond traditional administrative territories and, in the case of Copenhagen, even across national borders. The Nordic capital regions are also closely interconnected with each other and other global cities around the world, forming what could usefully be termed a 'Nordic capital megaregion'. This is particularly clear from a business perspective, but is also evident from a policy perspective where it is generally recognized that the Nordic capital regions need to cooperate with each other through new informal ways of territorial governance arrangements and strategic regional representations.

7.5   TRANSNATIONAL GOVERNANCE IN THE BALTIC SEA REGION

Since the fall of the Iron Curtain, the Nordic countries (with the exception of Iceland) have engaged in a number of transnational governance arrangements relating to the larger Baltic Sea Region. The dissolution of the Eastern Bloc opened the way for revitalizing transnational cooperations around the Baltic Sea, which have been expressed through symbolic terms such as 'Baltic Europe', 'Mare Balticum', the 'Scanno-Baltic Space' and, in particular, 'The New Hansa' (Joenniemi, 1993). As noted by Metzger and Schmitt (2012), the following activities generated various forms of networks and institutions and gave birth to a significant number of pan-Baltic governmental and non-governmental organizations. Although the exact number is difficult to define, at present we can count approximately 40 active pan-Baltic organizations forming a 'sea of acronyms' with partly overlapping agendas and activities (Löwendahl and Pursianen, 2009, p. 614). Examples include the Council of the Baltic Sea States (CBSS), the Baltic Sea States Sub-Regional Cooperation (BSSSC), the Union of Baltic Cities (UBC), Baltic 21, the Helsinki Commission (HELCOM), the Baltic Metropoles Network, the B7 Baltic Island Network, the Baltic Development Fund (BDF) and Visions and Strategies around the Baltic Sea (VASAB) (Metzger and Schmitt, 2012).

With respect to spatial planning and territorial development the VASAB network is worthy of particular emphasis. VASAB is an intergovernmental multilateral cooperation network consisting of eleven countries. Since its formation in 1992, the aforementioned four Nordic countries (Denmark, Finland, Norway and Sweden), the three Baltic States (Estonia, Latvia and Lithuania), the northern part of Germany (the Länder of Bremen, Hamburg, Schleswig-Holstein, Mecklenburg-Vorpommern, Brandenburg and Berlin), and, perhaps most notably, Belarus and the north-western part of Russia (Saint Petersburg City, Republic of Karelia and oblasts – the Russian autonomous provinces – of Kaliningrad, Leningrad, Murmansk, Novgorod and Pskov) have been permanent members of this transnational network. This is particularly noteworthy because in 1992 only

Denmark and Germany were full members of the EU. Norway, Sweden and Finland were in the process of joining the EU (only the latter two did so in 1995); Poland had signed a treaty of association with the EU; while other countries in the Baltic Sea Region were still seeking different ways of cooperation with the EU. Due to the vast EU enlargement in 2004, the Baltic Sea became akin to an internal 'EU lake' except for the northwestern edge of Russia. Inevitably, this challenges transnational cooperation between EU member countries and non EU member countries (Russia and Belarus), although some specific programmes (for example the EU Neighbourhood Programme) and specific EU strategies (for example the Northern Dimension) have been installed to support networking activities between the two groups of countries (and partly beyond).

Throughout the years, the VASAB network has initiated a number of conferences on spatial integration and transnational cooperation in the field of spatial planning and territorial development, and elaborated three main strategy documents which have been adopted by the national governments of all the member countries. The first strategic policy paper is from 1994, entitled *Vision and Strategies around the Baltic Sea 2010 – Towards a Framework for Spatial Development in the Baltic Sea Region.* With this document VASAB established general principles for spatial planning in this transnational area, which, at least in Europe, can be considered as an early forerunner for this sort of transnational strategic policy paper. It has also inspired the on-going elaboration of the European Spatial Development Perspective (ESDP) during the 1990s (Faludi and Waterhout, 2002). In 2001, a follow-up policy document, the so-called 'VASAB 2010 PLUS paper', was adopted and this put more emphasis on the development of transnational cooperation projects than its predecessor. To this end, it has served as an inspirational source for initiating projects which are politically supported in the national states around the Baltic Sea. In the meantime, some of these projects have been co-financed by the INTERREG initiative, an EU instrument to support cross-border and transnational cooperation.

Finally, in 2009 the *VASAB Long-Term Perspective for the Territorial Development of the Baltic Sea Region* was issued with a particular focus on the increasing demand for spatial integration and transnational networking within the Baltic Sea Region on the one hand, and with its global role on the other. For this purpose, the strategy is tasked with leading the transformation of the Baltic Sea Region into a well-integrated and coherent European model to become a 'macro-region' by 2030, by overcoming the intraregional socioeconomic development divides (VASAB, 2009a, p. 12). Urban regions in particular are expected to play a critical role in unlocking the potentials that exist within the Baltic Sea Region.

In doing so, urban regions can contribute to what is, in the current EU spatial policy discourse, a territorial cohesion perspective. Part of this process involved a background study, which was undertaken to identify the most important territorial assets, analysing socioeconomic disparities and challenges which affect the long-term spatial development of the Baltic Sea Region (Schmitt and Dubois, 2008; VASAB, 2009b). The policy paper, 'VASAB Long-Term Perspective', identifies three pillars for policy attention – (1) 'Promoting urban networking and urban–rural cooperation', (2) 'Improving internal and external accessibility', and (3) 'Enhancing maritime spatial planning and management' – which form the thematic scope of an action plan that consists of 22 initiatives (VASAB, 2009a). Furthermore, due to the character of this intergovernmental transnational network, the 'Long-Term Perspective' also addresses specific actions for integrating north-west Russia and Belarus into the Baltic Sea Region. These normative intentions have also been illustrated in a number of strategic maps. Figure 7.3 illustrates a synthesis of these by using a number of cartographic elements to depict notions of spatial integration, networking, relational or even soft spaces, as alternatives to those that are associated solely with political jurisdictions.

In the same year that the VASAB 'Long-Term Perspective' was adopted, another major strategic policy document outlining the territorial future of the Baltic Sea Region was released: *The European Union Strategy for the Baltic Sea Region* (EUSBSR) (CEC, 2009a, 2009b [2013]). This so-called 'macro-regional strategy' represents a still relatively novel approach within the various strands of the EUs territorial policy agenda. The EUSBSR is the first arrangement of its kind, followed by similar strategies that have been subsequently initiated, including for the Danube Basin (adopted in 2011), for the Adriatic–Ionian Region (to be adopted before the end of 2014), for the Alpine Region (adoption scheduled for autumn 2015) and for the North Sea–English Channel Area (still under negotiation).

The EUSBSR collects and highlights a number of existing and new action areas or potential projects for the Baltic Sea Region. It has been made very explicit when launching the EUSBSR that no new legislation, instruments or institutions will be set up. Instead, the existing framework of actors and institutions and funding opportunities within the EU and beyond should be consulted for the implementation of the intended activities. In 2013, an updated action plan was presented that proposes three general objectives ('save the sea', 'connect the region' and 'increase prosperity'), which are further specified by the selection of 17 priority areas and five cross-thematic horizontal actions (CEC, 2009b [2013]).

Like the 'Long-Term Perspective', the EUSBSR also identifies possible

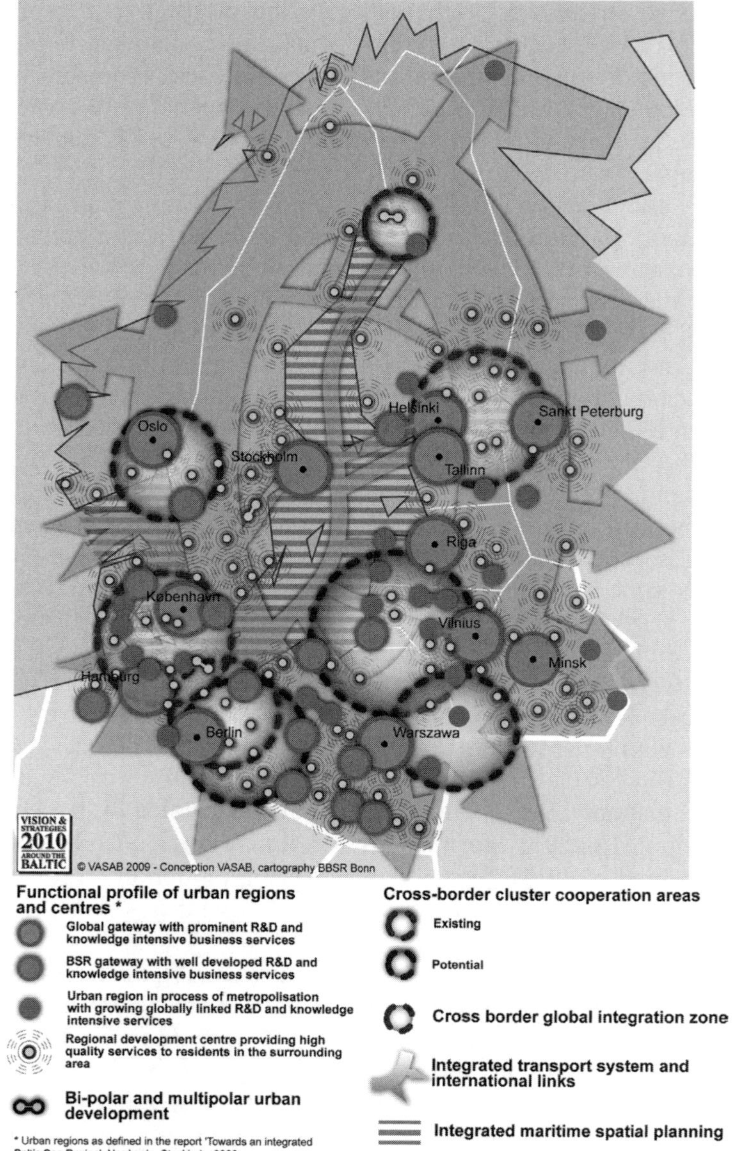

Source:　VASAB (2009a, p. 13). Reproduced by permission.

Figure 7.3　A territorial development perspective for the Baltic Sea region

stakeholders – both governmental and non-governmental – who might take responsibility and promote such actions and thus become enrolled as both the carriers and constitutors of the Baltic Sea Region. Another similarity is that both set a framework for a number of jointly agreed initiatives designed to strengthen transnational territorial cooperation around the Baltic Sea. A major difference between the two strategic documents lies in the different starting points of their authors. While the EUSBSR addresses the inter-sectoral challenges of the Baltic Sea Region, without mentioning where they occur or where such actions should best be tackled, the VASAB strategy is the product of a more 'place-based' perspective developed by civil servants of national ministries responsible for spatial planning. This is surprising, since the EUSBSR has been mainly promoted by the Directorate-General for Regional and Urban Policy within the European Commission, who is usually concerned, to at least some extent, with the spatial implications of various kinds of policies emerging from the EU (for example CEC, 2008, 2010). What is also noteworthy is the fact that the European Commission, who is the main driver behind the EUSBSR (cf. Metzger and Schmitt, 2012), does not seek to pursue an exact geographic demarcation. In this they hope to avoid the impression that such a macro-regional strategy might replace the well-established and territorially predefined INTERREG programme for transnational cooperation projects, which has existed since 1998 for the Baltic Sea Region.

In conclusion, since the early 1990s various regionalization efforts have been undertaken to solidify the Baltic Sea Region as a megaregion (even though the prefix 'macro' seems to be the prevailing term used here). Today the living heritage of a wide organizational patchwork and various initiatives – VASAB, the many projects generated from the EU INTERREG initiative and more recently the macro-regional approach – support the normative vision of a globally established Baltic Sea Region. In this light, the associated and intended actions, by both governmental and non-governmental actors and institutions, appear to demonstrate another episode of spatial rescaling – in this case between the nation state and the EU (Dubois et al., 2009; Stead, 2014). Furthermore, the Baltic Sea Region is a prime example of 'soft spaces' due to the fuzziness of its geography and the predominance of informal and non-statutory relations between actors and institutions, which transcend formally established boundaries and scalar levels (Stead, 2011). However, as argued by Metzger and Schmitt (2012), this notion seems to be an appropriate term to describe the spatiality of the existing patchwork and juxtaposition of initiatives, policy-networks and institutional arrangements in the Baltic Sea Region in general. But with the introduction of the EUSBSR, it appears that a process of solidification has been set in motion through the consolidation of a number of related articulations of the Baltic Sea Region and by providing a stabilization of institutional arrangements. An eye-catching example is that VASAB, together with HELCOM, form the 'action leader' of the horizontal action 'spatial planning' and thus comply themselves with the agenda set by the EUSBSR. Here the installation, or maybe better, self-nomination, of a spokesperson for the Baltic Sea Region, in form of the European Commission, seems to be a crucial aspect. In fact, the European Commission, which otherwise tends to deny its central role in this, asserts a strong coordinating and controlling role within the emerging meta-governance that is also related to the implementation of the EUSBSR (Metzger and Schmitt, 2012; EUSBSR, 2013).

7.6   SCOPE AND LIMITATIONS OF MEGAREGIONS AS OBJECTS FOR POLICYMAKING

In this chapter we have illustrated and problematized how (mega)regions are being constructed and at the same time challenged and deconstructed through various relations, processes and mechanisms from a North European perspective. The examples have clearly underlined our earlier assumption that megaregions seem to be a complex and partly fuzzy spatial concept that tends to mean different things in different contexts and to different people. Most eye-catching is the tension between 'hard spaces', such as spatialities that are based on political jurisdictions (nation states, administrative regions, municipalities), and 'soft spaces', functionally or otherwise defined regions which expand or even bypass territorially-embedded politico-administrative units. A key challenge in both theory and practice is how to reconcile these partly contradictory relations, processes and mechanisms, and manage the gap between transnational flows of ideas and capital, products and people, and (still) territorially-based politics in general, and urban planning and regional development in particular.

The importance of understanding on-going regionalization and urbanization processes through both the territorial approach and a relational perspective on regions has, of late, become less controversial (Jonas, 2012; Jones and Paasi, 2013; Varró and Lagendijk, 2013). However, the inter-linked processes are normally studied independently. A number of urban researchers focus on the external relations of cities and regions through mapping transnational (business) networks (for example Hoyler et al., 2008; Taylor et al., 2011). Conversely, many planning and policy oriented scholars centre the debate on place-based competitiveness and emphasize the importance of local contexts in regards to issues such as participation of civil society, democratic legitimacy or mobilizing other local stakeholders (for example Healey, 2010). Our empirical evidence indicates that some national, regional and local policymakers in the Nordic states are (at least) aware of these challenges. Norden seems to be an experimentation ground for adapting urban and regional planning and policymaking to globalization at different scales and through different forms of (new) transnational territorial governance and policymaking.

When reflecting on our empirical examples, some conclusions can be distilled in view of the scope and limitations of the megaregions concept in general and as objects for policymaking in particular. First we can see that there is a political and economic rationale for re-imagining urban-regional economic spaces. This rationale demonstrates that the Nordic urban/metropolitan centres are not only in a process of spatial clustering, but also embedded within (transnational) inter-city linkages. These underline the notion of interdependency, but also of robustness in view of international territorial competition. Likewise it can help to emphasize specific 'territorial commonalities' between the four Nordic capital regions and thus give a sense of common purpose. Potentially one could even imagine that this can be the base for mobilizing mutually agreed informal strategies or forming discourse alliances, for example, in relation to the EU or the Nordic Council of Ministers. However, in view of identifying corresponding policies, programmes and projects that help to shape megaregions, at the same time it might be challenging to ascertain which parts of economic and social life a megaregion influences (or not) and who might be the addressees of such interventions. This brings us inevitably to the question who is, and who is not, actually affected by megaregions (cf. Harrison and Hoyler, 2015a, 2015b; Schafran, 2014)?

The example of the emerging Baltic Sea macro-region shows that an upscaling of spatial policies, and at the same time overcoming local rivalries, is possible in principle once a common denominator or challenge is identified (for example pollution of the Baltic Sea, overcoming the east–west divide in terms of accessibility) and a framework under which to work and cooperate is developed. However, as the example of the Baltic Sea Region also shows, one can speculate that a certain heritage of transnational cooperation is helpful here, since recent regionalization efforts have built upon two decades of experiences in transnational and cross-border cooperation within different institutional and organizational arrangements. Similarly, the Öresund region has a long and winding development trajectory, supported by the relatively institutionalized Nordic transnational cooperation, such as the Nordic Council of Ministers, and the integrated history of Norden, emphasizing that regionalization is a collective historical process (Paasi, 2001; Painter, 2010). Nonetheless, caution must be taken regarding the extent to which decision-makers (not necessarily policymakers) can escape from their political jurisdictions and jump between different scales and/or (mega) regions. Decision-makers will be conscious of the potential threats this brings to their democratic legitimacy and accountability. As the example of VASAB has shown, another risk with the politically mobilized construction of recently created 'soft megaregions' is that the scope of political interventions is often limited. In the end, normative notions such as city-networks, overcoming socioeconomic divides or improving accessibility are easy to agree; the question is whether practitioners have the necessary mechanisms to intervene in delivering on these aspirations. For this, other vehicles have to be mobilized (for example INTERREG), which demand even more policy negotiation and bear the risk that some of the good intentions might wither away over time, that is, once the funding ends.

The future challenges of spatial planning and development are not limited to reconnecting the unbound fluid capital with bounded territorial politics, however. It is also a matter of grounding this in the everyday life and the local, to the people living in the cities and towns as well as in the rural areas within these megaregions. With place-based competitive entrepreneurial planning currently being pursued in the Nordic states, there is a clear risk of sidelining and bypassing other places both outside the megaregions (that is, the sparsely populated areas of Norden), and places inside megaregions, that is, those places not accredited with contributing to the attractiveness or competitiveness of the megaregion. It is thus also important to consider the cultural identity (or better, identities) of places and regions *within* megaregions (cf. Fleming, 2015; Schafran, 2015), and not only the most suggestive strategic representations provided by the policy community or the obsessive analysis of functional networks stemming from regional research.

ACKNOWLEDGEMENTS

The authors wish to express their thanks to their colleague Mitchell Reardon for proofreading and providing further useful comments on an earlier version of the text. We would also like to thank our colleague Linus Rispling for creating the map of the Nordic countries with capital cities and autonomous regions (Figure 7.1).

REFERENCES

8 Million City (2013), 'The Scandinavian 8 million city', available at http://www.8millioncity.com/welcome-onboard (accessed 4 November 2013).

Alestalo, M., S.E.O. Hort and S. Kuhnle (2009), 'The Nordic model: conditions, origins, outcomes, lessons', Hertie School of Governance – Working Papers, No. 41, available at http://www.hertie-school.org/fileadmin/images/Downloads/working_papers/41.pdf (accessed 23 September 2013).

Allmendinger, P. and G. Haughton (2009), 'Soft spaces, fuzzy boundaries, and metagovernance: the new spatial planning in the Thames Gateway', *Environment and Planning A*, **41** (3), 617–633.

Allmendinger, P. and G. Haughton (2010), 'Spatial planning, devolution, and new planning spaces', *Environment and Planning C*, **28** (5), 803–818.

Baeten, G (2012), 'Normalising neoliberal planning: the case of Malmö, Sweden', in T. Taşan-Kok and G. Baeten (eds), *Contradictions of Neoliberal Planning*, Dordrecht: Springer, pp. 21–42.

Bengtsson, B. and H. Ruonavaara (2010), 'Introduction to the special issue: path dependence in housing', *Housing, Theory and Society*, **27** (3), 193–203.

Berg, P-O., A. Linde-Laursen and O. Löfgren (eds) (2000), *Invoking a Transnational Metropolis: The Making of the Øresund Region*, Lund: Studentlitteratur.

Bergh, A. and G.O. Erlingsson (2009), 'Liberalization without retrenchment: understanding the consensus on Swedish welfare state reforms', *Scandinavian Political Studies*, **32** (1), 71–93.

Blomqvist, P. (2004), 'The choice revolution: privatization of Swedish welfare services in the 1990s', *Social Policy & Administration*, **38** (2), 139–155.

Boje, T.P. and S.E. Olsson Hort (eds) (1993), *Scandinavia in New Europe*, Oslo: Scandinavia University Press.

Brenner, N. (2004), *New State Spaces: Urban Governance and the Rescaling of Statehood*, Oxford: Oxford University Press.

Bukve, O., H. Halkier and P. de Souza (eds) (2008), *Towards New Nordic Regions: Politics, Administration and Regional Development*, Aalborg: Aalborg Universitetsforlag.

Castells, M. (2002), 'The cultures of cities in the information age', in I. Susser (ed.), *The Castells Reader on Cities and Social Theory*, Oxford: Blackwell, pp. 367–389.

CEC (Commission of the European Communities) (2008), *Turning Territorial Diversity into Strength – Green Paper on Territorial Cohesion*, COM (2008) 616, Brussels: CEC.

CEC (Commission of the European Communities) (2009a), *European Union Strategy for the Baltic Sea Region*, COM (2009) 248, Brussels: CEC.

CEC (Commission of the European Communities) (2009b [2013]), *European Union Strategy for the Baltic Sea Region Action Plan*, SEC (2009) 712, Brussels: CEC.

CEC (Commission of the European Communities) (2010), *Investing in Europe's Future – Fifth Report on Economic, Social and Territorial Cohesion*, available at http://ec.europa.eu/regional_policy/sources/docoffic/official/reports/cohesion5/pdf/5cr_en.pdf (accessed 31 October 2013).

Deas, I. and A. Lord (2006), 'From a new regionalism to an unusual regionalism? The emergence of non-standard regional spaces and lessons for the territorial reorganisation of the state', *Urban Studies*, **43** (10), 1847–1877.

Dickinson, R.E. (1964), *City and Region: A Geographical Interpretation*, London: Routledge & Kegan Paul.

Dosenrode, S. and H. Halkier (eds) (2004), *The Nordic Regions and the European Union*, Aldershot: Ashgate.

Dubois, A., S. Hedin, P. Schmitt and J. Sterling (2009), 'EU macro-regions and macro-regional strategies – a scoping study', Nordregio Working Paper, 2009:4, available at http://www.nordregio.se/Publications/Publications-2009/EU-macro-regions-and-macro-regional-strategies/ (accessed 23 September 2013).

EUSBSR (European Union Strategy for the Baltic Sea Region) (2013), *Roles and Responsibilities of the Implementing Stakeholders of the EUSBSR and a Flagship Project Concept*, available at http://files.groupspaces.com/EUSBSR/files/6 28857/RhAnpv6hMhb04mvuoLES/EUSBSR+roles+and+responsibilities.pdf (accessed 10 September 2013).

Evers, D. and J. de Vries (2013), 'Explaining governance in five mega-city regions: rethinking the role of hierarchy and government', *European Planning Studies*, **21** (4), 536–555.

Faludi, A. (2005), 'Polycentric territorial cohesion policy', *Town Planning Review*, **76** (1), 107–118.

Faludi, A. (2009), 'The megalopolis, the blue banana, and global economic integration zones in European planning thought', in C.L. Ross (ed.), *Megaregions: Planning for Global Competitiveness*, Washington, DC: Island Press, pp. 35–52.

Faludi, A. (2013), 'Territorial cohesion, territorialism, territoriality, and soft planning: a critical review', *Environment and Planning A*, **45** (6), 1302–1317.

Faludi, A. and B. Waterhout (2002), *The Making of the European Spatial Development Perspective: No Masterplan*, London: Routledge.

Femern (2013), 'Homepage' available at www.femern.com (accessed 4 November 2013).

Fleming, B. (2015), 'Towards a megaregional future: analysing progress, assessing priorities in the US megaregion project', in J. Harrison and M. Hoyler (eds), *Megaregions: Globalization's New Urban Form?* Cheltenham, UK and Northampton, MA, USA: Edward Elgar, pp. 200–229.

Florida, R. (2008), 'The rise of the mega-region', *Wall Street Journal*, available at http://online.wsj.com/article/SB120796112300309601.html (accessed 18 February 2013).

Galland, D. (2012), 'Understanding the reorientations and roles of spatial planning: the case of national planning policy in Denmark', *European Planning Studies*, **20** (8), 1359–1392.

Garcia-Alvarez, J. and J.-M. Trillo-Santamaria (2013), 'Between regional spaces and spaces of regionalism: cross-border region building in the Spanish "state of the autonomies"', *Regional Studies*, **47** (1), 104–115.

Graham, S. and S. Marvin (2002), *Splintering Urbanism: Networked Infrastructures, Technological Mobilities and the Urban Condition*, London: Routledge.

Gustafsson, H. (2006), *Nordens Historia: En Europeisk Region Under 1200 år*, Lund: Studentlitteratur.

Hall, P. (2008), 'Opportunities for democracy in cross-border regions? Lessons from the Øresund region', *Regional Studies*, **42** (3), 423–435.

Hall, P. and K. Pain (eds) (2006), *The Polycentric Metropolis: Learning from Mega-City Regions in Europe*, London: Earthscan.

Harrison, J. (2014), 'Rethinking city-regionalism as the production of new non-state spatial strategies: the case of Peel Holdings Atlantic Gateway Strategy', *Urban Studies*, **51** (11), 2315–2335.

Harrison, J. and M. Hoyler (2014), 'Governing the new metropolis', *Urban Studies*, **51** (11), 2249–2266.

Harrison, J. and M. Hoyler (2015a), 'Megaregions: foundations, frailties, futures', in J. Harrison and M. Hoyler (eds), *Megaregions: Globalization's New Urban Form?* Cheltenham, UK and Northampton, MA, USA: Edward Elgar, pp. 1–28.

Harrison, J. and M. Hoyler (2015b), 'Megaregions reconsidered: urban futures and the future of the urban', in J. Harrison and M. Hoyler (eds), *Megaregions: Globalization's New Urban Form?* Cheltenham, UK and Northampton, MA, USA: Edward Elgar, pp. 230–255.

Harvey, D. (2005), *A Brief History of Neoliberalism*, Oxford: Oxford University Press.

Healey, P. (2010), *Making Better Places: The Planning Project in the Twenty-First Century*, Basingstoke: Palgrave Macmillan.

Hedin, K., E. Clark, E. Lundholm and G. Malmberg (2012), 'Neoliberalization of housing in Sweden: gentrification, filtering, and social polarization', *Annals of the Association of American Geographers*, **102** (2), 443–463.

Hermelin, B. (2011), 'Nordic cities', in P.J. Taylor, P. Ni, B. Derudder, M. Hoyler, J. Huang and F. Witlox (eds), *Global Urban Analysis: A Survey of Cities in Globalization*, London: Earthscan, pp. 300–306.

Hesse, M. (2015), '*Mega*urban regions: epistemology, discourse patterns, big urban business', in J. Harrison and M. Hoyler (eds), *Megaregions: Globalization's New Urban Form?* Cheltenham, UK and Northampton, MA, USA: Edward Elgar, pp. 29–50.

Hospers, G.-J. (2006), 'Borders, bridges and branding: the transformation of the Øresund region into an imagined space', *European Planning Studies*, **14** (8), 1015–1033.

Hoyler, M., R.C. Kloosterman and M. Sokol (2008), 'Polycentric puzzles – emerging mega-city regions seen through the lens of advanced producer services', *Regional Studies*, **42** (8), 1055–1064.

Jensen, O. and T. Richardson (2004a), *Making European Space: Mobility, Power and Territorial Identity*, London: Spon Press.

Jensen, O. and T. Richardson (2004b), 'Constructing a transnational mobility region – on the Øresund region and its role in the European Union spatial policy', in S. Dosenrode and H. Halkier (eds), *The Nordic Regions and the European Union*, Aldershot: Ashgate, pp. 139–158.

Jessop, B. (2010), 'From hegemony to crisis? The continuing ecological dominance of neoliberalism', in K. Birch and V. Mykhnenko (eds), *The Rise and Fall of Neo-Liberalism: the Collapse of an Economic Order*, London: Zed Books, pp. 171–187.

Jessop, B. (2012), 'Dynamics of regionalism and globalism: a critical political economy perspective', *Journal of Ritsumeikan Social Sciences and Humanities*, **11** (1), 3–24.

Joenniemi, P. (1993), 'Regionalization in the Baltic Sea area: actors and policies', in P. Joenniemi (ed.), *Cooperation in the Baltic Sea Region*, New York: Taylor and Francis, pp. 161–178.

Jonas, A.E.G. (2012), 'Region and place: regionalism in question', *Progress in Human Geography*, **36** (2), 263–272.

Jones, M. and J.C. Hansen (2008), 'The Nordic countries: a geographical overview', in M. Jones and K.R. Olwig (eds), *Nordic Landscapes: Region and Belonging on the Northern Edge of Europe*, Minneapolis, MN: University of Minnesota Press, pp. 543–567.

Jones, M. and K.R. Olwig (eds) (2008), *Nordic Landscapes: Region and Belonging on the Northern Edge of Europe*, Minneapolis, MN: University of Minnesota Press.

Jones, M. and A. Paasi (2013), 'Regional world(s): advancing the geography of regions', *Regional Studies*, **47** (1), 1–5.

Keating, M. (1997), 'The inventions of regions – political restructuring and territorial government in Western Europe', *Environment and Planning C*, **15** (4), 383–398.

Lidström, A. (2007), 'Territorial governance in transition', *Regional and Federal Studies*, **17** (4), 499–508.

Lindeborg, L. (2011), 'The Baltic Sea region: a global region – no macroregion', in T. Herrschel and P. Tallberg (eds.), *The Role of Regions? Networks, Scale, Territory*, Kristianstad: Kristianstads Boktryckeri, pp. 281–289.

Löfgren, O. (2008), 'Regionauts: the transformation of cross-border regions in Scandinavia', *European Urban and Regional Studies*, **15** (3), 195–209.

Löwendahl, B. and C. Pursianen (2009), 'Multilateral cooperation and spatial development', *Informationen zur Raumentwicklung*, Heft 8/9, pp. 613–620.

Lujanen, M. (2001), *Boende och Bostadspolitik I Norden*, Copenhagen: Nordisk Ministerråd.

Lund Hansen, A. (2006), *Space Wars and the New Urban Imperialism*, Lund: Lund University.

Mäntysalo, R., I.-L. Saglie and G. Cars (2011), 'Between input legitimacy and output efficiency: defensive routines and agonistic reflectivity in Nordic land-use planning', *European Planning Studies*, **19** (12), 2109–2126.

Medeiros, E. (2011), '(Re-)defining the Euroregion concept', *European Planning Studies*, **19** (1), 141–158.

Medeiros, E. (2013), 'Euro-meso-macro: the new regions in Iberian and European space', *Regional Studies*, **47** (8), 1249–1266.

Metzger, J. and P. Schmitt (2012), 'When soft spaces harden: the EU strategy for the Baltic Sea region', *Environment and Planning A*, **44** (2), 263–280.

Nordic Council of Ministers (2011), 'Nordic co-operation', available at http://www.norden.org/en/publications/publikationer/2010-792 (accessed 13 September 2013).

OECD (2003), *OECD Territorial Reviews: Öresund, Denmark/Sweden*, Paris: OECD.

OECD (2009), *OECD Territorial Reviews: Copenhagen, Denmark*, Paris: OECD.

OECD (2012), *OECD Territorial Reviews: Skåne, Sweden*, Paris: OECD.

Olesen, K. and T. Richardson (2012), 'Strategic planning in transition: contested rationalities and spatial logics in twenty-first century Danish planning experiments', *European Planning Studies*, **20** (10), 1689–1706.

Paasi, A. (1986), 'The institutionalization of regions: a theoretical framework for understanding the emergence of regions and the constitution of regional identity', *Fennia*, **164** (1), 105–146.

Paasi, A. (2001), 'Europe as a social process and discourse: considerations of place, boundaries and identity', *European Urban and Regional Studies*, **8** (7), 7–28.

Paasi, A. (2011), 'The region, identity, and power', *Procedia – Social and Behavioral Sciences*, **14** (1), 9–16.
Paasi, A. (2013), 'Regional planning and the mobilization of "regional identity": from bounded spaces to relational complexity', *Regional Studies*, **47** (8), 1206–1219.
Painter, J. (2010), 'Rethinking territory', *Antipode*, **42** (5), 1090–1118.
PricewaterhouseCoopers (PwC) (2012), 'Northern lights: the Nordic cities of opportunity', available at http://www.pwc.com/en_GX/gx/psrc/pdf/northern-lights-2012.pdf (accessed 13 September 2013).
Ross, C.L. (ed.) (2009), *Megaregions: Planning for Global Competitiveness*, Washington, DC: Island Press.
Sager, T. (2011), 'Neo-liberal urban planning policies: a literature survey 1990–2010', *Progress in Planning*, **76** (4), 147–199.
Schafran, A. (2014), 'Rethinking mega-regions: sub-regional politics in a fragmented metropolis', *Regional Studies*, **48** (4), 587–602.
Schafran, A. (2015), 'Beyond globalization: a historical urban development approach to understanding megaregions', in J. Harrison and M. Hoyler (eds), *Megaregions: Globalization's New Urban Form?* Cheltenham, UK and Northampton, MA, USA: Edward Elgar, pp. 75–96.
Schmitt, P. and A. Dubois (2008), 'Exploring the Baltic Sea region – on territorial capital and spatial integration', *Nordregio Report*, 2008:3, available at http://www.nordregio.se/Publications/Publications-2008/Exploring-the-Baltic-Sea-Region/ (accessed 23 September 2013).
Schmitt, P. and L. Smas (2012a), 'Multi-scalar "intercity connectivities" from a Northern European perspective', *GaWC Research Bulletin*, 411, available at http://www.lboro.ac.uk/gawc/rb/rb411.html (accessed 13 September 2013).
Schmitt, P. and L. Smas (2012b), 'Nordic "intercity connectivities" in a multi-scalar perspective', Nordregio Working Paper, 2012:7, Stockholm: Nordregio, available at http://www.nordregio.se/en/Publications/Publications-2012/Nordic-intercity-connectivities-in-a-multi-scalar-perspective/ (accessed 13 September 2013).
Stead, D. (2011), 'European macro-regional strategies: indications of spatial rescaling?', *Planning Theory and Practice*, **12** (1), 163–167.
Stead, D. (2014), 'European integration and spatial rescaling in the Baltic region: soft spaces, soft planning and soft security', *European Planning Studies*, **22** (4), 680–693.
Storper, M. (1997), *The Regional World: Territorial Development in a Global Economy*, New York: Guilford Press.
Taylor, P.J., P. Ni, B. Derudder, M. Hoyler, J. Huang and F. Witlox (eds) (2011), *Global Urban Analysis: A Survey of Cities in Globalization*, London: Earthscan.
Van Houtum, H. and A. Lagendijk (2001), 'Contextualising regional identity and imagination in the construction of polycentric urban regions: the cases of the Ruhr area and the Basque Country', *Urban Studies*, **38** (4), 747–767.
Van Well, L. (2012), 'Conceptualizing the logics of territorial cohesion', *European Planning Studies*, **20** (9), 1549–1567.
Varró, K. and A. Lagendijk (2013), 'Conceptualizing the region – in what sense relational?', *Regional Studies*, **47** (1), 18–28.
VASAB (Vision and Strategy around the Baltic Sea) (2009a), *VASAB Long-Term Perspective for the Territorial Development of the Baltic Sea Region,*

available at http://www.vasab.org/conference/upload/dokumenti/vasab_ltp_ final.pdf (accessed 6 September 2013).

VASAB (Vision and Strategy around the Baltic Sea) (2009b), *VASAB Long-Term Perspective for the Territorial Development of the Baltic Sea Region – Background Synthesis Document*, available at http://www.vasab.org/index.php/ long-term-perspective (accessed 06 September 2013).

Wooldridge, A. (2013), 'Northern lights: special report – the Nordic countries', *The Economist*, **406** (8821), 1–16.

Zimmerbauer, K. (2013), 'Unusual regionalism in Northern Europe: the Barents Region in the making', *Regional Studies*, **47** (1), 89–103.

8. Globalization and the megaregion: investigating the evolution of the Pearl River Delta in a historical perspective

Xu Zhang

8.1 INTRODUCTION

Since the 1990s, global city-regions, mega-city regions and megaregions have attracted extensive attention in both academic and policy circles (Florida et al., 2008; Hall and Pain, 2006; Hoyler et al., 2008; Ross, 2009; Scott, 1998, 2001). Contrary to the views that predicted the 'death of distance' (Cairncross, 1997) or the 'end of geography' (O'Brien, 1992), many scholars believe that globalization does not lead to a simple dispersal of economic activities. On the contrary, globalization has reasserted the agglomerative tendency in many parts of the world, making large cities and urban regions even more important. On the one hand, while advances in technologies of transportation and communication enable some highly routinized economic activities to be transferred over ever-greater distances, the leading sectors of contemporary post-Fordist economy (namely high-tech production, neo-artisanal manufacturing, advanced professional services, cultural industries, see Scott, 2008), characterized by high levels of uncertainty, instability and complexity, actually raise the necessity of instant mutual interaction and the need for spatial proximity. Large city-regions, benefiting from the concentration of flexibly networked production systems and close integration with the world market, are primary choices for most modern economic activities (Scott, 2001, 2008; Scott and Storper, 2003). On the other hand, with increasing cross-border economic activities and intensified uncertainty gradually eroding (perhaps more accurately, restructuring) the capability (and willingness) of the nation state to protect all regional and sectoral interests within their jurisdictions, regions are directly confronted with increasing global competition and forced to take greater responsibility for their own prosperity. This fosters a widespread transfer of power and resources towards the sub-national tier followed by a resurgence of region-based forms of economic and political organizations, that is, the rise of new regionalism (Brenner, 2004; Rodríguez-Pose, 2008; Scott, 2001, 2008). Both trends, the concentration of post-Fordist economy and the restructuring of spatial governance and institution-building in favour of the regional scale, are commonly used to explain the growing importance of megaregions within a new world system (Harrison and Hoyler, 2015).

Starting from this assumption, most research on megaregions tends to be framed by the conditions of the current specific form of globalization and worldwide capitalist restructuring that began to unfold in the 1970s. It also explains why economic phenomena and governance practices prefixed by 'post' or 'neo' always become the focus of analysis (cf. Hesse, 2015). However, this conceptualization of megaregions as the spatial product of a combination of recent technological progress and (neo-liberal) capitalist development is contested.

One line of argument emphasizes the historical continuity in the developmental processes of regions (Kloosterman and Lambregts, 2007; Lambregts, 2006). Accordingly urban systems with high sunk costs (in physical, social and politico-institutional terms) tend to display strong path-dependent characteristics. The current developmental trajectories and fates of regions in the modern world are, as a consequence, still significantly affected by their particular local histories as well as by their insertion centuries ago in national and international economies (Schafran, 2015; Wachsmuth, 2015).

Another critique denounces the (implicit) 'EuroAmerican hegemony' in theorizations of megaregions. As Roy (2009) points out, much of the dominant theoretical work on city-regions is firmly located in the urban experience of North America and Western Europe. This 'normalized narrative of global city-regions' has devalued the fast-growing regions of the global South and has concealed 'the heterogeneity and multiplicity of metropolitan modernities' (Roy, 2009, p. 821).

These two perspectives in fact reflect a more essential question about the geography of megaregions: whether the rise of megaregions predicts a convergence, even homogenization, of urban forms in the 21st century. In this chapter I will contribute to this discussion on the basis of an empirical study of such a megaregion in China. Without denying the uniqueness of contemporary global capitalist economy and the new qualities of modern city-regions as its spatial expression, I want to argue that the pattern of a megaregion can only be adequately understood through referring to its long-term developmental trajectory within broader political economic processes. Although the current wave of globalization shows unprecedented power to include ever more parts of the world into a seemingly single capitalist economic system, the way that a region is integrated in this system is still deeply influenced by its unique developmental path and contingent local context. Moreover, such a historical and context-sensitive perspective is especially important in understanding regions outside the western world, where quite different regional and national histories and contexts may exist and, therefore, the applicability of mainstream theories should be questioned and tested.

To achieve this purpose, this chapter takes the Pearl River Delta (PRD), a megaregion with a history going back at least two millennia and with dramatic changes in the last three decades, as the case to investigate its formation and evolution in the context of changing globalization and state policies in a historical perspective. The central question is how the PRD has been continuously (re)shaped in terms of global linkages, national status and regional urban system by the national and global political economic changes during different historical periods. In the next section, I will give a brief introduction to both the Pearl River Delta region and the analytical framework. After that, empirical data will be presented to substantiate the claim that 'history matters' in a more concrete way. In the conclusion, I will discuss the implications of this study and make an evaluation of two available frameworks, 'accumulation and concentration of capital' (Kloosterman and Lambregts, 2007) and 'state–city relationship' (Taylor, 1995, 2004), for analysing the long-term evolution of cities and regions in the global economy.

8.2   THE PEARL RIVER DELTA: A BRIEF HISTORY

Located on the southern coast of China (Figure 8.1), the PRD is known as the country's 'Southern Gate' with a history of more than 2000 years. In 214 BC this region was unified into the Qin Empire (China's first centralized empire) with the administration centre at Panyu (now Guangzhou). Since then the PRD started increasing communications with Central China, accelerated remarkably after a new route to the North was created (in 716) in the Tang Dynasty (Xu et al., 1994, p. 28). More and more immigrants from the North arrived, especially during eras when Central China was suffering from war. Meanwhile, due to its strong foreign maritime trade, this region began to develop in a way rather different from most other parts of the country. Guangdong province was set up in 1370 under the regime of Ming with Guangzhou as its capital. The 'Canton System' (Van Dyke, 2005) in early Qing brought

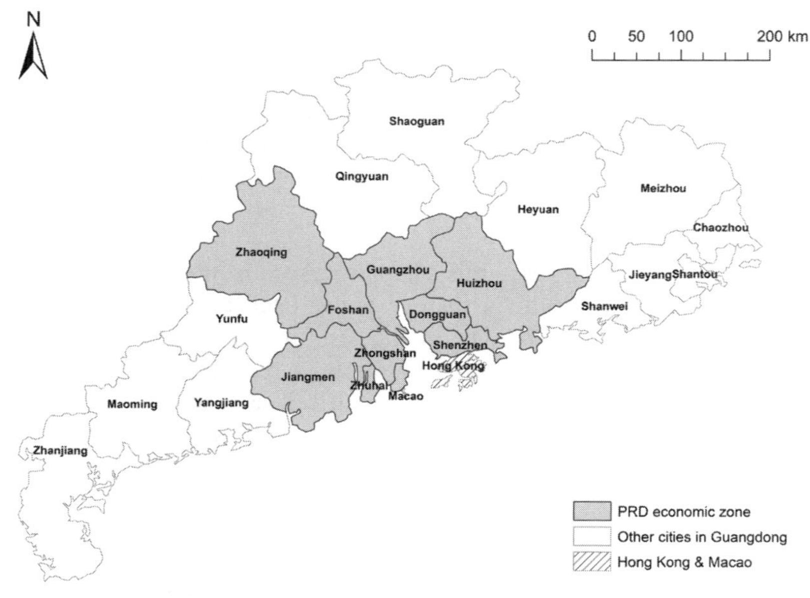

Source: Author

Figure 8.1   The geography of the Pearl River Delta

this region rapid prosperity within a short time. However, after the Opium Wars (1840–1842, 1856–1860) it experienced nearly one century of turbulence together with the whole country. The founding of the communist regime in 1949 and the establishment of a centrally planned economic system thereafter turned out to be the start of a period of slow development for this region. After 1978, Guangdong regained a special status in China's reform and opening up practice and entered a period of dramatic economic growth. In merely three decades it was transformed into the famous 'workshop of the world' and turned into a major 'regional powerhouse' in China (Enright et al., 2005). Since the late 1990s, we can observe a new development, namely a process of industrial upgrading and economic transition in the region.

Combining a rich history with global connections and periods of radical changes, the PRD provides a valuable case to explore the evolution of the megaregion from a long-term perspective. In addition, China's political context, represented by a strong (but constantly changing) central state and historical patterns of urbanization, make it a topical case to examine the impacts of national policies on regional

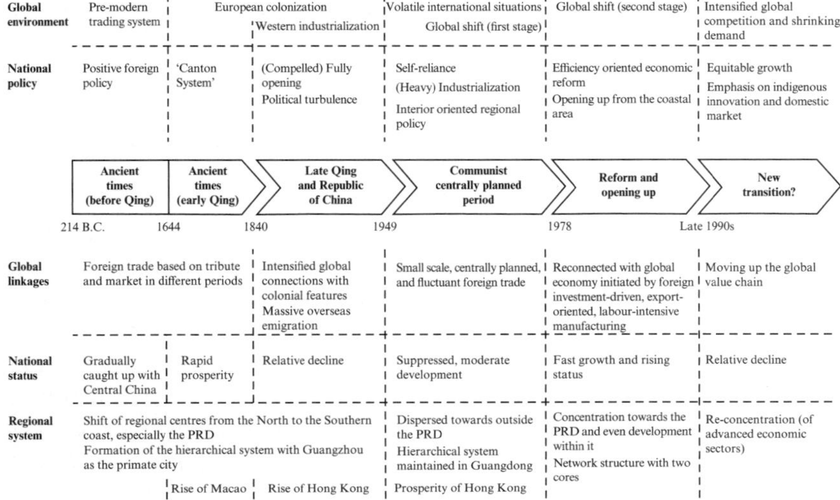

Source: Author

Figure 8.2 Historical framing of megaregion development in the Pearl River Delta

development across different stages of globalization. To undertake this type of historical megaregional analysis, an analytical framework was developed, linking the transformations of the PRD's global connections, its economic status within China and its internal urban system to the changes in the global and national political economic contexts within different historical periods. This framework is used to structure this chapter (Figure 8.2).

Since the concept of the PRD economic zone is relatively new, the following analysis is not limited to nine municipalities in this special zone, but also includes other parts of Guangdong province and even Hong Kong and Macao. This area is more similar to the so-called Greater PRD. The information for mapping the developments before 1949 comes mainly from local histories and relevant studies. Such data are relatively sketchy and mostly descriptive. More recent data are collected from various national and regional official statistics. Municipality is the main unit of analysis because data are more easily available and consistent at this level.

8.3　RISES AND FALLS: TRACING THE LONG-TERM EVOLUTION OF THE PEARL RIVER DELTA

8.3.1　Towards the Sea: Booming of Guangdong in Ancient Times (214 BC–1840)

The analysis begins with the period from 214 BC, when the region was first unified into China's national system, to the onset of the First Sino-British Opium War (1840). This is commonly regarded as the ancient period of China's history, ruled (although with interruptions) by powerful empires with a centralized bureaucratic system. The process of globalization during this period can be roughly divided into two stages: a pre-modern, merchant-led trading system based on overlapping regional city networks before the 16th century (Abu-Lughod, 1991; Taylor, 2012) and European expansion and colonization after that. China was at the heart of the East-Asian power system and trading network in the first stage and still maintained a high degree of autonomy until 1840.

As an agriculture-based economic entity with a huge territory, China did not have a strong need to involve itself in foreign trade in ancient times. However, since foreign trade provided an important way to acquire rare luxury goods and to increase national revenue, most royal courts adopted positive foreign policies and sometimes even actively participated in the tribute-type trade before the Ming Dynasty (Xu et al., 1994). Benefiting from its geographical location at the estuary of the Pearl River system and the starting point of maritime business routes to southern and eastern Asia and the Arabian world (China's major trading partners before the 16th century) Guangdong gained importance in the country's trading system (ibid.). China's first ancient foreign trade department (Shibo Si) was established in Guangzhou in the Tang Dynasty (661). The Ming (1368–1644) and Qing (1644–1911) authorities treated foreign trade with suspicion due to the concern of coastal safety and difficulties of managing foreigners. Foreign trade was restricted, sometimes even completely banned, by several emperors. However, the regulation in Guangdong was relatively relaxed. As the farthest port from the 'heart' of the empire, Guangzhou even became the only place designated by the Qing government for foreign trade under the highly regulated *Cohong* trading system between 1757 and 1842, monopolizing China's foreign trade for more than 80 years (Huang, 1988).[1]

Against this background, Guangdong gradually became China's major centre of foreign trade and connected with many ancient civilizations through the pre-modern trading networks. Major imports were rare luxury goods at first. Later, after Europeans became the main trading partner, raw cotton, woolen products and opium also became important. Exports were largely handicraft products and tea (Xu, et al., 1994). Following the Southern Dynasty (420–589), Guangzhou became the largest port city in China and one of the world's most famous ports. Except for being shortly surpassed by Quanzhou (in Fujian) during the Yuan Dynasty (1271–1368), Guangdong maintained its dominant status in China's foreign trade for about 1400 years (Xu et al., 1994).

Foreign trade, in turn, promoted Guangdong's social and economic development. Since far away from China's traditional political-economic centre, for a long time this region developed very slowly and lagged behind the central area. Guangdong's economic potential only started to emerge after transportation was improved and maritime trade started to thrive. During the Ming Dynasty, Guangdong caught up with Central China in terms of its overall economic level (Ye, 2007). The monopoly on foreign trade during the early Qing Dynasty brought the region prosperity based on commercial economy within a short time span. Its commercial networks spread to most major cities across the country (CCLCG, 2004). By 1839, Guangdong became the most populous province in China with nearly 23 million residents (Zhu, 1988).

There were three major changes in the regional spatial structure over this time. Firstly, the regional demographic and economic centre gradually shifted from the north of Guangdong, where immigrants first arrived, to the southern coastal part, where commercial economy and trade were more prosperous (Zhu, 1988). Secondly, a distinct, hierarchical, regional system was formed. At the top of the hierarchy was the political and economic centre Guangzhou. With approximately 900 000 residents Guangzhou was the second largest city (after Beijing) in China and the third largest city in the world by 1825 (Chandler, 1987). Below Guangzhou were several smaller commercial and handicraft towns or ports, including Foshan, Jiangmen, Chaozhou and Dongguan (CCLCG, 2004; Xu et al., 1994). The remainder of the region was mainly rural. The third remarkable change was the rise of Macao after being occupied by the Portuguese in 1573. Benefiting from Portuguese maritime power and Ming/Qing's dependence on Guangdong for foreign trade, Macao quickly grew from a small fishing village (with only 400 residents in 1555) to become an international trans-shipment centre on several important shipping routes: Guangzhou–Macao–Goa–Lisbon, Guangzhou–Macao–Manila–Mexico and Guangzhou–Macao–Nagasaki. At its peak, the population of Macao rose to 40 000 in 1640 (Huang, 1999).

8.3.2   Decline from Eminence: Turbulent Eras During the Late Qing and the Republic of China (1840–1949)

The industrial revolution started in England at the end of the 18th century and other major European countries followed in her wake. This economic development underpinned an acceleration of European colonial expansion in Asia. The balance of power between China and the Western world was gradually altered and the Qing Empire was defeated by the British in the Opium Wars. This defeat turned out to be a major break in China's history. After the war the Qing authority was compelled to open five ports for foreign trade according to the Treaty of Nanking (Nanjing), and more ports (including inland ones) were added over time. China also lost much of its sovereignty in affairs concerning foreign trade, tariffs and judiciary. Of more consequence, after the Opium Wars China experienced nearly one century of significant sociopolitical and socioeconomic turbulence: the collapse of the Qing Dynasty and the establishment of the Republic of China, the Warlord Era, the Sino-Japanese War and the Civil War. These subsequent political-economic changes had great impacts on the PRD.

With the penetration of European power into China, Guangdong was drawn further into the fast emerging international capitalist system. However, such intensified international connections were characterized by colonial features. Foreign capital became an important power in the region, not only controlling its foreign trade, but also heavily investing in manufacturing, shipping, railway and financial sectors. Guangdong became a main supplier of raw materials and handicraft products as well as a market for exporting industrial products for European countries, which means its specific position in the international division of labour was not very advantageous. From the beginning of the Republic of China (1912) to the end of the Sino-Japanese War (1945), Guangdong had a trade surplus in only three years (CCLCG, 2004). In addition, local domestic industries were severely restrained in the face of foreign competitors.

Political economic changes also shaped the region's global connections in another way: large-scale overseas emigration. Migrating to nearby countries had been a long history in Guangdong, but due to the unstable political economic environment, emigration entered a new stage after the Opium Wars. According to records, in 1941 there were about 5.42 million Chinese from Guangdong living overseas, mainly in Southeast Asia (79 per cent), Hong Kong (14 per cent), Macao (2.5 per cent) and North America (2.6 per cent) (CCGY, 1941). This large diaspora expanded Guangdong's overseas connections and contributed to its development through remittances and investment in local industry.[2] Their active role in the region, as we will see later, was further displayed after China implemented its Open Door policy in 1978.

At the national scale, Guangdong lost the predominant status in foreign trade due to the fierce competition from other opened regions, especially the Yangtze River Delta (YRD). Benefiting from its geographical location at the central point of China's coast and the estuary of the Yangtze River network, as well as a broad economically developed hinterland (including China's main producing areas of silk and cotton products), Shanghai replaced Guangzhou as the prime gateway for foreign products entering China. Between 1844 and 1867, Shanghai's share in China's imports and exports increased from 9 per cent to 67 per cent. At the same time, Guangzhou's share declined from 90 per cent to only 15 per cent.[3] Guangzhou's foreign trade volume further dropped to 7 per cent of that of Shanghai in 1947 (Yan, 1955). The loss of advantage in relation to foreign trade and the unstable political economy (especially due to the damage caused by war) severely constrained Guangdong's development. Indeed, from 1840 to 1947, Guangdong's population only increased from 25.3 million to 28.6 million (Zhu, 1988).

The most impressive change in the regional system during this period was the rise of Hong Kong under British rule. For a long time Hong Kong was only a small harbour (Tuen Mun) in Guangdong. After the Opium Wars, the British acquired it from the Qing government and made it part of their colonial empire. Excellent port conditions, its strategic geopolitical location, the free port status and its sociopolitical stability provided by the colonial government made Hong Kong a very attractive port for international trade, especially for trade with China. Hong Kong quickly replaced Macao as China's most important entrepôt centre. Between 1865 and 1900, 41 per cent of China's imports and 27 per cent of its exports were with Hong Kong (Keller et al., 2011). Trade-related activities, such as shipping and financial services, also grew very fast. Gradually, Hong Kong became a major provider of business services to Guangdong. Although located in two very different political systems, the fortunes of these two places were closely intertwined with each other. This unique geopolitical relationship has had very profound consequences, which are highly relevant even today.

8.3.3 Suppressed Development During the Centrally Planned Economy Period (1949–1978)

The establishment of the communist regime in 1949 led to fundamental political, economic and ideological reorientations in China. The communist leaders abolished the market-based private economy and replaced it with a centralized economic system characterized by public ownership and a high degree of state control and planning. They gradually retreated from the outside world and turned to self-reliance, partly for ideological reasons and partly because of the volatile international situations (the Cold War, the Korean War, Western embargo on China, worsening Sino-Soviet relations, the Vietnam War). Therefore, regional development in China was tightly bound up with national policies during the planned economy period.

Similar to the USSR, the Chinese central government placed a great emphasis on industrialization with exceptional prominence given to heavy industries. Meanwhile, the priority of investment turned to inland areas, which were considered to be closer to natural resources and energy, less vulnerable to foreign military power and beneficial for the 'balance' of national economy. As a traditional region focusing on trade, commerce and consumption, and lacking a robust industrial base and natural resources, Guangdong was not well-positioned in this national developmental strategy. The region's location at the coastal 'front line' also made it a very low priority for receiving state interior-oriented investment. From 1949 to 1978, Guangdong only received 2.5 per cent of national investment in state-owned enterprises (Zhang, 1992).

Under such circumstances, the role of Guangdong (and the PRD in particular) as a commercial and trade centre was deeply suppressed. Its connection with the global economy was limited to a small-scale, volatile foreign trade, which was seldom over 10 per cent of the national volume (Table 8.1). Foreign capital was excluded. Overemphasizing industrialization and self-reliance prevented Guangdong from exploiting traditional advantages in commerce and trade. Even worse, it disturbed the balance among different economic sectors. Therefore, fast industrialization[4] did not lead to corresponding economic development in the region. During the centrally planned period, Guangdong's importance in the national economic system was not prominent.

Following the national policy Guangdong's most important investments were targeted at the interior municipalities, such as Shaoguan and Qingyuan. Consequently, regional growth hotspots shifted from the PRD, where most industrial assets and outputs concentrated before 1949, to the northern mountainous and the western resource-rich areas (Figure 8.3). As the 'planning centre' of the region, the capital city Guangzhou maintained (even strengthened) its dominant status in the state-led growth. But development among the other municipalities showed a dispersed spatial pattern. By the end of this period, the spatial structure of Guangdong was featured by a strong core plus several administrative centres relatively evenly distributed over space (Figure 8.4).

Table 8.1 *Economic indicators of Guangdong (1952–2010)*

Items		1952	1955	1960	1965	1970	1975	1978	1985	1990	1995	2000	2005	2010
Population (million)	Guangdong	29.1	31.5	34.7	38.7	43.8	48.6	50.6	56.7	63.5	73.9	86.5	91.9	104.4
	% of National Total	5.1	5.1	5.2	5.3	5.3	5.3	5.3	5.4	5.6	6.1	6.8	7.0	7.8
GDP (RMB billion)	Guangdong	2.95	4.76	7.28	8.70	11.21	15.77	18.59	57.7	155.9	593.3	1074.1	2255.7	4601.3
	% of National Total	4.3	5.2	5.0	5.1	5.0	5.2	5.1	6.4	8.4	9.8	10.8	12.2	11.5
Capita GDP (RMB)	Guangdong	101	152	210	227	258	326	370	1026	2484	8129	12736	24647	44736
	% of National Total	84.9	101.3	96.3	94.6	93.5	99.1	97.1	119.6	151.1	161.1	162.1	173.8	149.2
FDI (USD billion)	Guangdong	–	–	–	–	–	–	–	0.5	1.5	10.2	12.2	12.4	20.3
	% of National Total	–	–	–	–	–	–	–	26.3	41.9	27.1	30.1	20.5	19.2
Imports and Exports (USD billion)	Guangdong	–	–	–	0.35	0.48	1.26	1.59	5.2	41.9	104.0	170.1	428.0	784.9
	% of National Total	–	–	–	8.1	10.5	8.5	7.7	7.4	36.3	37	35.9	30.1	26.4

Note: Due to changes in the statistical method, the absolute value of FDI since 2004 cannot be compared with that before it.

Sources: GSB (1984–2011, 1999); NBS (2010, 2011).

185

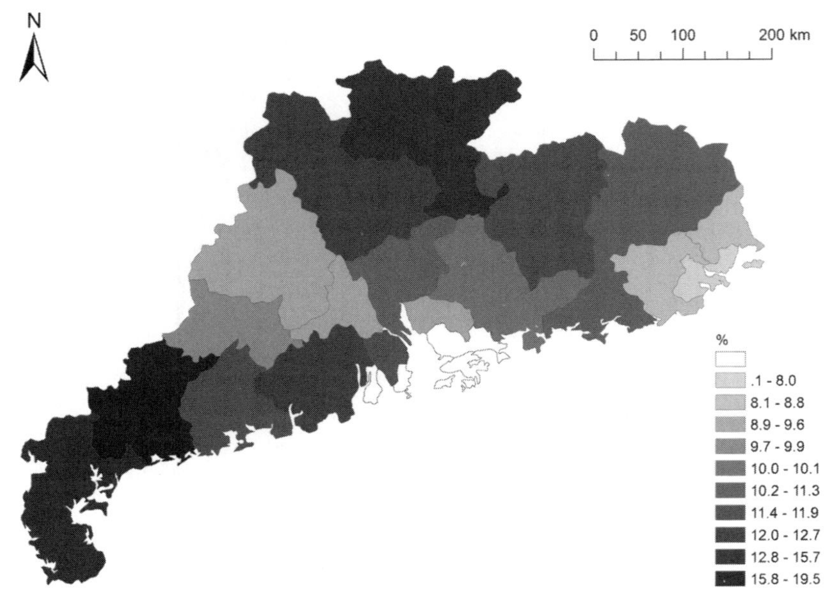

Notes:
1. Calculated by the author based on data in two years (current price).
2. No data for Shenzhen, Zhuhai.

Sources: DSB (2004); GSB (1999); SSB (2011).

Figure 8.3   *Average annual growth rate of industrial output in Guangdong (1952–1978)*

While mainland China gradually fell behind international competitors, Hong Kong entered a period of fast industrialization in the 1950s. This colonial city lost its role as the entrepôt centre after western countries imposed a blockade against China after the outbreak of the Korean War (Vogel, 1989). However, refugees from the mainland during the civil war (1945–1949) brought entrepreneurs (mainly from Shanghai), capital, technology and a large, cheap supply of labour to this land, which promoted the first wave of industrial growth based on textile industry. Later, industrialization diversified into clothing, plastics, toys and other labour-intensive export-oriented manufacturing in the late 1950s and early 1960s, and further moved to low-grade electronics in the late 1960s after Japan started to transfer some low end production activities to Asian neighbours (Schenk, 2008; Vogel, 1989). Hong Kong's average annual growth rate of real GDP reached 9.9 per cent between 1961 and 1981, and even in

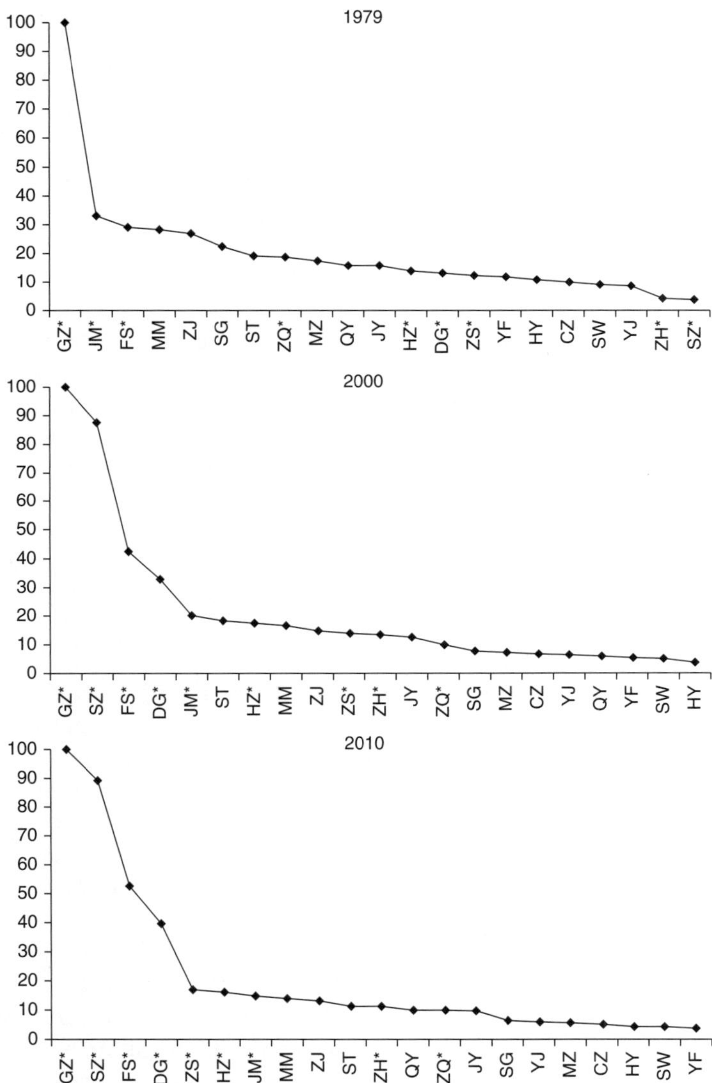

Notes: CZ-Chaozhou, DG-Dongguan, FS-Foshan, GZ-Guangzhou, HY-Heyuan, HZ-Huizhou, JM-Jiangmen, JY-Jieyang, MM-Maoming, MZ-Meizhou, QY-Qingyuan, SG-Shaoguan, ST-Shantou, SW-Shanwei, SZ-Shenzhen, YF-Yunfu, YJ-Yangjiang, ZH-Zhuhai, ZJ-Zhanjiang, ZQ-Zhaoqing, ZS-Zhongshan.
* Cities in the PRD.

Source: GSB (1984–2011, 1999).

Figure 8.4   GDP ranking of cities in Guangdong (1979, 2000, 2010)

terms of GDP per capita the growth rate was 7.4 per cent (Chen, 1987). Hong Kong's population had more than doubled from 2.25 million to 4.61 million between 1952 and 1978 (UN, 1953, 1979), with many immigrants arriving from mainland China (mostly from Guangdong). Hong Kong transformed from a pure entrepôt into a successful industrial city. Notwithstanding the spatial proximity, its interaction with the Guangdong region was limited until the end of the 1970s.

8.3.4   One Step Ahead: Re-Engaging the World After 1978

The economic transition that started from 1978 turned out to be another important break in China's history. To improve productivity and raise the basic living standard of the nation, the Chinese central government incrementally launched a series of reforms and opening up measures in the economic domain; including introducing market mechanisms, reducing state planning and intervention, actively attracting foreign investment and promoting exports to the global market. The state also abolished the 'balance' ideology and introduced an efficiency-oriented developmental strategy which gave more priority to coastal areas (Yang, 1990). Almost at the same time, a new 'global shift' of manufacturing activities from Asian Newly Industrialized Economies (Hong Kong, Taiwan, South Korea, Singapore) to their less developed neighbours started (Dicken, 2011). These two parallel processes triggered rapid industrialization and economic growth in China, with profound regional implications.

Guangdong was chosen by the central government as the first place to practice flexible economic policies. The region was close to Hong Kong and had extensive social network connections with overseas Chinese entrepreneurs. It was far away from Beijing and only contributed modestly to China's treasury therefore its change would have a lower risk of causing unrest in the central government. Local officials in Guangdong were also more open-minded and receptive to new programs and technologies (Vogel, 1989). As a result, three of the four earliest Special Economic Zones (SEZs), Shenzhen, Zhuhai and Shantou, were established in Guangdong in 1980, Guangzhou and Zhanjiang became the first group of 'Open Coastal Cities' in 1984, and one year later, the entire PRD was designated an 'Open Economic Zone'. Instead of investing heavily in Guangdong through top-down, state-led projects, the central government gave it preferential policies and greater autonomy to make economic decisions. Local governments, private entrepreneurs and foreign capital became major actors in regional development after 1978.

Guangdong regained its role as the 'Southern Gate' of China and started to re-connect with the global economic system. Foreign investment-driven, export-oriented, labour-intensive manufacturing was the most important linkage between the region and the outside world in the 1980s and early 1990s (Sit and Yang, 1997). Hong Kong played a crucial role in this process. This city recovered its status as mainland China's entrepôt centre. Meanwhile, as its economy started to transform from manufacturing to services-based, Hong Kong firms began to transfer their low-end, labour-intensive production to Guangdong (mainly the PRD) to take advantage of its cheaper labour, land resources, flexible policies, as well as the similar cultural and linguistic environment. By the end of 1997, the cumulative value of FDI from Hong Kong in Guangdong was estimated at 48 billion USD, accounting for nearly 80 per cent of the total FDI there. Hong Kong companies and joint ventures employed about 5 million workers in Guangdong, most of whom were working in labour-intensive assembly for export (Schenk, 2008). A 'front shop, back factory' style cross-border spatial division of labour between Hong Kong and Guangdong was formed (Sit and Yang, 1997). Following Hong Kong, investment from Western countries, as well as Japan, Taiwan and Singapore also grew rapidly. Guangdong became the largest recipient of FDI among all provinces in mainland China, attracting over 40 per cent of total FDI and contributing to a similar scale of export/import in the peak years (Table 8.1). The PRD was quickly transformed into the famous 'workshop of the world' and home to many world-leading manufacturing clusters (Enright et al., 2005).

The intensive inflow of foreign investment induced rapid industrialization in Guangdong after 1978 (Sit and Yang, 1997), which was further boosted by more diversified forces in the mid 1990s (Lu and Wei, 2007). The average annual growth rate of industrial output reached 21.6 per cent during the period 1979–2008, that is, 10.5 percentage points higher than the three decades before 1979.[5] Guangdong entered a new period of economic prosperity and acquired a rising status in the national system. By the end of the 1990s, Guangdong contributed to more than 10 per cent of mainland China's economy, with a much higher GDP per capita than the national average (Table 8.1).

This particular type of industrialization also caused a strong reconfiguration of the regional urban system. In contrast to the balanced developmental pattern during the planned economy period, a new process of concentration towards the PRD happened (Figure 8.5). Benefiting from advantages in policy, human capital, transportation condition and proximity to Hong Kong (the de-facto regional growth pole), the PRD was more attractive to foreign (especially Hong Kong) investors in the early years of opening up. Therefore cities in this region grew faster than inland areas. However, within the delta, since small-scale, processing-type

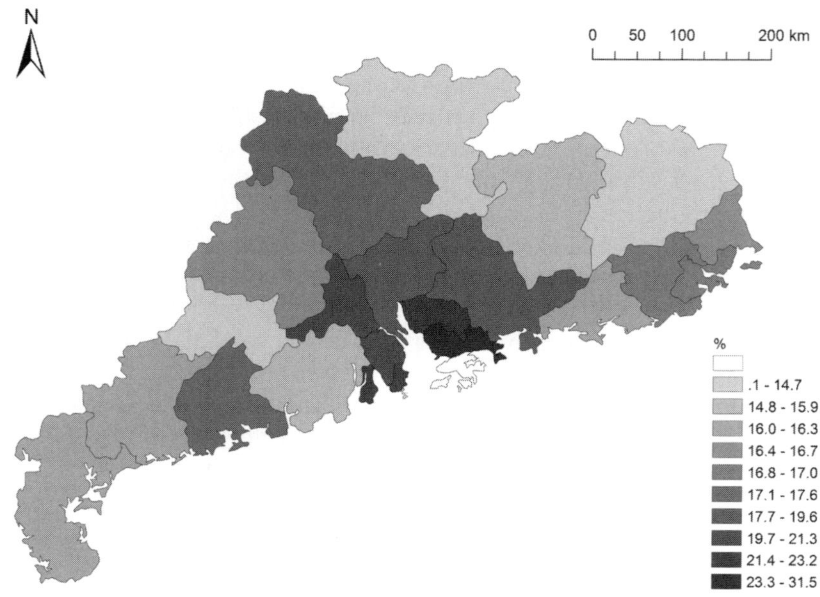

Note: Calculated based on data in two years (current price).

Source: GSB (1984–2011, 1999).

Figure 8.5   *Average annual growth rate of GDP in Guangdong (1979–2000)*

industrial investments were biased towards smaller cities and counties, where they could find cheaper labour, large undeveloped land and flexible, active local governors, these small urban places and rural areas experienced the fastest growth (Sit and Yang, 1997). In contrast, the capital city Guangzhou, constrained by its rigid administrative system and industrial burdens inherited from the centrally planned era, grew relatively slowly and lost many regional growth pole functions. Shenzhen experienced the most dramatic changes. Within just three decades, Shenzhen grew from a small town into an international metropolis with millions of residents. Many other cities in the PRD (Zhuhai, Dongguan, Foshan and Zhongshan) also grew faster than Guangzhou. In short, a trend of more even development occurred *within* the PRD while there was a spatial concentration towards the PRD at the provincial scale. As a result, the regional system evolved from a hierarchical structure dominated by Guangzhou into more of a horizontal urban system with two principal centres.

8.4   THE UNFINISHED STORY: TOWARDS A NEW TRANSITION?

In the 21st century, the PRD has encountered enormous challenges with its export-oriented economic growth model. The region suffers from a shortage of labour and, hence, rising labour costs in conjunction with price rises of raw materials, and an appreciation of RMB (Yang, 2012). This situation is further exacerbated by changes at the global scale as the PRD has to face shrinking demand in the industrialized world and intensified global competition from other lower-wage developing countries (Asia Business Council, 2011). Alongside this, to narrow the gap between the coastal and the inland areas, the Chinese central government has adjusted its regional policies from 'coast-preferred' to 'equitable growth', which pushes forward reform and opens up more regions and sectors, and promotes the development of inland provinces (ibid.). It has also given more emphasis to indigenous innovation, sustainable growth, internal demand and the domestic market. The advantageous position of Guangdong, based on export-oriented, labour-intensive industries, has thus been eroded.

Against this background, a new trend of industrial upgrading and transition promoted by the local government is emerging in the region. Both provincial and municipal governments have initiated relevant policies, such as *teng long huan niao* ('replacing the bird but keeping the cage'; in other words, removing the outdated, low value-added sectors to make room for innovative, high value-added activities) and 'withdrawing secondary (industries) and promoting tertiary (industries)' in their plans to promote the development of high value-added manufacturing and knowledge-based service sectors (Asia Business Council, 2011, p. 2). To realize these goals, local governors have also put great effort into constructing a modern transport and communication infrastructure together with launching hundreds of mega-projects through government-led investment, attracting companies in high-tech, capital-intensive industries, and enhancing cooperation with actors based in Hong Kong and Macao after they became part of China again.

At the moment, it is only possible to give a preliminary evaluation of the impacts of these changes. First of all, the region is showing some signs of upgrading in the global value chain. For example, between 2000 and 2010 the share of heavy industry in Guangdong's gross industrial output increased from 47.1 per cent to 61.7 per cent. Export of high- and new-tech[6] products grew from 17 billion USD to 175 billion USD, which means from 18.5 per cent to 38.7 per cent of total exports (GSB, 2011). In service sectors, 75 per cent of realized FDI among all services (27 per cent among all sectors) went into producer services[7] during 2006–2010. Employment in producer services almost doubled from 2.41 million to 4.65 million between 2003 and 2010 (GSB, 1984–2011). However, the region's ambition to transform from the 'workshop of the world' into a leading global city-region in the 21st century is not without pitfalls (see Liao and Chan, 2011; Yang, 2012).

At the national scale, although Guangdong still maintains a high-speed growth economy, its leading position in the country has declined in relative terms due to the faster development of other provinces and the fierce competition from China's other two major powerhouses: the YRD and the Bohai Economic Rim. This is reflected, firstly, in the fall of Guangdong's share in FDI and imports/exports. Since 2005, Guangdong's contribution to the national GDP, although remaining the largest among all provinces, has also started to drop (Table 8.1).

The regional urban system has not been significantly affected by these new changes (Figure 8.4). However, it is worth noting that advanced economic activities are more inclined to concentrate in the two core cities (Table 8.2). As the historical political, cultural and transportation centre, Guangzhou has a leading position in scientific research, technical services, logistics, cultural and recreational industries. Shenzhen, benefiting from its financial centre status, is more attractive to business services, real estate

Table 8.2   Guangzhou and Shenzhen's share of employment in Guangdong in selected economic sectors (2010)

Sector	Guangzhou (%)	Shenzhen (%)	Combined (%)
Scientific Research, Technical Services and Geological Prospecting	50	29	79
Leasing and Business Services	26	41	67
Real Estate	24	37	62
Information Transmission, Computer Services and Software	27	30	57
Finance	19	27	46
Transport, Storage and Postal Services	25	17	42
Culture, Sports and Recreation	24	13	37
Manufacture	14	17	31
All Sectors	14	12	26

Sources: GSB (2011); SBG (2011); SBS (2011).

and financial sectors. Their different comparative advantages are obviously related to distinct developmental paths. In the long run, economic transition and the new trend of concentration may shift the fortunes of different cities in the PRD and cause another restructuring of the regional system. However, when, how and to what extent this will happen is still undetermined.

8.5   CONCLUSION

This chapter has reviewed the evolution of the PRD through unpacking its global linkages, national status and regional system in the context of changing globalization and state policies from the pre-modern to the current era. Undoubtedly, for a region with a history of more than two millennia, the above analysis is necessarily brief and reductionist. I chose to organize the analysis based on five major stages in the region's history and focus on important structural forces driving regional changes in different periods. This leaves little space for variations within each stage and the internal dynamics. That said the analysis still generates some clues towards a better understanding of the development of the megaregion.

Firstly, the formation of a megaregion is a long-term process. Although globalization and worldwide capitalist restructuring in the past three or four decades have profoundly altered the fortunes of many regions and cities, history still matters in terms of indicating possible directions for change. In the case of the PRD, the external-oriented features of its economy have already been formed centuries ago. Its revitalization in the current stage of globalization should be treated as the continuation of this long-term trajectory, albeit adding some new elements. Historical legacies from former periods, such as colonial heritage (Hong Kong), diaspora (overseas investment), institutional arrangement (Shenzhen) and cultural legacy (Guangzhou), still have significant impacts on the patterns currently observed in the PRD megaregion. Based on the particular combination of these elements, cities within the same region (for example, Guangzhou and Shenzhen) may find different opportunities in the contemporary global economy.

Secondly, this process is constantly shaped and reshaped by political economic changes at supraregional scales, which (through re-organizing a region's natural, economic, social and geopolitical conditions) may provide possibilities for fundamental path breaks for the region. Several such breaks can be identified in the PRD's evolutionary trajectory: some brought it rapid prosperity within a short time, such as the Canton System in the early Qing Dynasty and the Reform and Opening Up after 1978, while others seriously constrained its development, including the invasion of foreign colonial forces and political turbulence between 1840 and 1949 and the excessive intervention of the central state during the communist centrally planned period. The transition from one stage to another is the result of interaction between the continuing global capitalist restructuring (pre-modern world system, industrialization and global capitalist expansion, global shifts) and the transformation of the state (centralized empires, semi-colonial sovereignty, communist regime, reforming state).

Therefore, it is proper to conclude that the formation and evolution of megaregions may not follow the same pattern, but reflect the local specific combination of historical legacies and contingent political economic contexts. There are two available frameworks for analysing the long-term evolution of cities and regions in the world economy, but both of them have limited applicability in the case of this chapter. Kloosterman and Lambregts (2007) have set up a framework for comparing long-term trajectories of regional urban systems through examining the accumulation (the quantity of capital that is accumulated in the regional economy) and concentration (the extent to which a region's capital stock is concentrated in the major cities) of capital according to different stages (which they divide into pre-industrial, industrial and post-industrial) of capitalism (cf. Phelps and Ozawa, 2003). However, China's unique history makes the three-phase division seem over-simplified. For example, the PRD has experienced at least three identifiable stages of industrialization. The first stage happened in the late 19th and early 20th centuries, in which colonial investment and demand played a major role. The second stage took place during the communist centrally planned period, which was characterized by over-industrialization with great emphasis on heavy industries. Both processes were to a large extent the outcomes of interventions from outside and, due to either the control of colonial power, or the ignorance of basic regional conditions, none of them was able to bring sustainable accumulation of capital in the region. It was only in the third stage that a significant accumulation and redistribution of capital took place in the PRD. This time, it was the foreign investment-induced fast industrialization after 1978, which was also initiated by forces at higher levels, but 'strategically coupled' with local interests and motivations (Yang, 2009). Therefore, the process of industrialization in the PRD is not a simple linear path, but accompanied with several ruptures and even retrogresses. In addition, considering its unique legacies of industries, capital and labour, there seems to be little reason to believe that the region will follow a similar route of de-industrialization or post-industrialization as most western megaregions in the near future.

The second framework, as developed by Peter Taylor (1995, 2004), tries to understand the rises and falls of cities and regions in the world system through the lens of their relationship with nation states. Taylor distinguishes three phases in the evolution of the historical world system. First, a mercantilism-based, city-centred, pre-modern transcontinental 'world system' up to the end of the European medieval age. Second, the rise of territorial nation states and the nationalization of cities from the 17th to the mid 20th century, which surrendered cities to a state-centred modern world system. Third, the undermining of states and the rise of a worldwide network of cities and regions as the major spatial organization of the world economy since the 1970s. Opting for such a prominent role to opposing city–state relationships is deeply rooted in what is arguably the rather idiosyncratic history of European political-territorial fragmentation and mercantilist tradition; thereby it tends to treat the fortunes of cities and states as opposite to each other. In my view, this approach has underestimated the power and influence states have had in cities and regions, at least in the Chinese context. As the PRD shows, the central state has always played a key role in regional development, not only influencing a region's internal structure (spatial developmental pattern), but also shaping its connections (flows of goods, capital, knowledge and people) with the outer economic systems. Only in very rare and short periods (like the end of the Qing Dynasty) can we observe a weakening or absence of state power in a limited number of cities and regions. In most times, the destinies of the state and its cities and regions are closely intertwined with each other. Instead of the 'state versus cities' metaphor, state regulation, policy, strategy, even direct intervention, set up one of the most important preconditions for regional development in China.

The experience of the PRD may be a unique case. Even in China, we can find regions with quite different developmental trajectories and diverse ways to integrate with the national and global systems. However, the story of the PRD shows that a full consideration of local history and context can enrich our understanding of the megaregion as 'globalization's new urban form'. Moreover, in a world with increasing similarities and growing inter-regional competition, concepts like 'global city', 'global city-region' or 'megaregion' are quite easily overused by local policymakers and managers as an ideal model to guide city and regional development, as well as a marketing strategy to highlight regions on the map of the global economy. This urges both the academic and the policy world to rethink the applicability of these 'fashionable' concepts in different local contexts, and to look for the specific mode of development which fits the unique path, conditions and identity of a place. In this sense, our search has just begun.

ACKNOWLEDGEMENTS

I would like to thank Robert C. Kloosterman for his helpful and constructive comments on earlier drafts of this chapter. The comments from the editors of this volume are also much appreciated.

NOTES

1. A similar policy was also adopted by the Ming government during the period 1523–1566 (CCLCG, 2004).
2. Between 1864 and 1948 remittance flows into Guangdong reached 2.87 billion USD, accounting for 82 per cent of the national total volume. It is estimated that 40 per cent of domestic industries in Guangdong was invested by overseas Chinese capital in 1949 (CCLCG, 2004).
3. Calculated based on Yao (1962).
4. For example, the share of the secondary sector (manufacturing and construction) in regional GDP increased from 13 per cent to 47 per cent between 1949 and 1978 (NBS, 2010).
5. Source: report from Guangdong Statistics Bureau, available at http://www.gdstats.gov.cn/tjfx/t20091009_74223.htm (accessed 18 July 2013).
6. 'Biotechnology', 'Life Sciences Technology, Photoelectric Technology', 'Computer and Communication Technology', 'Electronic Technology', 'Computer Integrated Manufacturing Technology', 'Material Technology', 'Aerospace Technology', 'Others'.
7. 'Transport, Storage and Postal Services', 'Information Transmission, Computer Services and Software', 'Finance', 'Real Estate', 'Leasing and Business Services', 'Scientific Research, Technical Services and Geological Prospecting'.

REFERENCES

Abu-Lughod, J.L. (1991), *Before European Hegemony: The World System AD 1250–1350*, Oxford: Oxford University Press.
Asia Business Council (2011), 'Economic transformation of the Greater Pearl River Delta: moving on up the value chain', Pearl River Delta Briefing available at www.asiabusinesscouncil.org/docs/PRDBriefing.pdf (accessed 18 July 2013).
Brenner, N. (2004), *New State Spaces: Urban Governance and the Rescaling of Statehood*, Oxford: Oxford University Press.
Cairncross, F. (1997), *The Death of Distance: How the Communications Revolution is Changing Our Lives*, Boston, MA: Harvard Business School Press.
CCGY (Compilation Committee of Guangdong Yearbook) (1941), *Guangdong Nianjian* [Guangdong Yearbook], Guangdong: Guangdong Archives.
CCLCG (Compilation Committee of Local Chronicles of Guangdong Province) (2004), *Guangdong Shengzhi: Jingji Zongshu* [History of Guangdong Province: Review of Economy], Guangzhou: Guangdong People's Publishing House.
Chandler, T. (1987), *Four Thousand Years of Urban Growth: An Historical Census*, Lewiston: St. David's University Press.
Chen, E.K.Y. (1987), 'Foreign trade and economic growth in Hong Kong: experience and prospects', in C.I. Bradford Jr. and W.H. Branson (eds), *Trade and*

Structural Change in Pacific Asia, Chicago, IL: The University of Chicago Press, pp. 333–378.

Dicken, P. (2011), *Global Shift: Mapping the Changing Contours of the World Economy*, 6th edition, London: Sage.

DSB (Dongguan Statistical Bureau) (2004), *Dongguan Statistical Yearbook*, Beijing: China Statistics Press.

Enright, M.J., E.E. Scott and K.M. Chang (2005), *Regional Powerhouse: The Greater Pearl River Delta and the Rise of China*, Chichester: Wiley.

Florida, R., T. Gulden and C. Mellander (2008), 'The rise of the mega-region', *Cambridge Journal of Regions, Economy and Society*, **1** (3), 459–476.

GSB (Guangdong Statistical Bureau) (1984–2011), *Guangdong Statistical Yearbook*, Beijing: China Statistics Press.

GSB (Guangdong Statistical Bureau) (1999), *Guangdong Wushi Nian* [Fifty Years of Guangdong], Beijing: China Statistics Press.

Hall, P. and K. Pain (eds.) (2006), *The Polycentric Metropolis: Learning from Mega-City Regions in Europe*, London: Earthscan.

Harrison, J. and M. Hoyler (2015), 'Megaregions: foundations, frailties, futures', in J. Harrison and M. Hoyler (eds), *Megaregions: Globalization's New Urban Form?* Cheltenham, UK and Northampton, MA, USA: Edward Elgar, pp. 1–28.

Hesse, M. (2015), '*Mega*urban regions: epistemology, discourse patterns, big urban business', in J. Harrison and M. Hoyler (eds), *Megaregions: Globalization's New Urban Form?* Cheltenham, UK and Northampton, MA, USA: Edward Elgar, pp. 29–50.

Hoyler, M., R.C. Kloosterman and M. Sokol (eds) (2008), 'Special issue: Globalization, city-regions and polycentricity in north-west Europe', *Regional Studies*, **42** (8), 1055–1217.

Huang, Q. (1988), 'Qingdai qianqi Guangdong de duiwai maoyi' [The foreign trade of Guangdong in the early stage of the Qing Dynasty]', *Researches in Chinese Economic History*, (4), 73–88.

Huang, Q. (1999), *General History of Macao*, Guangzhou: Guangdong Education Publishing House [in Chinese].

Keller, W., B. Li and C.H. Shiue (2011), 'China's foreign trade: perspectives from the past 150 years', *The World Economy*, **34** (6), 853–892.

Kloosterman, R.C. and B. Lambregts (2007), 'Between accumulation and concentration of capital: toward a framework for comparing long-term trajectories of urban systems', *Urban Geography*, **28** (1), 54–73.

Lambregts, B. (2006), 'Polycentrism: boon or barrier to metropolitan competitiveness? The case of the Randstad Holland', *Built Environment*, **32** (2), 114–123.

Liao, H.F. and R.C. Chan (2011), 'Industrial relocation of Hong Kong manufacturing firms: towards an expanding industrial space beyond the Pearl River Delta', *GeoJournal*, **76** (6), 623–639.

Lu, L. and Y.D. Wei (2007), 'Domesticating globalisation, new economic spaces and regional polarisation in Guangdong province, China', *Tijdschrift voor Economische en Sociale Geografie*, **98** (2), 225–244.

NBS (National Bureau of Statistics) (2010), *China Compendium of Statistics 1949–2008*, Beijing: China Statistics Press.

NBS (National Bureau of Statistics) (2011), *China Statistical Yearbook*, Beijing: China Statistics Press.

O'Brien, R. (1992), *Global Financial Integration: The End of Geography*, New York: Council on Foreign Relations Press.

Phelps, N. and T. Ozawa (2003), 'Contrasts in agglomeration: proto-industrial, industrial and post-industrial forms compared', *Progress in Human Geography*, **27** (5), 583–604.

Rodríguez-Pose, A. (2008), 'The rise of the "city-region" concept and its development policy implications', *European Planning Studies*, **16** (8), 1025–1046.

Ross, C.L. (ed.) (2009), *Megaregions: Planning for Global Competitiveness*, Washington, DC: Island Press.

Roy, A. (2009), 'The 21st-century metropolis: new geographies of theory', *Regional Studies*, **43** (6), 819–830.

SBG (Statistical Bureau of Guangzhou) (2011), *Guangzhou Statistical Yearbook*, Beijing: China Statistics Press.

SBS (Statistical Bureau of Shenzhen) (2011), *Shenzhen Statistical Yearbook*, Beijing: China Statistics Press.

Schafran, A. (2015), 'Beyond globalization: a historical urban development approach to understanding megaregions', in J. Harrison and M. Hoyler (eds), *Megaregions: Globalization's New Urban Form?* Cheltenham, UK and Northampton, MA, USA: Edward Elgar, pp. 75–96.

Schenk, C.R. (2008), 'Economic history of Hong Kong', in R. Whaples (ed.), *EH.Net Encyclopedia*, available at http://eh.net/encyclopedia/economic-history-of-hong-kong/ (accessed 18 July 2013).

Scott, A.J. (1998), *Regions and the World Economy: The Coming Shape of Global Production, Competition, and Political Order*, Oxford: Oxford University Press.

Scott, A.J. (ed.) (2001), *Global City-Regions: Trends, Theory, Policy*, Oxford: Oxford University Press.

Scott, A.J. (2008), *Social Economy of the Metropolis: Cognitive-Cultural Capitalism and the Global Resurgence of Cities*, Oxford: Oxford University Press.

Scott, A.J. and M. Storper (2003), 'Regions, globalization, development', *Regional Studies*, **37** (6–7), 549–578.

Sit, V.F. and C. Yang (1997), 'Foreign-investment-induced exo-urbanisation in the Pearl River Delta, China', *Urban Studies*, **34** (4), 647–677.

SSB (Shantou Statistical Bureau) (2011), *Shantou Statistical Yearbook*, Beijing: China Statistics Press.

Taylor, P.J. (1995), 'World cities and territorial states: the rise and fall of their mutuality', in P.L. Knox and P.J. Taylor (eds), *World Cities in a World-System*, Cambridge: Cambridge University Press, pp. 48–62.

Taylor, P.J. (2004), *World City Network*, London: Routledge.

Taylor, P.J. (2012), 'Historical world city networks', in B. Derudder, M. Hoyler, P.J. Taylor and F. Witlox (eds), *International Handbook of Globalization and World Cities*, Cheltenham, UK and Northampton, MA, USA: Edward Elgar, pp. 9–21.

UN (United Nations) (1953), *Demographic Yearbook*, New York: UN.

UN (United Nations) (1979), *Demographic Yearbook*, New York: UN.

Van Dyke, P.A. (2005), *The Canton Trade: Life and Enterprise on the China Coast, 1700–1845*, Hong Kong: Hong Kong University Press.

Vogel, E.F. (1989), *One Step Ahead in China*, Cambridge, MA: Harvard University Press.

Wachsmuth, D. (2015), 'Megaregions and the urban question: the new strategic terrain for US urban competitiveness', in J. Harrison and M. Hoyler (eds), *Megaregions: Globalization's New Urban Form?* Cheltenham, UK and Northampton, MA, USA: Edward Elgar, pp. 51–74.

Xu, D., D. Huang, Y. Liang and Y. Cheng (1994), *Guangdong Duiwai Jingji Maoyi Si* [The Foreign Economic and Trade History of Guangdong], Guangzhou: Guangdong People's Publishing House.

Yan, Z. (1955), *Zhongguo Jindai Jingji Si Tongji Ziliao Xuanbian* [Compilation of Statistics of China's Modern Economic History], Beijing: Science Press.

Yang, C. (2009), 'Strategic coupling of regional development in global production networks: redistribution of Taiwanese personal computer investment from the Pearl River Delta to the Yangtze River Delta, China', *Regional Studies*, **43** (3), 385–407.

Yang, C. (2012), 'Restructuring the export-oriented industrialization in the Pearl River Delta, China: institutional evolution and emerging tension', *Applied Geography*, **32** (1), 143–157.

Yang, D. (1990), 'Patterns of China's regional development strategy', *The China Quarterly*, **122**, 230–257.

Yao, X. (1962), *Zhongguo Jindai Duiwai Maoyi Si Ziliao 1840–1895* [Information on China's Modern Foreign Trade History 1840–1895], Beijing: Zhonghua Book Company.

Ye, X. (2007), 'Zhujiang sanjiaozhou de kaifa yu jindaihua jincheng' [The process of development and modernization of the Pearl River Delta], *South China Review*, (1), 53–61.

Zhang, X.R. (1992), 'Jingji tizhi gaige yu duiwai kaifang de jincheng' [Progress of reforms of economic system and opening up], in T. Maruya (ed.), *Guangdong: 'Open Door' Economic Development Strategy*, Tokyo: Institute of Developing Economics, pp. 1–17.

Zhu, Y.C. (1988), *Chinese Population: Volume of Guangdong*, Beijing: Chinese Financial Publishing House [in Chinese].

9. Towards a megaregional future: analysing progress, assessing priorities in the US megaregion project

Billy Fleming

9.1 INTRODUCTION

For the first time in recorded history the majority of the planet's population resides in cities. In the United States alone, nearly two-thirds of Americans are projected to live in urbanized areas by the year 2050 (Yaro, 2005). This will not just be in urban centres, for 'most of the nation's population growth and an even larger share of its economic expansion will occur in ten or more emerging megaregions' (Regional Plan Association, 2006, p. 12). As the US population migrates towards these urban regions, the 21st century is poised to become the 'century of the city' on both a national and a global scale (Peirce et al., 2008). The implications for this (re)inhabitation of the city are profound. Water resources will become increasingly stretched and denuded while aging and under-built infrastructural systems will need to be reconsidered in entirely new and innovative configurations. Meanwhile, the American promise of social mobility – seen by many to be dependent on access to quality education and high-wage employment – will become more and more difficult to fulfill. Complicating matters is what Rybczynski (2010) recently referred to as the 'makeshift metropolis', a term which can be considered in this context as a description for the fractious, often ad-hoc, nature of highly localized planning in the US. In the face of these seemingly intractable challenges, how then might one hope to plan for and accommodate the massive (re)inhabitation of US cities and urban regions? If Yaro and his colleagues at the Regional Plan Association (RPA) are to be believed, that hope rests on a renewed interest in regionalism in general, and more specifically, the concept of the megaregion (Yaro, 2005; Ross, 2009; Steiner, 2011).

In pursuit of the promise imbued by a megaregional future, this chapter poses three key questions about the megaregion concept and its potential practical applications: (1) how and why did the concept of megaregions emerge and evolve in the US?; (2) what are the current opportunities and challenges for advancing the US megaregion project?; and (3) how might the megaregional construct be applied to future planning research and training in the US and beyond? To achieve this, the chapter begins by expanding on the standard megaregional literature and exploring the work of two prescient cultural geographers: Donald Meinig and Wilbur Zelinsky. As I will show, their work is particularly revealing when positioned alongside the work of the more recognized proponents of the megaregion concept for the way in which it elucidates the evolutionary nature of megaregional research, and begins to deconstruct the argument that megaregional thinking is an entirely new enterprise.

After briefly reviewing the megaregional literature, this chapter employs a pair of research methods to begin ameliorating gaps in our current understanding. To contextualize the provenance, evolution and potential future trajectories of megaregional planning, semi-structured interviews were conducted with key proponents and architects of the megaregion concept. One of the themes identified by these key informants – economic development – is then explored between the Texas Triangle and Gulf Coast megaregions. Several key findings arise, including how data limitations, gaps in federal and state policy frameworks and the prevalence of anti-government/anti-intellectual sentiment have served to impede the progress of megaregional research and planning. The findings serve to confirm a number of preconceptions about the economic structure and strength of the Texas Triangle and Gulf Coast while providing some new insight into the role Houston plays as the functional link between the twin urban systems. The chapter concludes with a brief discussion of this study's relevance to megaregional planning research and pedagogy.

9.2   BETWEEN MEGALOPOLIS AND MEGAREGIONS

9.2.1   Key Megaregional Proponents

Megaregional literature reviews have generally focused on the works of Jean Gottmann, the European Union's Spatial Development Perspective (ESDP) and, in more recent publications, the RPA's America 2050 initiative (Harrison and Hoyler, 2015a). Taking each in turn, Gottmann's (1961) book, *Megalopolis: The Urbanized Northeastern Seaboard of the United States*, wove more than 250 illustrative forms of analysis into one compendium positing that the entire northeastern seaboard of the US had grown into a singular functional region. Although the work was largely ignored outside of the discipline of geography, Gottmann's analysis still provides a robust framework for contemporary megaregional inquiry.

More recently, Faludi (2009) has provided a comprehensive review of the ESDP's evolution and potential applications for megaregional planning in the US. In this he recounts the role of geographer Roger Brunet and his research team in convincing, first, French Minister François Cheregue, and eventually the whole of the European Union to adopt a megaregional spatial development strategy. Faludi also discusses the internal arguments over nomenclature – an issue that would later hamper megaregional discourse in the US as well. Adoption of the ESDP led to the identification of global economic integration zones within Europe as well as so-called 'lagging regions' that could be bolstered through EU structural funds (Faludi, 2009). Indeed, while the focus is often on the events of the late 1980s and 1990s it should not be forgotten that European planning at the megaregional scale continues today (albeit as a very 'weak' form of strategic planning) and the business of delineating and supporting the continent's economic engines is continuously adapting.

In the US, numerous proponents of megaregions have each provided their own thorough review and take on Gottmann's 'megalopolis' and how the acceptance of megaregional planning efforts in Europe and Asia are forcing the hand of planners to address this deficit in their own national context (Florida, 2009; Nelson and Lang, 2011; Ross, 2009; Steiner, 2011; Yaro, 2005, 2011). There are five main threads to megaregion analysis in the US: (1) Bob Yaro (2005, 2011), President of the RPA and America 2050 initiative, has focused largely on megaregional transportation issues; (2) Catherine Ross, the Harry West Professor of City and Regional Planning at the Georgia Institute of Technology, has focused on delineating the hierarchical structure of megaregions with a particular focus on the Piedmont Atlantic megaregion of the southeast US (Dablanc and Ross, 2012; Ross, 2008, 2009; Ross et al., 2015); (3) Richard Florida and colleagues (Florida et al., 2008, 2012) attempt to delineate megaregional space across the globe using light emissions as a proxy for economic integration; (4) Robert E. Lang and colleagues draw heavily on US Census data to identify what they determine to be the geography of 'megapolitan America' (Lang and Dhavale, 2005; Nelson and Lang, 2011); and finally (5) Frederick Steiner (2011), the Dean of the University of Texas School of Architecture, has worked on a variety of issues, primarily within the Texas Triangle. Rather than review each of these oft-cited authors comprehensively – a task that would occupy the bulk of this chapter – a particular emphasis is placed on a selection of work which emerged between the publication of Gottmann's (1961) book, *Megalopolis: The Urbanized Northeastern Seaboard of the United States*, and the re-emergence of debates on megaregions over the past decade. While there are other literatures which megaregionalists may benefit from re-engaging with (for example spatial economics, the new regionalism, urban economics at the megaregional scale), my focus here is specifically on the contribution of certain aspects of cultural geography.

9.2.2   The Cultural Geography of an Imperialistic Republic

> Texans have long been taught to think of their homeland as an empire, and to use that word as something more than just a grandiose name for a large area . . . it implies not only a relative size, but a history of conquest, expansion, and dominion over a varied realm . . . not only an outward movement of people, but the thrust of a self-confident, aggressive people driven by a strong sense of superiority and destiny. (Meinig, 1969, p. 7)

One of the nation's most culturally distinct areas, Texas provides a wealth of opportunities for exploring the role of cultural identity at the mega-regional scale. The work discussed in this section was produced in the 1960s and 1970s, shortly after Gottmann's (1961) book was published and well before any of the contemporary megaregionalists began their work. This is significant because in each contemporary conception of the term megaregion, cultural geography is poised to play a prominent role in crafting a method for delineating this spatial scale.

The author of a number of studies into the cultural geography of the US, Wilbur Zelinsky (1973) actually post-dates and builds on the work of Donald Meinig. However, for the current purpose it is more apposite to consider them in reverse chronological order, for the work of Zelinsky provides the context for Meinig's study of Texas. This is because drawing on the work of Meinig, Zelinsky generalized and upscaled Meinig's findings and methods to the national scale. Zelinsky's attempt to delineate the cultural geography of the US begins by identifying four quintessentially American themes: (1) rugged individualism; (2) the inexorable quest for upward mobility and change; (3) a mechanistic worldview, especially with regard to nature; and (4) the constant pursuit of messianic perfection (Zelinsky, 1973, pp. 41–63). Zelinsky applies these themes across the entire US to produce a map of cultural regions that captures megaregions such as the Texas Triangle, Sun Corridor and the Midwest (Figure 9.1).

Focusing exclusively on Texas, Meinig (1969) variously examines the historical migration patterns to/through the state, the racial tensions that have persisted since the land was settled, and the role that the imperialistic vision of the state's founders played in shaping the various

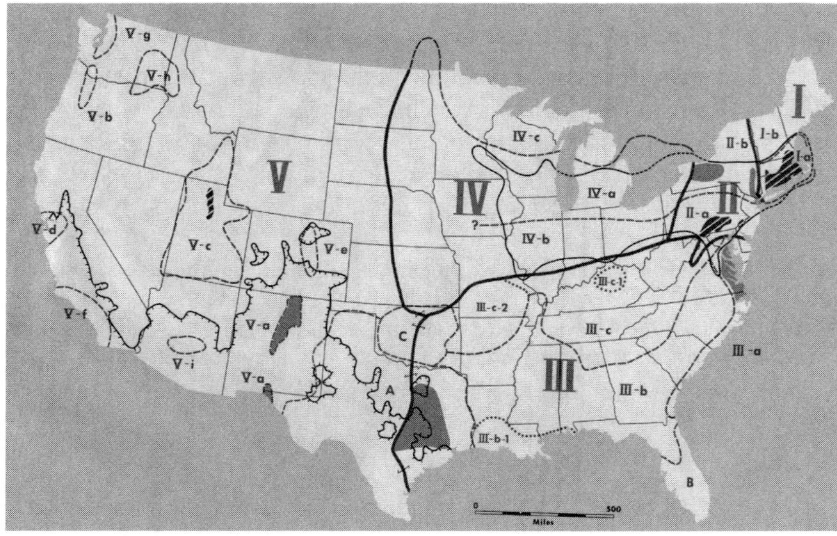

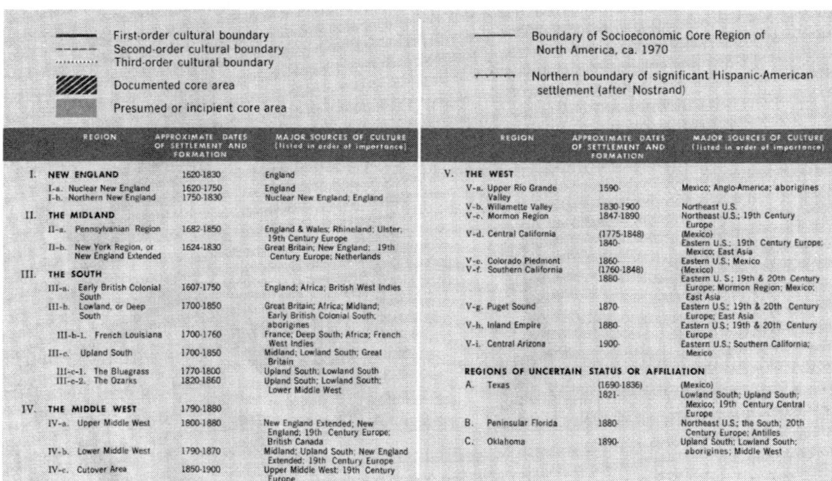

	First-order cultural boundary
	Second-order cultural boundary
	Third-order cultural boundary
	Documented core area
	Presumed or incipient core area

	Boundary of Socioeconomic Core Region of North America, ca. 1970
	Northern boundary of significant Hispanic-American settlement (after Nostrand)

REGION	APPROXIMATE DATES OF SETTLEMENT AND FORMATION	MAJOR SOURCES OF CULTURE (listed in order of importance)
I. NEW ENGLAND	1620-1830	England
I-a. Nuclear New England	1620-1750	England
I-b. Northern New England	1750-1830	Nuclear New England; England
II. THE MIDLAND		
II-a. Pennsylvanian Region	1682-1850	England & Wales; Rhineland; Ulster; 19th Century Europe
II-b. New York Region, or New England Extended	1624-1830	Great Britain; New England; 19th Century Europe; Netherlands
III. THE SOUTH		
III-a. Early British Colonial South	1607-1750	England; Africa; British West Indies
III-b. Lowland, or Deep South	1700-1850	Great Britain; Africa; Midland; Early British Colonial South; aborigines
III-b-1. French Louisiana	1700-1760	France; Deep South; Africa; French West Indies
III-c. Upland South	1700-1850	Midland; Lowland South; Great Britain
III-c-1. The Bluegrass	1770-1800	Upland South; Lowland South
III-c-2. The Ozarks	1820-1860	Upland South; Lowland South; Lower Middle West
IV. THE MIDDLE WEST	1790-1880	
IV-a. Upper Middle West	1800-1880	New England Extended; New England; 19th Century Europe; British Canada
IV-b. Lower Middle West	1790-1870	Midland; Upland South; New England Extended; 19th Century Europe
IV-c. Cutover Area	1850-1900	Upper Middle West; 19th Century Europe

REGION	APPROXIMATE DATES OF SETTLEMENT AND FORMATION	MAJOR SOURCES OF CULTURE (listed in order of importance)
V. THE WEST		
V-a. Upper Rio Grande Valley	1590-	Mexico; Anglo-America; aborigines
V-b. Willamette Valley	1830-1900	Northeast U.S.
V-c. Mormon Region	1847-1890	Northeast U.S.; 19th Century Europe
V-d. Central California	(1775-1848) 1840-	(Mexico) Eastern U.S.; 19th Century Europe; Mexico; East Asia
V-e. Colorado Piedmont	1860-	Eastern U.S.; Mexico
V-f. Southern California	(1760-1848) 1880-	(Mexico) Eastern U.S.; 19th & 20th Century Europe; Mormon Region; Mexico; East Asia
V-g. Puget Sound	1870-	Eastern U.S.; 19th & 20th Century Europe; East Asia
V-h. Inland Empire	1880-	Eastern U.S.; 19th & 20th Century Europe
V-i. Central Arizona	1900-	Eastern U.S.; Southern California; Mexico
REGIONS OF UNCERTAIN STATUS OR AFFILIATION		
A. Texas	(1690-1836) 1821-	(Mexico) Lowland South; Upland South; Mexico; 19th Century Central Europe
B. Peninsular Florida	1880-	Northeast U.S.; the South; 20th Century Europe; Antilles
C. Oklahoma	1890-	Upland South; Lowland South; aborigines; Middle West

Source: Zelinsky (1973, p. 118). Copyright © 1992. Reproduced by permission of Pearson Education, Inc., Upper Saddle River, NJ.

Figure 9.1   The cultural regions of the United States

cultural regions of the state. Meinig's (1969) book, *Imperial Texas – An Interpretative Essay in Cultural Geography*, is divided into six chapters that range in focus from the state's Spanish settlers, to the expansionary vision of Sam Houston and his colleagues, to the eventual differentiation of the fragmented cultural landscape that comprises contemporary Texas. Charting the various periods and locations of migration into Texas, Meinig (1969) identifies three periods of settlement within the state: (1) the pioneers who moved to Texas from the northeast and the Ohio River Valley; (2) the second stream of in-migrants, most of whom came from the Carolinas, Tennessee, Virginia and Arkansas; and (3) the final stream of settlers who came from the swamplands of Louisiana, Mississippi and Alabama. Due to the state's reliance on large, rapid developments in the north and east, four broad regions began to emerge in the 1860s. Houston and Galveston, the only true pair of proximate major cities at the time, helped to anchor the Gulf Coast part of the state, while San Antonio emerged as the largest city of South Texas. The two remaining regions – North and West Texas – were without major cities at the time and defined primarily by the provenance of their early settlers. By the 1960s the rapid growth and accumulation of wealth – especially in its burgeoning metropolises – led Meinig to identify nine distinct cultural areas within Texas (Figure 9.2).

What Zelinsky and Meinig help to elucidate is the notion that mega-regional thought is less novel than it is often portrayed. Interestingly both Meinig and Zelinsky cite Gottmann's work on the northeastern 'Megalopolis' when discussing the need for studies of cultural geography at the state and regional scales. Meinig and Zelinsky also implicitly iden-tify many of the same megaregions to 'emerge' in the early 2000s, making a compelling case for exploring the cultural cohesions and cleavages that persist at this expansive scale. Areas like the Gulf Coast, for example, may struggle to find an identity in economic or infrastructural terms but there is great potential for defining the megaregional extent through patterns of cultural cohesion.

Recognizing the contributions of understudied megaregionalists such as Meinig and Zelinksy is vital to the continued growth of the mega-regional construct. In less than a decade, contemporary researchers have produced an impressive body of literature on the emerging concept of megaregions in the US. But work on the subject has stalled in recent years. As the concept approaches its decennial, it is also impor-tant to note that new ideas are beginning to gain traction. Richard Weller, the Australian landscape architect and newly-appointed chair of Penn's Landscape Architecture Department, recently published *Made in Australia: The Future of Australian Cities* – a vision for a megaregional Australia (Weller and Bolleter, 2013). With his colleague Julian Bolleter, Weller weaves urban design, landscape architecture and regional plan-ning into a compendium of analysis and future growth scenarios at the continental scale. It provides a compelling framework for others aiming

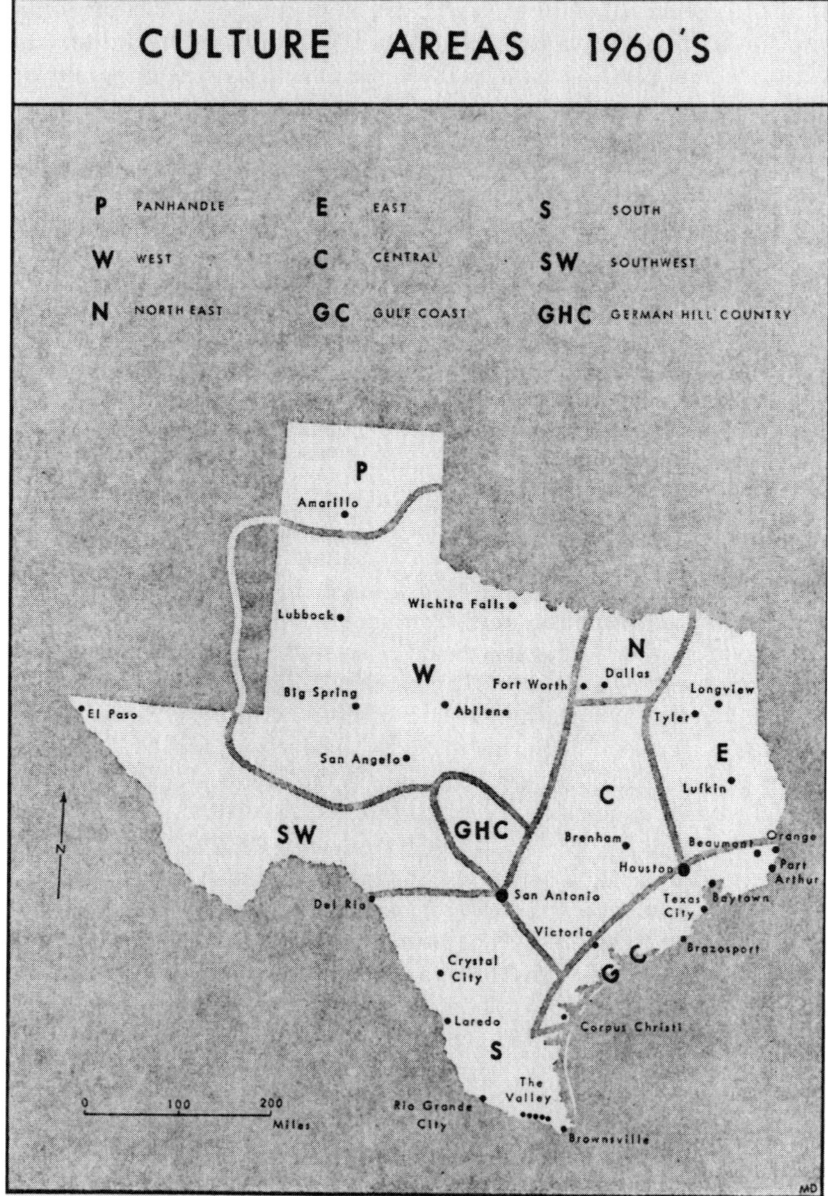

Source: Meinig (1969, p. 93). Copyright © 1969, renewed 1997. Reproduced by permission of the University of Texas Press.

Figure 9.2   The cultural areas of Texas

to make the case for megaregional planning in their own respective territories.

Nonetheless, the megaregional thesis still offers many more questions than it provides answers. It is for this reason that this chapter is based on research which seeks to engage the key proponents, that is, those responsible for advancing the megaregion in academic and public debates, in discussion over the foundations, frailties and futures of megaregion research (Harrison and Hoyler, 2015a). To this end, the next section outlines a number of these as yet unanswered questions, including the evolution and fate of megaregional planning.

9.3   RESEARCH DESIGN

This triptych of megaregional theory – antecedents, ancillaries and contemporaries – generates three distinct problems that are investigated within this chapter. The first problem identified is that there are a limited number of issues and relationships pertaining to megaregions. Research has centred on the topics of high-speed rail (HSR) and, to a lesser extent, large landscape conservation (Ross, 2009; Pirani et al., 2011; Seltzer and Carbonell, 2011; Todorovich and Hagler, 2011). A second problem is derived from the relatively small number of researchers working on the topic of megaregions. In their fervent efforts to identify the complexities of planning at such an expansive scale, there has been little in the way of reflection on the evolution of, or future trajectories for, megaregional research. As the megaregion project begins to expand and diversify its disciplinary base, understanding precisely how and why the concept and framework has evolved will be critical to charting its future applications. Finally, if megaregions are indeed the new scale of global economic competition – as, among others, Florida et al. (2008), Ross (2009) and Nelson and Lang (2011) would have us believe – it stands to reason that they must be competing against one another for public and private investments, highly skilled workers and innovation. As the only physically conjoined pair of megaregions in the US (see Harrison and Hoyler, 2015a, Figure 1.1) the Texas Triangle and Gulf Coast provide an ideal pairing for testing this notion of inter-megaregional relationships.

9.3.1   Research Goals and Questions

There are three primary goals of this chapter. The first is to provide an initial evaluation of the provenance, progress, barriers and future trajectories of megaregional planning. The second goal is to provide a first statistical assessment of the broad socioeconomic and industry-driven variables traversing the borders between two of these megaregions. While some work has been done within the Texas Triangle, very little has been completed within the Gulf Coast and none has broached the intersection of the megaregional pair. The final goal is to begin identifying the research challenges and pedagogical reforms necessary to address megaregional issues in the US.

9.3.2 Research Methods

The research reported here builds upon an earlier research project which involved a mixed-methods approach to the questions and goals performed in two sequential phases (see Fleming, 2012). First, semi-structured interviews were conducted with key informants – that is, those at the centre of US megaregional debate and responsible for its ascendancy in academic and political debate – to deduce the provenance, progress and future trajectories of planning for megaregions. By its very nature this population is limited to a relatively small group of individuals. Therefore to select these key informants a purposive sampling strategy was applied to reflect their impact on the intellectual development of the megaregion concept as well as their significant contribution to megaregion debate over the past decade – and in some cases longer still. In other words, many of the leading progenitors and proponents of the megaregion concept were identified and interviewed for this chapter. These interviews have been transcribed, coded and analysed using HyperRESEARCH software. Interviews were divided into three parts: (1) portals of entry into the megaregion project; (2) lingering questions and perceptions of progress in megaregional research; and (3) the anticipated trajectory of near future academic research and political intervention. Interviews lasted approximately one hour, with quotes used here for the purpose of expressing the key points of concern raised.

The second part of the study employed a descriptive statistical analysis and GIS-mapping of nine socioeconomic and industry-driven variables to develop a foundational understanding of the broad economic trends permeating the Gulf Coast and Texas Triangle's boundaries. Metropolitan Statistical Areas (MSAs) were utilized as the units of analysis in this phase of the study. There are 25 MSAs between the Texas Triangle and Gulf Coast megaregions. Each is listed in Table 9.1 according to their 'megaregional membership'. Datasets were all three-year American Community Survey (ACS) samples, drawn from SF1, SF2, SF4 and S701 forms in 2005, 2007, 2009 and 2011. This time period was important

Table 9.1   The 25 MSAs of the Texas Triangle and Gulf Coast

Metropolitan Region	Megaregion Membership
Alexandria, LA	Gulf Coast
Austin-Round Rock, TX	Texas Triangle
Baton Rouge, LA	Gulf Coast
Beaumont-Port Arthur, TX	Gulf Coast + Texas Triangle
Brownsville-Harlingen, TX	Gulf Coast
College Station-Bryan, TX	Texas Triangle
Corpus Christi, TX Metro Area	Gulf Coast
Dallas-Fort Worth-Arlington, TX	Texas Triangle
Gulfport-Biloxi, MS	Gulf Coast
Houma-Bayou Cane-Thibodaux, LA	Gulf Coast
Houston-Sugar Land-Baytown, TX	Gulf Coast + Texas Triangle
Killeen-Temple-Fort Hood, TX	Texas Triangle
Lafayette, LA	Gulf Coast
Lake Charles, LA	Gulf Coast
Longview, TX	Texas Triangle
McAllen-Edinburg-Mission, TX	Gulf Coast
Mobile, AL	Gulf Coast
New Orleans-Metairie-Kenner, LA	Gulf Coast
Pascagoula, MS	Gulf Coast
Pensacola-Ferry Pass-Brent, FL	Gulf Coast
San Antonio, TX	Texas Triangle
Sherman-Denison, TX	Texas Triangle
Texarkana, TX-Texarkana, AR	Texas Triangle
Tyler, TX	Texas Triangle
Waco, TX	Texas Triangle

Source: Author

because it included pre- and post-Katrina economic trends along the Gulf Coast. All datasets were cleaned and compiled in Microsoft Excel. Descriptive statistics were calculated utilizing 'R', an open sourced statistical modeling software program. For the final component of this phase, each MSA was compared along each individual variable to the mean of all 25 MSAs. They were then assigned an over-performing, under-performing or baseline value in order to gauge MSA performance on an individual and aggregated basis.

9.4 TOWARDS A MEGAREGIONAL FUTURE: IMPEDIMENTS TO PROGRESS AND OPPORTUNITIES FOR GROWTH

> The other part about all of this – whether intentional or unintentional – is that you are essentially identifying a limited number of places where we *think* the majority of the nation's growth is going to occur. That means a majority of the nation, at least geographically, will have to ask 'what's in it for us'. (Interview #1 2012)

Drawn from the key informant interviews, more than 40 distinct themes were identified to contextualize the formulation of what we today identify as megaregional research. The aim was to bring clarity to its progress and evolution, and to posit likely trajectories for near-future megaregional planning. Four 'gateway' themes were identified: (1) the ESDP; (2) an affinity for regionalism; (3) prior work and familiarity with the US Census Bureau; and (4) the 2004 Penn Graduate Planning Studio, *Plan for America*. Respondents also identified an ongoing discussion over the nomenclature of megaregions, megapolitans and megapolitan clusters.

Respondents revealed a number of broad themes describing the evolution of megaregional thought. The first theme, that little or nothing had changed since the early 2000s, appeared in each interview. Interviewees, however, were then quick to acknowledge the areas of progress. These included: (1) the approach to delineation, both in terms of defining megaregional extents and whether or not elucidating these boundaries is important; (2) the unexpected synergies between megaregions and large landscape conservation; and (3) the possibility of common action at the megaregional scale. Despite these themes of progress, respondents were

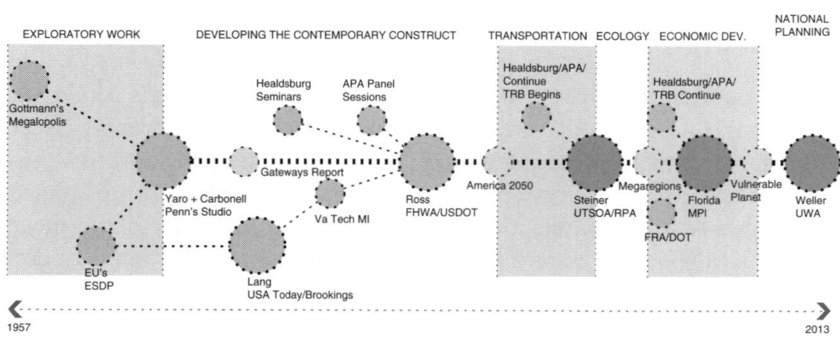

Source: Author

Figure 9.3 A megaregional timeline: Gottmann to Weller

equally quick to identify a series of barriers. These included: (1) a lack of synthesis for the abundant datasets provided by the US Census Bureau, Bureau of Economic Analysis, Bureau of Labor Statistics and many other statistical agencies; (2) the rise of the Tea Party and anti-government sentiment in certain areas of the US; (3) various gaps in federal and state policies that prevent or discourage planning at the megaregional scale; and (4) the lack of a national agenda for infrastructure, transportation systems or regional planning.

To punctuate their interviews, respondents were then asked to address the future of megaregional planning. With striking uniformity, each key informant discussed potential applications in the practice of planning for resiliency and climate change adaptation as well as economic development at the megaregional scale. Other themes identified by the respondents included the further development of large landscape conservation practice, augmented transportation and infrastructure planning, and the elusiveness of governance structures at the megaregional scale. The remainder of this section is focused on two components of these extensive findings: the barriers to progress and the future trajectories of megaregional planning.

9.4.1   Barriers to Progress in Megaregional Planning

> You also have people out there . . . who [are] fundamentally anti-metropolitan . . . pro-sprawl even . . . suggesting there's no reason to believe that all these tiny little places not highlighted by us aren't going to be our next economic beacons . . . So people are getting a pretty mixed message and what that means is that it will take a bunch of studies to change policy at the national level coupled with a clear set of objectives and a strong lobbying effort to incorporate them wherever possible . . . This is never going to be something to gain prominence in the US, because it is *right*; it just doesn't work that way here. (Interview #1, 2012)

Despite the rapid growth and evolution of megaregional planning in the US, a number of impediments have been encountered. Chief among these is the data gap, both in terms of readily available secondary data and the governmental unit at which the datasets are collected. In other words, key informants largely agreed that more types of data – particularly those related to economic exchange and travel behaviour – are necessary. As one of the interviewees stated:

> Some of the biggest gaps are in metro-to-metro transportation networks. There is no systematic tracking of long-distance automobile travel and this could give us a fuller picture of how many people are taking very long commutes from the fringe of one metro to another. (Interview #3, 2012)

In contrast, another interviewee discussed how work being done in cognate disciplines can begin to address the data gap. They noted how:

> There are people with such sophisticated knowledge of the country, like infectious disease which requires face to face exchange. So it's about people contacting people and they do simulations about what happens if someone is infected with smallpox in Portland; they can model how that spreads through the whole country, first to Seattle and then throughout the rest of the region. (Interview #5, 2012)

Some of these gaps – particularly those involving the unit of collection or analysis – could be addressed by Lang's megapolitan statistical area concept (Lang and Dhavale, 2005; Nelson and Lang, 2011). As one interviewee noted, the Census Bureau has left the methods in place for a megapolitan statistical area and many of the career staff that were in place during the Clinton Administration are still working there. It is merely a matter of mustering the political. The other gaps, however, would likely need to be addressed through additions to the American Community Survey or another Census-driven effort. Given the current political environment, this seems like a tall order in the near term.

Perhaps the greatest point of consensus amongst all respondents was the barrier posed by the political moment ushered in by the conservative electoral wave of 2010 and the rise of the Tea Party. Mentioned by most of the respondents, it is clear that the pervasiveness of these anti-science, anti-intellectual forces will continue to challenge state-led planning efforts at all scales, especially at the regional and megaregional scale. One interviewee captured the respondents' pessimistic outlook succinctly:

> It's something that's political ... because you need the resources from the national level. There are a lot of priorities at the national level right now, none of which have to do with this, perhaps with the lone exception being HSR, and most of those have been shelved or rejected. Unless we have a transportation reauthorization bill that explicitly directs attention to that issue, it's not going to change much. So at the end of the day, to add that kind of cultural-historical threads needed will require direction at the national level and I think you've got a very tough environment to work in there. (Interview #1, 2012)

This thematic area evoked the most despair from the respondents, leading many to look beyond the Obama Administration for progress on regional policy. Here is where the work of Meinig and Zelinsky holds the greatest promise. Armed with an understanding of the breadth and depth of anti-government sentiments that are permeating the American landscape, megaregional planners could better understand where opposition to this scale is likely to occur, to what degree that opposition will approach consensus (versus the appearance of consensus through existing power structures) and to begin identifying megaregional identities and iconography.

Blind spots in the federal policy and regulatory framework also emerged as one of the greatest barriers to advancing megaregional research. In some cases the gaps are relatively small, such as the establishment of a megapolitan statistical area within the Census Bureau through Congressional action. Others, however, are much more significant:

> Only the policy work remains. In other words, the geography is fine. Because now I'm interested in the[se new] question[s], which is in supply chains, distant commuters that don't reach the CSA threshold but nonetheless show enough affinity to consider how all that integration works with the world economy. So I'm actually interested in the [megaregional] scale, but only through the public policy lens and what we know to be exchanges: air commuting, goods flows, supply chain, water sharing, and environmental impacts. (Interview #5, 2012)

With dozens of bureaus in the federal government tasked with collecting and distributing statistical information, one might assume that closing this gap is relatively simple. However, as long as the authority to collect and disseminate information is controlled by Congress this appears to be a tall order. One interviewee punctuates the discussion of policy gaps in the megaregional realm by raising a different sort of impediment: antiquated institutional policy amongst the foundations working with cities and regions. They note that:

> There's always a shortage of researcher dollars. It's always under-funded because foundations don't think at this scale and most government agencies don't either. A number of foundations, particularly at the national scale, think about metropolitan areas or issues, but when we've framed an infrastructure or transportation agenda at the megaregional or national scale they routinely tell me 'We don't operate there; we just do Philly or Boston or New York. We can't be bothered by this stuff'. (Interview #2, 2013)

The final barrier identified provides an apt segue to the next section of this chapter's findings, which is focused on future trajectories and deals with the absence of a national agenda at the regional or megaregional scale. One interviewee addresses this failing by saying that:

> The interesting thing is this field is still unsettled, and it's lost some momentum too . . . I don't think it has the same push it did back in 2006, 2007 or 2008 when it was a really hot topic. . . . But I'm glad we held back. We had time to reflect on some of this so none of it was offered as the hottest concept in planning; it was more of a codification of a body of literature that establishes a reasonable basis for a geography larger than the current metro. (Interviewee #5, 2012)

However, not all of the respondents' perspectives were quite as critical. Yaro and his colleagues at the RPA often note that in the early days of the Obama Administration, their conception of megaregions played an outsized role in the President's *Vision for High-Speed Rail* plan, with some of their work permeating Secretary LaHood's (2011) National Rail Plan as well. This was noted by one of the interviewees who struck an optimistic note in the conclusion:

> I'm kind of glad it's not – that it's pretty dorky and that only people who are geeks care about this stuff and are raising it at this stage in the game, because that probably means it's on the routine path to implementation. (Interview #5, 2012)

9.4.2 Opportunities to Advance Megaregional Planning

> In the short run we're going to capitalize on the political moment and what appears to be bipartisan interest in dealing with the climate and energy. We think folks will still be interested by the end of the year and there may be some national potential for this [resiliency planning], and there's a feeling that Sandy was a real eye-opener. (Interview #4, 2012)

Respondents identified six thematic areas they hope or believe will drive megaregional planning in the near future. These included: (1) planning for climate change and resiliency; (2) the practice of economic development; (3) merging green infrastructure with large landscape conservation; (4) further developing work with transportation infrastructure; (5) the potential governance structures; and (6) the policy reforms necessary to plan at this scale. Some of these have already been broached, including megaregional transportation planning and the notion of governance at this scale. Others, however, are in uncharted territory and should provide robust research lines and opportunities for practitioners in the near and long-term. This section recounts the respondents' discussion of these new trajectories for megaregion research.

Perhaps the most striking revelation to come from the interviews with key informants was their consensus regarding a pending shift towards megaregional resiliency and climate change adaptation. With many of the interviews taking place in the immediate aftermath of Superstorm Sandy, it is certainly possible that overly optimistic mega-regionalists envisioned an opportunity that was less attainable than they let on. However, this theme was more prominent in interviews than transportation, energy infrastructure and economic development. One interviewee elucidated the focus on coastal and megaregional resiliency, noting that:

> We are just [beginning] the process of reorienting a lot of the work we [previously] planned to do on energy to have a more specific focus on what has come out of the experience in the New York metropolitan area after [Superstorm] Sandy. It's a really terrific policy opportunity and people are saying we can't let this opportunity pass us by. (Interview #4, 2012)

As many others have noted, crisis begets planning at the regional and megaregional scale (Dewar and Epstein, 2007; Ross, 2009; Yaro, 2011). Another interviewee echoed this sentiment:

> [Superstorm] Sandy affected an area stretching from North Carolina to Maine, which is a larger definition for the Northeast [Megaregion], and the heart of it is the place that got the direct hit from New York to New Jersey and parts of Connecticut. It's interesting because Congress said 'let's look at the most urbanized area of the country' and that's probably not a bad frame for thinking about how to prevent future storm damage. (Interview #2, 2013)

This major appropriation for regional planning along the northeastern seaboard did not come without a fight, however. The process of appropriating these relief funds – once a perfunctory action within Congress – took more than three months of negotiation, solicited calls from legislators to make commensurate cuts to other portions of the federal budget as an offset and, at $50 billion, was considerably less than the original funding request.

Two respondents also proffered advice on the route federal policymakers could (even should?) consider when thinking about coastal resiliency at the megaregional scale. In the words of one interviewee:

> Along came [Superstorm] Sandy and a lot of attention became focused on coastal resiliency, infrastructure vulnerability, deciding whether to replace damaged infrastructure that had become hazardous to the community, figuring out how to be more flood proof, how to have an electrical distribution system that is less vulnerable to outages. These are the challenges we are going to need to confront. (Interview #4, 2012)

Another interviewee went a bit further, outlining what could become a new federal agency tasked with planning for resiliency rather than picking up the pieces after a natural disaster:

> We still need to pursue some national thinking using the megaregion frame as a way to think about disaster prevention . . . [I]n the Netherlands, you know they don't have an agency comparable to FEMA [Federal Emergency Management Agency]. FEMA's role is to pick up the pieces after disaster strikes, and the Dutch approach is to figure out what the disasters are likely to be and then take the necessary steps to address them. (Interview #2, 2013)

The points raised here have salience outside of the northeast US as well. The fallout from hurricanes impacting the Gulf Coast, Texas Triangle and Florida could be reduced by a proactive approach to planning for natural disasters. Much the same could be said about earthquakes in California and wildfires in the Front Range. Whether or not this assemblage of mega-regionalists can capitalize on the political moment remains to be seen, but they do appear to have learned an important lesson from 2010's HSR disappointment: when a political window opens, it only remains ajar for a brief period. Therefore, one must be ready to act almost immediately, a principle which hindered their push for a national rail plan in the early days of the Obama Presidency. This time, however, the RPA seems poised to capitalize on the political opportunity.

Receiving considerable attention from the respondents, economic development is likely to continue to occupy a large space within the future of megaregional planning. Most remarks focused on the aspect of coordinating economic development policy across a larger scale, though each respondent provided their own unique applications, including interstate highway alignments, the extraction and refinement of natural resources and even megaregional networks of higher education institutions to foster economic competitiveness. That being said, opinion amongst the respondents was largely split on whether these future applications would be a positive or deleterious outcome. Some unsurprisingly struck an optimistic tone in regards to the future of economic development at the megaregional scale:

> We are looking at bringing the I-11 corridor around the west side of Phoenix and capturing some of the flow of logistics from the Port of Los Angeles or the new port near the Baja that would route around to Tucson and I-8. So it's interesting . . . big scale, regional governance questions about what is the level of cooperation. (Interview, #5 2012)

This perspective helps to highlight the epistemological differences between the megapolitanists – grounded in the Census – and the megaregionalists, who are aligned with the tradition of regional planning practiced by the RPA. Megapolitanists tend to approach the concept from an epistemic position based in measures of integration formulated by the US Census Bureau, which relies primarily on commuting patterns to delineate functional space. Megaregionalists, on the other hand, tend to approach the concept through the lens of 'new regionalism', which advocates for drawing boundaries at the scale of the problem being studied (for example, environmental degradation, high-speed rail service or water resource management). Perhaps most importantly, the megapolitanists appear to view economic development at the megaregional scale as a policy question for geographers at the Census Bureau and congressional staff members assigned to transportation issues in the US Congress.

Megaregionalists tend to conceive of megaregional economic development as a softer, less prescriptive tool for planners. They are already 'starting to think about economic development collaborations and research collaborations at the megaregion scale in the northeast' (Interview #2, 2013). Though less ambitious relationships already exist – such as the academic common market across the southern US – nothing like the sort of collaborative research environment described by this interviewee has been attempted at the megaregional scale. The notion of coordinating economic development practices is also developed further by this respondent:

> We have this silly business on the East Coast with four or five places in the southeast that are developing post-Panamax container terminals.[1] We don't need more than one! If the federal government were thinking at this scale, they might save a lot of money that they could then invest in other things. It's the same in the northeast. We have half a dozen cities doing the same thing and it would be nice to have someone thinking about this at a larger scale. The FAA [Federal Aviation Authority] does this for airports – that is how Dallas-Fort Worth happened. (Interview #2, 2013)

But optimism about the applications for megaregional economic development did not abound. Others expressed either disinterest in the application, or disbelief in its efficacy. This is significant because, despite abundant references to a positive outlook for the megaregion concept and megaregional planning, both clearly remain contentious subject matters. One interview expressed scepticism in the following way:

> Right now, people are begrudgingly willing to accept metropolitan areas as a unit for economic analysis, but economic development is still a predominantly local practice, particularly in places where local policy depends on things like tax incentives and the sales tax – almost as much as land use planning. So fundamentally you're dealing with something that is jealously guarded and very local. So building a megaregional strategy probably requires more than just linking what exists. (Interview #1, 2012)

This interviewee would go on to describe the inherent difficulties in identifying metropolitan areas within a megaregion that are proximate and functionally related. To illustrate this, they argued that Austin, TX is more closely linked economically to San Francisco, CA and Seattle, WA than Portland, OR, which is geographically closer. They did not discuss, however, the sociocultural commonalities between Austin and Portland. Without some movement from the Census towards recognizing megapolitan statistical areas, however, the conversation in an American context is moot. The type of analysis and planning necessary to coordinate economic development at the megaregional scale is not possible without this policy reform.

Punctuating the future trajectories for megaregional planning is the opportunity for innovative governance structures and policy reforms to incentivise planning at the megaregional scale. These thematic areas were often discussed as a necessary next step. One interviewee, however, was quick to distinguish between governance strategies and new governmental units, saying that:

> It leads to interesting debates because some people assume that when you show them a big region on a map that you're saying it should become some sort of governmental unit, and I don't think anybody has seriously proposed that because it just doesn't seem feasible and I'm not even sure it would be desirable. A promising approach to megaregional governance is not going to be about creating new layers of government; it's going to be about getting the Governor of New York and the Governor of New Jersey to agree on something. (Interview #4, 2012)

Another interviewee broached this theme through the lens of policy reform, noting that:

> The issue now is the focus on jobs, poverty and economic opportunity for which the megaregion is not a bad way to look at these things. . . . We did this work on the history of national planning and twice now there have been relatively comprehensive infrastructure plans. But the interesting thing is that they were both completed in the final year of a second term by very progressive, far-sighted Presidents. So it might be a nice opportunity for the Obama Administration to be thinking about what they want their legacy to be and maybe we can get them to organize a national long-range strategy for infrastructure and economic development and opportunity with the megaregional frame. (Interview #2, 2013)

Indeed, as President Obama's administration continues to pursue their 'ladders of opportunity' agenda outlined in the 2013 State of the Union Address, this interviewee's proposal for a megaregional approach to poverty and economic development may hold promise. The RPA report on underperforming regions arguably provides a workable framework (Todorovich and Hagler, 2009). Whether or not this becomes a viable lens for the federal government's view of poverty and economic opportunity, however, will likely hinge on policy reforms within the Census Bureau and Department of Transportation. These governmental units could codify the megapolitan statistical area and then demand that Metropolitan Planning Organizations plan at that scale for issues other than transportation. Nonetheless, this could become problematic where there is overlap between megaregions, such as the Texas Triangle and Gulf Coast.

9.5   TESTING ECONOMIC INTEGRATION: THE CASE OF THE TEXAS TRIANGLE AND GULF COAST MEGAREGIONS

Generating a foundational analysis for testing economic integration between the Texas Triangle and Gulf Coast required two relatively simple steps: developing baseline data for both megaregions, and comparing individual MSAs within each megaregion to this baseline. For the former, Census Bureau information on median income, population growth, educational attainment (bachelor's and advanced degrees) and unemployment rates were analysed for the time period 2005–2011. The industrial classifications of agriculture, manufacturing, transportation/warehousing, information technology and professional services were also examined. This produced a library of descriptive statistics for the Texas Triangle–Gulf Coast megaregional pair across nine distinct variables (samples of which are presented in Tables 9.2 and 9.3).

What this enables is a metro-by-metro comparison of urban regions within the study area to the baseline levels generated by the preceding analysis. To achieve this, metropolitan areas were first stratified against one another to produce 'top' and 'bottom' performing urban regions. As one might expect, the Texas Triangle generally outperformed the Gulf Coast in terms of economic growth, wages and population growth. Each MSA was then compared to the baseline data and given an indicator based upon its performance (less than, equivalent to, or greater than the baseline) across the 2005–2011 study period. This produced a data pool for the megaregional pair (samples of which are illustrated in Tables 9.4 and 9.5).

Table 9.2   Median household income in the Texas Triangle and Gulf Coast

	Range (−)	Range (+)	Mean	Median
2005	$36551	$68191	$52165	$51427
2007	$41002	$74105	$57206	$56205
2009	$44792	$77673	$60508	$59001
2011	$47208	$61718	$61718	$60570
Change	29%	−9%	18%	18%

Source: Author

Table 9.3   Share of workers in the manufacturing industry in the Texas Triangle and Gulf Coast

	Range (−)	Range (+)	Mean	Median
2005	2.49%	11.14%	5.79%	5.43%
2007	5.00%	18.20%	9.63%	9.70%
2009	4.30%	17.50%	9.36%	9.90%
2011	4.60%	19.30%	9.06%	8.90%
Change	0.74%	8.17%	3.33%	2.96%

Source: Author

The descriptive statistical analysis tends to confirm the preconception that the Gulf Coast is a struggling, if non-existent economic unit – especially compared to the Texas Triangle. However, upon closer examination the Houston and Beaumont MSAs – the pair of regions shared by the Texas Triangle and Gulf Coast – appear to serve as a spatial, economic and functional bridge between the megaregional pair. On first viewing, they share economic characteristics with both the Texas Triangle and Gulf Coast. Though further analysis is needed to determine the significance and complexity of these relationships, several descriptive and intuitive links between Houston and this megaregional pair arose. Many of the economic trends within the Houston MSA – including educational attainment, population growth, and median income growth – are mirrored in the largest metropolitan areas of the Texas Triangle (Austin, Dallas, and San Antonio) and Gulf Coast (New Orleans, Baton Rouge, and Lafayette). Growth in the megaregions' key industries – Agriculture, Forestry, Fishing, and Hunting (AFFH), Transportation, Warehousing, and Utilities (TWU), Information Technology, and Professional Services – are mirroring the various patterns of growth, decline and stagnation within the Houston MSA. Given the descriptive nature of these findings, however, further study into the direct and indirect economic impacts of Houston on the Texas Triangle and Gulf Coast is needed.[2]

Resonating with calls for more macro- and micro-level research into megaregions (Harrison and Hoyler, 2015a, 2015b; Schafran, 2014, 2015) what this brief snapshot of testing economic integration between the Texas Triangle and Gulf Coast megaregions illuminates is the urgent need for further studies to discern precisely how, in this particular case, these two MSAs influence the megaregions they share and, more generally, the argument running through this chapter which is how coherent megaregional spaces actually are. In this spirit of scoping out near-future priorities for

Table 9.4   Economic indicators for the Baton Rouge (Gulf Coast) MSA

	Socioeconomic variables									
	Median Income		Population		Bachelor's		Advanced		Unemployment	
2005	$54 958	▲	706 909	▼	9.51%	▲	5.28%	▲	3.60%	▲
2007	$59 539	▲	753 299	▼	15.90%	▲	8.40%	▲	4.60%	▼
2009	$64 379	▲	779 442	▼	16.80%	▲	8.20%	▲	3.90%	▲
2011	$66 432	▲	808 242	▼	17.90%	▲	8.90%	▲	4.30%	▲
Change	20.88%	▲	14.33%	▲	8.39%	▲	3.62%	▲	1.80%	▲
	Industry-specific variables									
	AFFH		Manufacturing		TWU		Information		Professional	
2005	0.72%	▼	6.22%	▲	3.11%	▲	1.12%	▼	5.75%	▲
2007	1.10%	▼	9.70%	↔	4.80%	▼	1.80%	▼	9.80%	▲
2009	1.10%	▼	9.90%	▲	4.50%	▼	1.70%	▼	10.00%	▲
2011	1.20%	▼	9.10%	↔	4.60%	▼	1.70%	▲	9.60%	▲
Change	0.48%	▼	2.89%	▼	1.49%	▼	0.58%	▲	3.85%	▲

Source: Author

Table 9.5   Economic indicators for the Austin (Texas Triangle) MSA

	Socioeconomic variables									
	Median Income		Population		Bachelor's		Advanced		Unemployment	
2005	$68 191	▲	1 496 364	▲	16.58%	▲	8.24%	▲	3.70%	▲
2007	$74 098	▲	1 533 263	▲	25.20%	▲	13.00%	▲	4.40%	↔
2009	$77 079	▲	1 651 234	▲	25.20%	▲	13.30%	▲	4.50%	▼
2011	$77 994	▲	1 631 368	▲	26.10%	▲	13.80%	▲	5.80%	▼
Change	14.38%	▲	23.11%	▲	9.16%	▲	5.56%	▲	2.10%	▼
	Industry-specific variables									
	AFFH		Manufacturing		TWU		Information		Professional	
2005	0.33%	▼	7.25%	▲	2.29%	▲	1.86%	▲	9.00%	▲
2007	0.80%	▼	9.70%	↔	3.40%	▲	2.80%	▲	13.20%	▲
2009	0.07%	▼	9.10%	▼	3.50%	▲	2.60%	▲	13.80%	▲
2011	0.07%	▼	8.90%	▼	3.30%	▲	2.30%	▲	13.80%	▲
Change	0.04%	▼	1.65%	▼	1.01%	▲	0.44%	▲	4.80%	▲

Source: Author

megaregional research, the final section considers whether there are applications in academia and planning practice that can advance megaregional thinking.

9.6   PROSPECTS FOR MEGAREGIONAL PRAXIS

The findings presented in the previous section, in concert with the proposed additions to the body of megaregional literature, offer an initial agenda for the future of megaregional research and practice. The remainder of this chapter aims to outline the broad strokes of this potential agenda for academic research and pedagogy.

9.6.1   Towards a (Re)New(ed) Megaregional Research Agenda

If the US megaregion project is moving towards an ecological perspective, then defining precisely what constitutes megaregional ecology must be addressed. Green infrastructure concepts like Low-Impact Development (LID) and biomimicry have occupied a considerable amount of landscape architecture scholarship since the late 1990s. Sustainable SITES, an interdisciplinary, applied research endeavor organized by University of Texas–Austin's Lady Bird Johnson Wildflower Center with support from the American Society of Landscape Architects and the US Botanic Garden, has begun to unravel the impact of these design interventions through a number of performance metrics (Fleming et al., 2013). But this work has been focused on the project-scale impact of green infrastructure and the few categories with a city or regional perspective have been difficult to achieve or measure.

There is space in this discussion that megaregionalists are beginning to occupy. The key questions centre on: How do multiple projects employing, for example, alternative storm water treatment methods within the same city alter the aggregate performance of the area's various infrastructure systems? How do they impact regional water quality? What are the fiscal impacts of a city or region-wide green infrastructure system on the budget of a municipality or utility company? If the impact is positive, how might this return be monetized and for whom? These questions will require extraordinarily sophisticated modeling tools as well as interdisciplinary teams of designers, planners, ecologists, engineers and many others. Landscape architects have seized this topic, along with much of the field of physical planning over the past twenty years. Planners, ironically, have been in retreat; perhaps regional green infrastructure and megaregional ecology can be their return?

Universally decried as a barrier to the evolution of megaregions, the data gap merits attention from scholars operating at this scale. Despite the feedback from the key informants, there is not a dearth of data. Rather, there is a lack of willingness to mine or capture the copious amounts of digital data that exist. Meinig and Zelinksy utilized archival research to uncover the role of sociocultural sorting on regional and megaregional identity. Surely contemporary researchers can begin constructing more sophisticated understandings of the social dynamics driving or hindering megaregional development.

One potential source offers megaregional scholars an opportunity to query issues of cultural characteristics, travel behaviour and settlement patterns at once: social media, especially Twitter. Launched in 2006, Twitter has grown exponentially and is now the second-largest social media outlet, trailing only Facebook. It generates incredibly rich datasets within the 140-character tweets that its users generate. Geolocations of tweets can in many cases be tracked to generate time-series data. Tweets can also be categorized according to themes or key trends to begin elucidating the spatial relationships between users and their varying preferences and characteristics. Ed Manley, a doctoral student in geomatic engineering at University College London, has already begun exploring these phenomena using a combination of Twitter data and, when possible, GPS-tracking information from publicly owned vehicles (Manley, 2013, 2014; see also Graham, 2011; Graham and Zook, 2011; Reades and Smith, 2014). One can begin to imagine how such methods could also be used to generate maps and analysis of megaregional language, culture, colloquialisms and other distinctive traits. If megaregional planners are to pick up where Meinig and Zelinsky left off, unlocking the power of social media's datasets presents one of the most tractable and exciting opportunities to do so.

9.6.2   Crafting a Megaregional Curriculum

If megaregional planning is going to expand outside of academia and into practice, it will require a cadre of young planners trained in its principles. Ethan Seltzer's work at Portland State University, in collaboration with Daniel Carson at the University of Washington, provides an interesting framework engaging planning students in the conceptualization of megaregional development. In 2005, this professorial duo began teaching parallel, collaborative courses on the Cascadia/Ecolopolis megaregion of the Pacific Northwest. The class produced an extensive report (Seltzer, 2006), which was jointly published by Portland State University, the University of Washington, and the RPA and follow-up publications by Seltzer and his colleagues have been produced as a result (Seltzer, 2008, 2009, 2011). This approach merits consideration from universities in each of the US megaregions.

McSherry et al. (1993) also proffer an intriguing model for planning educators to consider. As professors in the Arizona State University (ASU) Environmental Planning program, the trio reflected on the results of a yearlong studio sequence that was developed for first year master's students at ASU. This approach is similar to the capstone experience of many landscape architecture programs, including the University of Arkansas, Virginia Tech and Kansas State University. Several graduate programs in public policy – including the LBJ School of Public Affairs at the University of Texas at Austin – employ a similar approach. In the first semester at ASU, students engage in various forms of site inventory, in quantitative and qualitative methods of analysis, and in various forms of visual representation and design communication (McSherry et al., 1993, pp. 122–123). This work takes place in small teams and results in a comprehensive report of the study area's opportunities and constraints by the end of the semester. To overcome the difficulties of interdisciplinary studio education, the second semester utilizes an 'iterative criticism model' in which plan-making questions are constantly posed, challenged and refined (McSherry et al., 1993, pp. 127–129). Recommendations are drawn from the first semester's exhaustive analysis and aim to overcome two additional difficulties of studio education: (1) that plan-making requires policy recommendations and physical interventions; and (2) the scientific method, though exceptionally valuable to planners, cannot be an end in and of itself (McSherry et al., 1993, p. 127). As planning educators continue to revive, reinvent and reimagine studio education in their respective curricula, this 1993 model still holds immense value for the issues facing regional and megaregional planners. It may even be an appropriate substitute for the current capstone experience at many planning programs: professional reports and theses.

Scholars at UT-Austin could develop their own 'Topics in the Texas Triangle' studio, workshop, or practicum courses akin to the Seltzer–Carson effort in Cascadia and the McSherry–San Martin–Steiner approach at ASU. The Texas Triangle is facing a particular set of challenges, including increasingly stressed water supplies and hyper-congestion along its highways, which will undoubtedly require input from the state's leading research institutions. Similar approaches merit consideration across the other megaregions of the US. With the addition of Richard Weller as the Chair of Landscape Architecture, the University of Pennsylvania's School of Design is positioned to once again blur the line between design and planning, this time at the megaregional scale. One of the most pressing concerns is to further extend the focus of teaching and research beyond the Northeast Megaregion (for example Glass, 2015 on the Great Lakes Megaregion; Schafran, 2014 and Wheeler, 2015 on Northern California). Some US megaregions lack an anchor institution that is actively engaged at this scale, providing opportunities akin to those of the Texas Triangle for University of Texas, Austin.

At the time of this chapter's submission, only one university – the University of Texas at Austin – offers annual coursework focused exclusively on the topic of megaregions. Scholars at the University of Pennsylvania offer a yearlong seminar and studio on regional infrastructure, which occasionally broaches the megaregional scale. Similarly, graduate students at Georgia Tech University are exposed to the issues, challenges and opportunities of megaregions through the case study of the Piedmont Atlantic megaregion (McCray et al., 2013). Developing coursework, similar to what has been proposed here (or otherwise), could accomplish two valuable feats within planning education. First, this could revive the 'regional' component of city/urban/community and regional planning programs across the country. Only a handful of programs – for example at Portland State University, the University of Illinois at Urbana-Champaign, the University of Michigan and the University of Pennsylvania – have remained focused on the region while many others have narrowed their scales of focus to that of the neighborhood or community. But regional issues and regionalism in general are not dwindling and planning as an academic discipline would be wise to retain its focus on this component of their curricula.

Planning education has also shifted away from the type of physical planning practiced by leading proponents of megaregionalism. At least as an academic discipline, it has moved closer to sociology, urban affairs and public policy in recent years and has ceded substantial ground to landscape architecture. Rather than abandoning physical planning, new curricula could renew focus on the art of plan-making at a scale that is exclusively their own: the region and, by extension, the megaregion.

9.7   CONCLUSION

This chapter has attempted to contextualize the US megaregion project and to discuss potential future trajectories. This involved reviewing new threads of megaregional literature, which, when taken alongside the findings presented as a result of key informant interviews, can begin charting a course towards a megaregional future. A number of opportunities were identified for researchers, educators and practitioners of regional and megaregional planning. These included identifying and utilizing untapped data sources, resiliency planning, and tools for examining the overlapping and integration of megaregional spaces. Alongside this, the chapter also reveals a number of (potential or real) barriers to advancing megaregional thinking. When taken together, just as megapolitans and megaregions can be thought of as components of the same system, so too can these seemingly disparate academic and practice-based challenges be considered interdependent pieces of the same megaregional future.

NOTES

1. Panamax ports are deep water ports capable of servicing a fully laden Panamax cargo vessel. Post-Panamax relates to the expansion of the Panama Canal to service the world's largest cargo vessels, which when it opens in 2015, will have a significant impact on world shipping lanes.
2. There is no space here to elaborate further on this integration, rather I raise it as a point of reference for considering the imperatives for near-future megaregional research. My own doctoral research on *Patterns of Integration – Houston's Link to the Texas Triangle and Gulf Coast* is developing this research and will outline in more detail the evidence supporting this claim.

REFERENCES

Dablanc, L. and C.L. Ross (2012), 'Atlanta: a mega logistics center in the Piedmont Atlantic Megaregion (PAM)', *Journal of Transport Geography*, **24** (S1), 432–442.
Dewar, M. and D. Epstein (2007), 'Planning for megaregions in the United States', *Journal of Planning Literature*, **22** (2), 108–124.
Faludi, A. (2009), 'The megalopolis, the blue banana, and global economic integration zones in European planning thought', in C.L. Ross (ed.), *Megaregions: Planning for Global Competitiveness*, Washington, DC: Island Press, pp. 18–34.
Fleming, W. (2012), *Towards a Megaregional Future: Prologue, Progress, and Potential Applications*, Master's Thesis, The University of Texas at Austin.
Fleming, W., F. Steiner and T. McCray (2013), *The Makeshift Texas Triangle: Building Resiliency Across a Vulnerable Landscape*, Austin, TX: Center for Sustainable Development, The University of Texas at Austin.
Florida, R. (2009), 'Foreword', in C.L. Ross (ed.), *Megaregions: Planning for Global Competitiveness*, Washington, DC: Island Press, pp. xvii–xix.
Florida, R., T. Gulden and C. Mellander (2008), 'The rise of the mega-region', *Cambridge Journal of Regions, Economy and Society*, **1** (3), pp. 459–476.
Florida, R., C. Mellander and T. Gulden (2012), 'Global metropolis: assessing economic activity in urban centers based on nighttime satellite images', *The Professional Geographer*, **64** (2), 178–187.
Glass, M.R. (2015), 'Conflicting spaces of governance in the imagined Great Lakes megaregion', in J. Harrison and M. Hoyler (eds), *Megaregions: Globalization's New Urban Form?* Cheltenham, UK and Northampton, MA, USA: Edward Elgar, pp. 119–145.

Gottmann, J. (1961), *Megalopolis: The Urbanized Northeastern Seaboard of the United States*, New York: Twentieth Century Fund.

Graham, M. (2011), 'Time machines and virtual portals: the spatialities of the digital divide', *Progress in Development Studies*, **11** (3), 211–227.

Graham, M. and M. Zook (2011), 'Visualizing global cyberscapes: mapping user-generated placemarks', *Journal of Urban Technology*, **18** (1), 115–132.

Harrison, J. and M. Hoyler (2015a), 'Megaregions: foundations, frailties, futures', in J. Harrison and M. Hoyler (eds), *Megaregions: Globalization's New Urban Form?* Cheltenham, UK and Northampton, MA, USA: Edward Elgar, pp. 1–28.

Harrison, J. and M. Hoyler (2015b), 'Megaregions reconsidered: urban futures and the future of the urban', in J. Harrison and M. Hoyler (eds), *Megaregions: Globalization's New Urban Form?* Cheltenham, UK and Northampton, MA, USA: Edward Elgar, pp. 230–255.

LaHood, R. (2011), *National Rail Plan: Moving Forward*, Washington, DC: USDOT.

Lang, R.E. and D. Dhavale (2005), 'Beyond Megalopolis: exploring America's new megapolitan geography', *Metropolitan Institute Census Report Series*, 05:01, Alexandria, VA: The Metropolitan Institute at Virginia Tech.

Manley, E. (2013), 'Analysing languages in the New York twittersphere', available at http://urbanmovements.co.uk/2013/02/21/analysing-languages-in-the-new-york-twittersp/ (accessed 7 October 2013).

Manley, E. (2014), 'Identifying functional urban regions within traffic flow', *Regional Studies, Regional Science*, **1** (1), 40–42.

McCray, T., L. Loftus-Otway, W. Fleming and D. Johnson (2013), 'Changing our scale of thinking: value of a megaregional planning course', *Journal of Planning and Urban Development*, **139** (4), 235–241.

McSherry, L., I. San Martin and F. Steiner (1993), 'Reflections on teaching a year-long graduate studio', in R. Ribe, R. Melnick and K. Cairn (eds), *Proceedings of the Council of Educators in Landscape Architecture Annual Conference*, Washington, DC: Landscape Architecture Foundation, pp. 120–137.

Meinig, D.W. (1969), *Imperial Texas: An Interpretive Essay in Cultural Geography*, Austin, TX: University of Texas Press.

Nelson, A.C. and R.E. Lang (2011), *Megapolitan America: A New Vision for Understanding America's Metropolitan Geography*, Washington, DC: APA Planners Press.

Peirce, N.R., C.W. Johnson and F.M. Peters (2008), *Century of the City: No Time to Lose*, New York: Rockefeller Foundation.

Pirani, R., R. Freudenberg and P. Winters (2011), *Landscapes: Improving Conservation Practice in the Northeast*, New York: RPA.

Reades, J. and D.A. Smith (2014), 'Mapping the "space of flows": the geography of global business telecommunications and employment specialization in the London mega-city-region', *Regional Studies*, **48** (1), 105–126.

Regional Plan Association (2006), *America 2050: A Prospectus*, New York: RPA.

Ross, C.L. (2008), *Megaregions: Literature Review of the Implications for US Infrastructure Investment and Transportation Planning*, Prepared for the USDOT by the Center for Quality Growth and Regional Development, Georgia Institute of Technology.

Ross, C.L. (ed.) (2009), *Megaregions: Planning for Global Competitiveness*, Washington, DC: Island Press.

Ross, C.L., D. Lee, E. Meijers and T. Welch (2015), *Megaregions, Prosperity and Sustainability*, London: Routledge.

Rybcyznski, W. (2010), *Makeshift Metropolis: Ideas About Cities*, New York: Scribner Press.

Schafran, A. (2014), 'Rethinking mega-regions: sub-regional politics in a fragmented metropolis', *Regional Studies*, **48** (4), 587–602.

Schafran, A. (2015), 'Beyond globalization: a historical urban development approach to understanding megaregions', in J. Harrison and M. Hoyler (eds), *Megaregions: Globalization's New Urban Form?* Cheltenham, UK and Northampton, MA, USA: Edward Elgar, pp. 75–96.

Seltzer, E. (2006), 'Ecolopolis 2.0: Cascadia', School of Urban Studies and Planning, Portland State University, available at http://dr.archives.pdx.edu/xmlui/handle/psu/8758 (accessed 4 November 2013).

Seltzer, E. (2008), 'Ecolopolis 3.0: Infrastructure and Sustainability in Cascadia', School of Urban Studies and Planning, Portland State University, available at http://dr.archives.pdx.edu/xmlui/handle/psu/8759 (accessed 4 November 2013).

Seltzer, E. (2009), 'Ecolopolis 4.0: Livability in Cascadia', School of Urban Studies and Planning, Portland State University, available at http://dr.archives.pdx.edu/xmlui/handle/psu/8760 (accessed 4 November 2013).

Seltzer, E. (2011), 'Ecolopolis 5.0: High-Speed Rail in Cascadia', School of Urban Studies and Planning, Portland State University, available at http://dr.archives.pdx.edu/xmlui/handle/psu/8761 (accessed 4 November 2013).

Seltzer, E. and A. Carbonell (2011), *Regional Planning in America: Practice and Prospect*, Cambridge, MA: Lincoln Institute of Land Policy.

Steiner, F. (2011), *Design for a Vulnerable Planet*, Austin, TX: University of Texas Press.

Todorovich, P. and Y. Hagler (2009), *New Strategies for Regional Economic Development*, New York: RPA.

Todorovich, P. and Y. Hagler (2011), *High-Speed Rail in America*, New York: RPA.

Weller, R. and J. Bolleter (2013), *Made in Australia: The Future of Australian Cities*, Crawley: University of Western Australia Press.

Wheeler, S. (2015), 'Five reasons why megaregional planning works against sustainability', in J. Harrison and M. Hoyler (eds), *Megaregions: Globalization's New Urban Form?* Cheltenham, UK and Northampton, MA, USA: Edward Elgar, pp. 97–118.

Yaro, R.D. (2005), *Global Gateway Regions: America's 3rd Century Strategy for Preserving the American Dream*, New York: RPA.

Yaro, R.D. (2011), 'Rebuilding and renewing America: a twenty-first century national infrastructure', in A.G.O. Yeh and J. Xu (eds), *China's Pan-Pearl River Delta: Regional Cooperation and Development*, Hong Kong: Hong Kong University Press, pp. 43–62.

Zelinksy, W. (1973), *The Cultural Geography of the United States*, New York: Prentice Hall.

10. Megaregions reconsidered: urban futures and the future of the urban

John Harrison and Michael Hoyler

10.1 AN INTRODUCTION TO (MORE THAN JUST) A DEBATE ON MEGAREGIONS

We live in a world of competing urban, regional and other spatial imaginaries. This book's chief concern has been with one such spatial imaginary – the megaregion. More particularly, its theme has been the assertion that the megaregion constitutes globalization's new urban form. Yet, what is clear is that the intellectual and practical literatures underpinning the megaregion thesis are not internally coherent and this is the cause of considerable confusion over the precise role of megaregions in globalization. This book has offered one solution through its focus on the *who, how* and *why* of megaregions much more than the *what* and *where* of megaregions. In short, moving the debate forward from questions of definition, identification and delimitation to questions of agency (who or what is constructing megaregions), process (how are megaregions being constructed), and specific interests (why are megaregions being constructed) is the contribution of this book.

The individual chapters have interrogated many of the claims and counter-claims made about megaregions through examples as diverse as California, the US Great Lakes, Texas and the Gulf Coast, Greater Paris, Northern England, Northern Europe, and China's Pearl River Delta. But, as with any such volume, our approach has offered up as many new questions as it has provided answers. In this concluding chapter, we identify some of these questions as part of an ongoing reconsideration of megaregions and reformulation of a programme of research for those of us interested in megaregions and global urban studies more broadly.

One of the main unresolved questions to arise out of this book is the status and position of the 'megaregion' within global urban studies. This extends much further than the immediate focus of this book, so one of our aims in this final chapter is to connect the contribution(s) of this collection to contemporary debates centred on urban futures and the future of the urban. The book has presented multiple pathways into the megaregion debate and we have identified four to develop further in this chapter, which are: (1) competing or complementary spatial imaginaries; (2) megaregional glocalization; (3) utopian/dystopian urban dreams; and (4) urban history, periodization and temporality.

To foreground this, we begin with three examples which caught our eye in the short period we were writing this chapter. They serve as an important reminder both of the continuing influence of megaregions within popular public discourses and the need for the type of more critical analysis that this book promotes.

10.1.1   The Cali Baja 'Megaregion'

In October 2013, David Mayagoitia, Chairman of the Tijuana Economic Development Corporation extolled the virtues of a megaregion spanning the US–Mexican border when officially launching the *Cali Baja Binational Megaregion Initiative* (http://www.calibaja.net/cbdb/p/):

> What we're trying to do is promote investment . . . We want to create a binational economic development entity that actually promotes the whole region as a single group. The [US–Mexican] border only represents a line that we have to cross on a daily basis. What we would like to do is expand our region to include Los Angeles, because why not? Why not create a picture of what we want to be, and strive for that picture. Why not be Hong Kong and Shenzhen? (quoted in Connor, 2013)

Looking beyond the goal of investment and the fact that this is clearly indicative of how the geoeconomic logic for promoting the competitiveness of megaregions is putting megaregionalism centre stage of political action, what marks this example out among the many others we could have chosen is that Cali Baja is a cross-border region. Located on the US–Mexico border, Cali Baja is geographically proximate to, but politically detached from, the US megaregions. This is important for two reasons. On the one hand, Tijuana, Mexico is only one mile from the US border so, for Mayagoitia, playing down the significance of the border while playing up the potential for a binational economic development entity favours Cali Baja's inclusion alongside Cascadia as a cross-border megaregion within the discursive framing of US megaregions.[1] On the other hand, Tijuana is located just 25 miles from San Diego and 140 miles from Los Angeles: expanding to include Los Angeles not only brings the outside in, to make the case stronger for a Cali Baja megaregion, it takes the inside out, because Cali Baja would by the same token become part of an already existing South California megaregion (Harrison and Hoyler, 2015, Figure 1.1).

Quite clearly, there are strong motivating factors for Mayagoitia, Tijuana and Cali Baja to pursue megaregionalism as both an economic and political strategy. But while they can seek to influence the discursive framing of megaregions what they cannot do is change it. They are on the fringes economically, while politically they are excluded. On the face of it they are disempowered by the discourse of US megaregions. Yet, in and through the creation of a megaregional space they are entering the possibility of engaging and exerting influence over other centres of social power. Facing up to this challenge, Mayagoitia goes on to add:

> There's really no rules, there's really no set manual to set up a mega-region. Things sort of evolve and happen, and you respond to those things. As you go through this process, you begin to realize that collaboration makes you stronger … It makes people listen to what you have to say. (Quoted in Connor, 2013)

If the earlier statement focused on the 'what' and 'where' of the Cali Baja megaregion, the remainder of this section has focused on the 'who', the 'why' and the 'how' in relation to megaregions. The opening to this second statement is pertinent because although megaregions have fast become an officially institutionalized task for policy elites the world over, megaregions are not universally accepted as 'official' state/governmental policy. The result is less prescription than might otherwise be the case, meaning the question of who constructs megaregions and why becomes even more important. In this way the final sentence becomes the most significant. It shines a light on what is the ultimate goal of megaregionalism as a political project – exerting influence in and through megaregions. The open question in this example and many others too are: who are the 'people', what is (and whose is) the message, and perhaps most critical of all, if successful, who, what and where is likely to gain/lose the most as a result?

10.1.2   The Hampton Roads–Richmond 'Megaregion'

In December 2013 the unfolding process of megaregionalism saw actors located in another space which currently finds itself 'off' the politically-constructed map of megaregions ponder its position within national and international circuits of globalized capital accumulation. Located in the US State of Virginia, Hampton Roads and Richmond are strategically positioned between two megaregions. One hundred miles to the north of Richmond is Washington, DC and the southern tip of the Northeast Megaregion (Gottmann's (1961) 'megalopolis'). To the south is Raleigh, the northernmost city in the Piedmont Atlantic Megaregion identified by the Regional Plan Association (RPA) (2006), located 180 miles from

Hampton Roads. As a result, Hampton Roads and Richmond find themselves located on the fringes of US megaregionalism as it is politically constructed. This has not gone unnoticed, particularly among local business leaders. More interesting is the response:

> Businesses can certainly do this on their own. We don't need the formality of a megaregion, but it's a perception. We certainly need to look united to be competitive to our brethren to the north and south who have already created those megaregions that are competing better than we are now. (Tom Frantz, Hampton Roads Business Roundtable, quoted in Bozick, 2013)

Unlike Cali Baja, where the modus operandi is to create a formal megaregion, the approach favoured by business leaders in Hampton Roads implies seeking the benefits of operating like a megaregion in an economic sense (and signified to the wider world through a merger of metropolitan statistical areas (MSAs)) but without the formality of being a megaregion in the political sense. This example demonstrates that the question is not always where, why and how actors choose to engage in the construction of megaregions but why some choose to engage more than others. In the case of Hampton Roads and Richmond do they choose not to engage in attempts to politically construct a megaregion because they recognize they will not be permitted into the exclusive club of 11 megaregions which the Regional Plan Association (2006) have placed on a pedestal as America's new urban hierarchy? Is it that business sees the whole megaregion idea as being somehow abstract and of no immediate consequence other than in marketing terms? Or is it that they can see the potential importance in terms of attracting business and infrastructure investment, thus engaging with the megaregion concept but only on their own terms? These are the important but often unanswered questions which we argue the more critical perspective promoted by this book can and need to avail answers to if we are to move forward with megaregions as a key component of global urban studies.

Cali Baja and Hampton Roads–Richmond appear to adopt very different strategies yet they both respond to the same feeling of being disempowered by megaregionalism, and globalized urbanization more broadly. Moreover, their different strategies aspire to much the same outcomes, that is, to create a mechanism which can lobby on behalf of certain capitalist interests. This neoliberal pro-growth model sees Cali Baja and Hampton Roads–Richmond both using the 'megaregion' to engage extra-regional actors and seek to exert influence over them, all in order to fix mobile capital investment within their region and facilitate growth. More specifically, local actors in Hampton Roads–Richmond have mobilized around one particular issue – securing money for local transportation projects. Irrespective of whether you are a national organization, such as the RPA with its America 2050 initiative, or a local group of business leaders, megaregions are a leveraging tool particularly when it comes to funding transportation projects:

> In terms of federal dollars, the bigger attention you attract, the more leverage you have. (Tom Frantz, Hampton Roads Business Roundtable, quoted in Bozick, 2013)

> The clout of a bigger region could bring more attention and help all of the things going on just snowball a little further. [Adding] If we're not in the top MSA regions, they're not thinking about us. (Russell Held, Senior Vice President, Virginia Port Authority, quoted in Bozick, 2013)

The appeal of megaregions is not only the end goal. Megaregions provide a narrative, a story board on which local issues are played out. The trend towards enlarged urban scales in policymaking is less about planning and governing at that scale and more about the creation of 'spaces of engagement' – the space in which the politics of defending and enabling certain place-specific, essential interests unfolds (Cox, 1998). From megalopolis to megaregion, European Spatial Development Perspective to America 2050, Cali Baja to Hampton Roads–Richmond, the story of megaregions is firmly rooted in the creation of a specific narrative and perception of place.[2] To reiterate our earlier point, the construction of megaregions should be seen as a spatial strategy and, by implication, a deeply politicized act. The creation of a megaregional space is a tactic employed by actors with place-specific interests; actors who are motivated at a particular moment in time to create a space to enhance or defend those very interests. We argue that timing is the important but often overlooked dimension of megaregional analysis – a mistake caused by too much focus on the *what* and *where* of megaregions, rather than the *who, how* and *why* – and it is also a key dimension in our third example.

10.1.3 A New PAR-LON 'Megaregion'?

In January 2014, an open letter to Boris Johnson, Mayor of London, saw Anne Hidalgo, Deputy Mayor of Paris and mayoral candidate in the March 2014 elections, claim that:

> London is a suburb of Paris and Paris is a suburb of London . . . From Tokyo, Shanghai, Lagos or Rio – cities that will have more than 20 million inhabitants by 2030 – Greater London and Paris Grand, with a combined population of 20 million, may well be seen as a single conurbation. Indeed, in this not-too-distant future, London and Paris together could be seen from Asia, Latin America or

> Africa as . . . possessing a critical mass of resources to reckon with. That's if we can find a way to collaborate effectively. (Hidalgo, 2014, p. 1)

There are two important aspects to this: the first is spatial, the second is temporal. Spatially, Hidalgo chooses the term conurbation over megaregion, yet the argument still holds that this is a further example of endeavours to politically construct a megaregional space of engagement in order to secure certain economic interests from external threats which seek to undermine or dissolve them. Paris is reaching out to London, much like Cali Baja is reaching out to San Diego and Los Angeles. Yet, what marks this example out is that by standard definitions Paris already has the critical mass to consider itself a megaregion (Florida et al., 2008). Two closely related questions immediately present themselves. The first is why 20 million? This is the global benchmark set by organizations such as UN-Habitat for megaregions, so this might be a valid reason were it not that Paris and London as metropolitan-scaled cities are both approaching a population of 20 million already. This suggests it must be something else, which is why the second question we must ask is why London?

Perhaps, ultimately, this example has more to do with French territorial politics and an awareness of Anne Hidalgo's position as the Socialist Party candidate for the 2014 mayoral elections. The challenge for Hidalgo was to position herself for the forthcoming elections as a future mayor with global outlook, against a background where the political party she represents is, under President François Hollande, implementing a 75 per cent 'super tax' on employers paying salaries over 1 million euros per annum. Among Parisian elites the fear is this super tax will spark an exodus of wealthy French millionaires and talented entrepreneurs from Paris to London (where the top rate of tax is currently 45 per cent) and undermine the status of Paris as a globally competitive city. Coming less than one month after Hollande's super tax was approved by France's highest court, the timing of Hidalgo's quotes are therefore not insignificant. Indeed, the timing of this very public courting of Johnson and London becomes even more important to this story when we consider they came just four days after she had told a gathering of Parisian-based Anglo-American reporters how 'London is in some ways a suburb of Paris' (quoted in Samuel, 2014, p. 1). What we arrive at is the competitive positioning of Paris vis-à-vis London clearly giving way to what can be interpreted as a conciliatory move to espouse a more cooperative spirit between London and Paris. This certainly appears to suggest Hidalgo's very public courting of Johnson and London owes much more to French politics than representing a genuine attempt to plan and govern at the scale of the megaregion. Put bluntly, the megaregion is not the story in this example; it is just the vehicle for communicating a particular story to its chosen audience. What we see is the use of the megaregion idea at a time that is politically expedient. The result is what will no doubt amount to a very fleeting, temporary attempt at constructing a megaregional space of engagement.

This example demonstrates that only in asking the 'why' question does the temporal dimension come to the fore. Therefore, it is not sufficient simply to ask the 'why' question in a spatial context (Why 20 million? Why London?), we need equally to be asking it in a temporal context (Why now?).

10.2 MEGAREGIONAL FUTURES AND THE FUTURE OF THE MEGAREGION

10.2.1 (Re)new(ed) Spatial Imaginaries: Competing or Complementary?

As we noted in our introductory chapter, megaregions are just one of an increasingly large number of competing spatial imaginaries which purport to reflect globalization's new urban form. There are four important aspects to this which this book has confronted. The first is why, from all the competing spatial imaginaries that exist to explain globalization's new urban form, megaregions have emerged to become one of the more powerful, persuasive and dominant imaginaries. The chapters in this book point to a divergence of opinion depending on whether you take geoeconomic or geopolitical arguments as your starting point. For some, megaregions *do* constitute globalization's new urban form. They are the spatial manifestation of economic activity, the economic motors in today's quicksilver global economy, the newest incarnation of what agglomeration economists argue is incontrovertible in globalized urbanization and that is the trend which sees an ever smaller number of increasingly large urbanized clusters surging ahead to dominate the global economy (Florida, 2014). The formula appears to be bigger is better (Hesse, 2015). While this may in part explain the emergence of some megaregions, for others, the new map of megaregions is constructed politically. While not denying the economic logic, our book highlights the presence of so many megaregions is the result of a more calculated act of political lobbying to ensure certain places appear on the map and are included alongside those urban economies they aspire to be considered with. Megaregions could arguably be seen as the latest example of a new regional theory being led, in large part, by policy developments (Lovering, 1999).

The second aspect follows on directly from the first. When is a megaregion a megaregion? The interventions in this book provide further illustration that megaregions mean different things, to different people, in different contexts. The politicized nature of megaregion formation leads to the definition becoming blurred. It is for this reason that our own contribution sought to reaffirm megaregions as comprising two or more interrelated urban systems (Harrison and Hoyler, 2015). This does not address the question of whether these megaregions are realities or imaginaries but it does help distinguish megaregions from other spatial forms (Harrison and Hoyler, 2015, Table 1.1). Defining the parameters is important because it ensures that as researchers we begin with the same objects under our consideration.

This leads straight to a third aspect. Although trying to distinguish megaregions from other spatial forms is important for analytical purposes, how social processes are spatially configured is highly complex, undeniably messy and always in a state of flux (Harrison, 2013; Taylor et al., 2013). While some megaregional spaces may well emerge from how those social processes are configured by globalizing forces, in many cases they are being imposed as part of strategic attempts by actors to make competitiveness-oriented interventions (for example funding large-scale infrastructure projects, establishing new forms of public–private partnerships) designed to change these patterns to the advantage of their location. The key point here is that some megaregions exist in institutional form but not in spirit, others exist in spirit but not in institutional form. One of the questions which require further research is uncovering where the evidence supports the creation of a megaregion as opposed to examples where evidence is being found to justify a megaregion. This is important because it raises the prospect of megaregional legitimacy, that is, the degree to which places can legitimately identify as a functioning megaregional space as opposed to a formal megaregional space where there is little evidence of actually existing processes of megaregionality.

The final point concerns when and where megaregions complement or contradict the many other imaginaries which exist to account for (different aspects of) globalization's new urban form. It might sound somewhat paradoxical to argue this but the danger with the 'brave new world of megaregions' (Smas and Schmitt, 2015) is we focus too much on the megaregion itself. We have observed a tendency in much of the work that has taken place on megaregions to – either consciously or subconsciously – neglect engaging with other competing urban and regional imaginaries. Privileging megaregions over other spatial imaginaries serves to boost the profile of megaregions, but in so doing it presents a compelling narrative that only tells part of the story. Very much akin to Jessop et al.'s (2008) account of the prevalence of 'one-dimensionalism' in social-scientific thinking over recent decades, one consequence of this privileging of megaregions is a megaregional world thesis which is guilty of overplaying its hand through exaggerated claims to its exceptionalism. This produces a somewhat insular, inward-looking, debate, which focuses on a single spatial imaginary – the megaregion. Our point is that it is wrong to study megaregions without considering them in the broader contours of global urban studies.

It goes without saying that the study of megaregions is not alone in this. In fact these four aspects point in the direction of a more general concern with contemporary studies of urban and regional formations. Too often it seems that the 'cult of newness' (Schafran, 2015) results in a tendency towards providing snapshots of a single fragment of the spatial configuration of urban-regional space at any one point in time. The failures rest in not considering the different fragments and whether they can be spatially aligned to form a coherent configuration or positioning the time-frame under consideration within longer historical trajectories. On the spatial aspect of this, it is becoming increasingly important to account for the space-times in which different urban and regional imaginaries are complementary, contradictory, overlapping, or competing. This is because endeavours to overcome the spatial tensions and contradictions inherent within the capitalist system are resulting in increasing numbers of (re)new(ed) spatial imaginaries (Harrison and Growe, 2014; Hoyler et al., 2006). We also see derivations, mutations and realignments of spatial concepts – such as Smas and Schmitt's (2015) idea of 'soft megaregions' – so the challenge is not simply to identify megaregions, but to recognize their position, role and status within the broader spectrum of urban-regional space. The following quote emphasizes this point and provides a useful framing for the context in which future studies of megaregions (and other spatial imaginaries) need to be considered:

> The overall configuration of regions within the world market cannot be planned with any certainty of success. On the contrary, given that there are many competing regional imaginaries (as well as other spatial or spatially-attuned imaginaries), the configuration is the unintended, unanticipated, and, indeed, 'messy' result of the pursuit of numerous regional projects in conjunctures that cannot be grasped in all their complexity in real time. (Jessop, 2012, p. 26)

This observation underpins our argument that megaregions always need to be considered within the broader contours of global urban studies. Moreover, it is why, for us, this book serves as an introduction to a debate around megaregions, while simultaneously contributing to broader debates centred on urban futures and the future of the urban. Put simply, in producing this book it has become clearer to us that focusing on one spatial unit or imaginary provides an ever decreasing lens on the totality of our globalizing urban world. The chapters in this volume provide an indication of what can be achieved when we position a single spatial unit/ imaginary within these broader configurations of urban-regional space. The difficulty of the task which lies ahead is not lost on us, but if we are to move forward in any meaningful way with global urban studies it is one we must confront conceptually, methodologically and empirically.

10.2.2 Megaregional Glocalization

Whether megaregions exist in space and time is one thing. It is another thing whether megaregions have any meaningful impact on society. Our starting point is to recognize that processes of globalized urbanization and megaregionality are far more partial than the narrative would suggest. Yet, accounts extolling the 'continuity' and 'interpenetration' of urban-economic processes across *all* geographic space abound (Scott, 2012), most notably Brenner's (2013) theory of 'planetary urbanization'. So what is going on? Here we turn to the work of Wachsmuth, who, in a critical exposé of the perseverance of the city as an ideological concept in globalization, argues that 'while urbanization might now be a planetary process, it is not lived or experienced as one' (2014, p. 78). We are particularly sympathetic to this perspective because, as this book has shown, the rise of megaregions 'brings us inevitably to the question who is, and who is not, actually affected by megaregions?' (Smas and Schmitt, 2015, p. 167). More to the point, it furthers our own contention that we need increasingly to focus on the questions of *who* (is affected), *how* (they are affected) and *why* (they are affected) in relation to megaregions.

In this section we want to broaden the spatial focus of megaregional research to consider the extent to which processes of megaregionality are being represented in a singular globalized form when in fact they appear to be experienced in distinctly localized ways. Schafran's (2015, p. 90) intervention is timely because it emphasizes the need to 'rethink the geography of megaregions'. He offers two heuristic devices to help advance the geography of megaregions. In the first, Schafran's distinction between 'megaregional spaces' and 'spaces of the megaregion' enables us to consider two distinct, yet interrelated, forces which are always present in, and in conflict across, megaregions. On the one hand, there are integrative forces which seek to reassert the coherence, legitimacy and validity of the megaregional space, often through an evolving discursive frame. This is also reflective of the argument that all (megaregional) space is exposed to urban-economic processes. On the other hand, there are differential forces which ensure the exposure to megaregionality is geographically uneven across the megaregional space. This calls for both macro- and micro-level

analysis of megaregions because the balance between these forces is important for recognizing how megaregionalism is experienced in places across
the megaregion at any point in time.[3]

In this book we see many examples of this type of macro- and micro-
level analysis of megaregions. Smas and Schmitt (2015), for example,
point to attempts in Northern Europe to establish 'Norden' across spaces
which share cultural, historical and political commonalities, yet are now
experiencing diverging development paths in respect of territorial policy
and politics, and urban and regional planning. Likewise Glass (2015)
draws attention to the reinvention of the US Midwest as the Great Lakes
megaregion in an attempt to preserve the legitimacy of this imagined space
as a viable political authority. However, these efforts neglect to consider
how the tens of thousands of extant spaces of local governance operating
across the Great Lakes mean the megaregional space is both fragmented
and – unlike some other megaregions, such as Gottmann's megalopolis –
discontinuously urbanized. Meanwhile Fleming (2015) shows how megaregionalists are reinventing the discursive framing of megaregions from a
singular logic of megaregional competitiveness to a more pluralized vision
where megaregions are deemed important for resilience, climate change
adaptation, and economic development in order to preserve megaregional
spaces. Then, later in his chapter, Fleming goes on to test economic integration between the Texas Triangle and Gulf Coast megaregions, observing how the Houston and Beaumont Metropolitan Statistical Areas – as
the only two regions which are included in both megaregions – appear
to share economic characteristics with both the Texas Triangle *and* Gulf
Coast megaregions. What we see in each of the three examples is how
megaregionalism is itself a reflection of the defining features of global
urbanization – namely, accelerated processes of global integration being
matched by greater local differentiation – hence the need for more macro-
and micro-level analyses which seek to understand the dynamics and
interplay between the integrative and differential forces impacting upon
megaregional space and spaces of the megaregion.

Schafran's (2015) second heuristic device is the recovery and extension of Taylor and Pain's (2007) framework for conceptualizing processes of urban expansion. Distinguishing between vertical (or primate)
megaregional systems ('Process A'), horizontal megaregional systems
('Process B') and hybrid megaregional systems ('Process A + B') is critical to understanding how megaregionalism is differentially experienced
because each has different material and infrastructural requirements.
Therefore, where capital is spatially fixed – and by implication who is
most affected – is dependent on the economic processes shaping the urban
fabric. But we should not forget that when, where and how capital is

spatially fixed remains a deeply politicized act. Megaregionality, real or otherwise, is clearly used to legitimize certain investment decisions relating to infrastructure, housing and social reproduction, and by implication who is being affected most/least by megaregionalism in action.

Our broader point is that the challenge to rethink the geography of megaregions needs to include the spatial and experiential geographies of megaregions. Put simply, the geographical map of megaregional space is fundamentally different to the geographical map of where megaregionality is experienced. Where the former appears relatively coherent and stable over time the latter is partial, fragmented, uneven and constantly in a state of flux. The important point to make is that being included on the politically-constructed map of megaregions does not mean you experience megaregionalism, likewise, just because you are not on the megaregional map does not mean you do not experience the effects of megaregionality. So although arguments pertaining to a world of megaregions – or even a '*mega*regional world' (cf. Storper, 1997) – might appear convincing when viewing a map of megaregional spaces, mapping spaces of megaregionality would appear to cast doubt on some of the claims made on behalf of megaregions representing globalization's new urban form.

10.2.3   Urban Dreams: Utopia or Dystopia?

In his latest book, *Keys to the City*, the influential economic geographer Michael Storper offers a revealing insight into the current state of global urban economic development:

> The geographical churn, turbulence, and unevenness of development, combined with the sheer scale of urbanization, will make city-region development more important than ever – to economics, politics, our global mood, and our welfare. And managing it will pose one of the most critical challenges to humanity. The winning side of the process will excite us and motivate talent, but the losing side will create displacement and anger, both within and between countries. (Storper, 2013, p. 4)

What drew our attention to this quote is the way in which it points to the type of megaregional research we advocate. In the opening few words, we see that the emphasis is firmly on the scale of urbanization and its resulting spatial form. Yet, what follows shows us how the question of what is the spatial form of large-scale urbanization and where are they located is largely inconsequential. These questions only become of consequence when we come to understand their impacts – on society, the economy, politics and the environment. But more than this, urban studies are at their most powerful when questions of agency and process are to the fore.

Storper's reference to 'managing it' is most revealing in this regard, as is his distinction between the capacity for globalized urbanization to excite us and to vex us, because the clear inference is that actors and agency are active in determining the winners and losers. They have a critical role in deciding when, where and at what pace development occurs, who benefits, and ultimately what the consequences are of globalized urbanization.

Although Storper stops short of adjudicating on what he sees as the balance between excitement and anger, winners and losers, the wider literature in global urban studies is reverberating with utopian and dystopian accounts of near urban futures. Briefly illustrating the former, Ed Glaeser (2011, pp. 9–10) argues in his book, *The Triumph of the City*, that 'not all urban poverty is bad' because cities attracting poor people 'demonstrates urban strength, not weakness . . . a fact of urban life that should be celebrated'. Alongside this, in his book *Extraordinary Cities*, Peter Taylor (2013) speaks of the 'unleashing of human potential' within cities across the ages, a picture which presents the city as the solution rather than the cause or the victim. We can contrast these accounts with those of Mike Davis (2006), in his book *Planet of Slums*, and David Harvey (2010) in *The Enigma of Capital*, who both offer up gruelling, often apocalyptic, depictions of contemporary global urbanization, reminiscent of Victorian Europe only on a vastly bigger scale. What this speaks to is a broader urban narrative, one which the geography of megaregions detailed in this book reflects, but also contributes to.

In our opening chapter we pointed to the clear difference among the forefathers of megaregional research on the future urban condition, with Patrick Geddes and Lewis Mumford both viewing large-scale urbanization as unsustainable, while Jean Gottmann held a progressive view of the economic and social potential of the expanded urban form. It was not lost on us as we worked to produce this volume that much of the new and emerging urban literature continues to be written through the megalopolis-tinged spectacles of these antecedent accounts. One example of this is *Planet of Slums*, in which Mike Davis (2006) opens with the following epigraph: 'Slum, semi-slum, and superslum . . . to this has come the evolution of cities'. These are the words of Patrick Geddes, quoted by Lewis Mumford in *The City in History* (1968, p. 464), and now used in the 21st century by Davis to underscore his despairing account of global urbanization. Indeed, it is not only the antecedent work on megaregions which gives inflection to these contemporary urban debates; much reference is also made to the foundational work on megaregions. Continuing with the example of *Planet of Slums*, Davis equates megaregions with the 'Leviathan', before proceeding to highlight an OECD account extolling the virtues of an embryonic West African megaregion that will soon be 'comparable to the U.S. east coast' (Cour and Snrech, 1998, p. 94; see also UN-Habitat, 2010), and declaring: 'Tragically, it probably will also be the biggest single footprint of urban poverty on earth' (Davis, 2006, p. 6).

Our own starting point was a reading of the megaregional literature which appeared, on the surface at least, to concur with Brendan Gleeson's recent commentary on the literature contributing to the 'urban age' thesis: 'The overall cast is . . . broadly similar – optimistic and generally of the view that cities have immanent trends, even laws, which define their possibilities' (Gleeson, 2012, p. 932). Certainly the foundational work on the resurgent interest in megaregions portrayed an unquestionable logic linking megaregions to global economic competitiveness. Our more critical approach to considering megaregions provides a different perspective. Nonetheless, it would be wrong to say that our book only offers criticisms and negative connotations. None of the contributions suggest the megaregion is an empty vessel. Each contribution highlights aspects of the megaregion thesis which are arguably in need of more thorough examination, exposing potential fault lines in the logics which have given rise to the more optimistic claims regarding the role of megaregions in globalization. Moreover, the authors endeavour to demonstrate through their own research new ways of thinking about megaregions; ways of thinking that develop the megaregion into a more robust concept and focused policy tool. Four points immediately present themselves across the chapters.

The first of these concerns competitiveness. Nearly all the work that has taken place on megaregions has concentrated on linking megaregions to competitiveness. Indeed it has been impossible to escape inherent notions of 'policy boosterism' dominant in megaregion analysis to date (Hesse, 2015). Nevertheless, Wachsmuth's intervention suggests how:

> [C]ontrary to the new prevailing wisdom . . . US megaregions are not emerging as competitive actors in the global economy, but rather are better understood as strategic terrains upon which a multitude of differently scaled competitiveness strategies are being enacted. (Wachsmuth, 2015, p. 52)

What follows from this line of thinking is that the 'unimpeachable logic' connecting megaregions to global economic competitiveness is in the process of being challenged, discredited, even broken (Glass, 2015). This has far reaching consequences for the future of the megaregion concept in both intellectual and practical debates because without the link to competitiveness the megaregion thesis lacks its 'big idea'. Nevertheless, what we have witnessed in recent years are proponents of the megaregion concept moving to broaden the evidence base for megaregions beyond the solely geoeconomic discourse of competitiveness (Regional Plan Association,

2013; Ross et al., 2015; Seltzer and Carbonell, 2011). This is particularly prevalent in the United States. Fleming (2015) details how Superstorm Sandy came to expose just how susceptible megaregional infrastructure was to external threats when it struck the US east coast in 2012. Yet the damage caused by the storm was to open up a new opportunity as proponents of megaregional planning moved to strategically position megaregions prominently within (re)emerging debates around resiliency planning, energy infrastructure and environmental/climatic change. This demonstrates one recurring feature of megaregional applications, which is they are not spatial, temporally, or thematically fixed. Like other spatial constructs and processes, megaregions and megaregionality have stronger/ weaker resonances in particular places, at particular times, and in relation to particular themes. It also demonstrates that megaregions do not just need to strategically position themselves in national and international circuits of capital accumulation; they also need to compete with other spatial imaginaries to embed themselves in a multi-level system of local, regional, national and international governance. This requires understanding both the geoeconomics and geopolitics of megaregionalism. Indeed, as Margit Mayer (2008, p. 416) so eloquently encapsulates:

> Put bluntly: it is never the spatial form that acts, but rather social actors who, embedded in particular (multidimensional) spatial forms and making use of particular (multidimensional) spatial forms, act. The relevance of a particular spatial form either for explaining certain social processes or for acting on them can be measured only from the perspective of the engaged actors. Thus, in order to define criteria for the relevance of (a specific form of) spatiality, we need to start, both in our theoretical endeavours as well as in political practice, from concrete social processes and practices rather than reifying spatial dimensions.

It is for these reasons that one of the main contributions of this book is its attempt to move the megaregional debate forward from questions of definition, identification and delimitation to questions of agency (who or what is constructing megaregions), process (how are megaregions being constructed), and specific interests (why are megaregions being constructed) through an analysis of the tactics, strategies and mechanisms employed by actors to put megaregions on the political-economic map.

The second of these concerns follows logically from the first. Successfully embedding megaregions geoeconomically and geopolitically does much to instil optimism that they are coming to represent globalization's new urban form. Yet, it is the inability of actors to successfully position megaregions within a globalizing world economy and political system which is intermixing this optimism with a strong dose of scepticism. One of the biggest concerns is always past failure. This concern is taken up by

Wheeler (2015, p. 99) especially, who quickly points out that in the United States experience tells us that 'we can hardly plan at the regional scale, let alone for megaregions'. Once again drawing on the US context – but none-theless with equal relevance to other geographic contexts – Glass develops this further, identifying two primary reasons *why* we are right to be scepti-cal about the rhetoric surrounding (mega)regional projects:

> [C]onditions within the US preclude enactment of grand visions such as the megaregion. There are two key exigencies preventing the megaregion becom-ing reality. First are the political exigencies of American life. . . . [P]roponents of the megaregion must be capable of continually reasserting the value and need for this geography over the likely long time it will take for the megaregion notion to be enacted and granted political legitimacy. Added to those chal-lenges are geographic exigencies. (Glass, 2015, p. 139)

These geographic exigencies are the thousands of extant politico-administrative units which comprise our increasingly complex, multi-scalar political systems; the very systems into which social actors have to embed megaregions before arguably the megaregion approach can begin to match some of the optimism held by its key proponents.

Our third concern returns us once again to this important distinction between 'megaregional spaces' and 'spaces of the megaregion' (Schafran, 2014). We are strong advocates of combining this type of macro- and micro-level analysis because adopting one or the other can result in an overly utopian or dystopian perception of megaregions. It might be argued that the evidence in support of megaregions being globalization's new urban form is at its strongest when considering megaregional spaces, because this is the lens through which megaregions are commonly pre-sented as being internally coherent spaces. Similarly, it might be argued that the evidence which opposes megaregions being globalization's new urban form is at its strongest when considering the more localized 'spaces of the megaregion', because this is the lens through which the unevenness of megaregionality processes across megaregional space come to the fore.

Our fourth and final concern is that for all of this, we find ourselves left with one very simple question. What, if anything, has changed? We are forced to ask this question because the contributions to this book almost always return to this particular concern. Feverishly attempting to portray megaregions as something distinctly 'new' is nothing new (Taylor and Lang, 2004), and yet the evidence points towards megaregions being the latest phase in a long-running urban saga. As we and others have noted, there is certainly a trend towards 'bigger is better' in global urban analysis (Harrison and Hoyler, 2015). Moreover, on competitiveness, it is argued that '[m]egaregions represent a *heightening* of the imperative towards interurban competition but at a *new spatial scale*' (Wachsmuth, 2015, p. 66; our emphasis), while on the environment it is being argued that 'rather than helping bring about more sustainable societies this *new scale* of [megaregional] planning is likely to *accelerate* what some climate change scientists have labelled BAU ("business-as-usual") forms of development' (Wheeler, 2015, p. 97; our emphasis). The key point here is that new narratives seem to echo the same old narrative. What is new about megaregions is, for the most part, the scale of analysis and intervention. Otherwise much, and this includes the outcomes, appears to remain the same – only more ubiquitous, more intense, and on a much grander scale.

10.2.4   The Missing Dimension: Urban History, Periodization and the Temporality of Megaregions

Taking stock of the 'urban age' thesis, Gleeson (2012, p. 942) concludes that 'popular urbanology reminds us that there is truly nothing new under the ever-glowing sun'. Certainly, feverish attempts by urbanists to account for globalization's evolving spatial form and function can lead to an unhealthy obsession with newness. Megaregions and the megaregion concept are illustrative of this trend: two of the founding intellectual contributions underpinning this resurgent interest in megaregions include claims to 'new data', 'new, natural economic units', 'new global terrain', 'new technology and innovation', 'new scale', 'new approach', 'new urbanism', 'new patterns', 'newly defined' and 'new agenda and paradigm' (Florida et al., 2008; Ross, 2009). While we do not wish to deny that some aspects of the megaregional thesis are indeed new, the trap is to over-emphasize what is new. One of the main aims of this book has therefore been to think about how to historicize the current situation with regard to megaregions.

In our introductory chapter we suggested the roots of today's megaregions concept go back to the beginning of the 20th century. One of the most pertinent points for us was to demonstrate the ebb and flow of the megaregion concept in the 20th century. This is important because it is easy to forget that the megaregion is one of the more durable spatial concepts in urban studies. Specifically in relation to functional urban areas, looking beyond the flotsam and jetsam of past and present experiments reveals 'world city', 'city-region' and 'megaregion' as the spatial imaginaries which are standing the test of time. At a time when we are being asked to consider why, when urbanization processes far exceed the city, the concept of 'the city' remains so tenacious (Wachsmuth, 2014), one of the aims of this book has been to consider why the megaregion concept continues to be renewed both intellectually and practically; withstanding the appearances and disappearances of so many other competing spatial imaginaries (cf. Taylor and Lang, 2004). In this way we agree with Hesse (2015, p. 30) that '[t]he more popular this term and the associated concept is becoming, the more it seems useful to explore the question of where it comes from, what its meanings are, and whether it brings urban-regional policies forward or not' – only we would go further and say it is not only useful, it is essential. Our one note of caution is deciding which historical trajectory to embed megaregions in plays a critical role in determining the extent to which current interest in megaregions is seen to reflect the continuity or discontinuity of longer-term trends relating to urban expansion, urban development, and urban studies. Four points emerge from the contributions to this book.

The first is the need for a more historical perspective of megaregions. In his contribution, Schafran (2015) claims contemporary megaregional research is 'ahistorical' and argues for a 'less economistic, more historical' – to which we would add, more political – approach to future studies of megaregions. The point being made is that too many studies concentrate exclusively on the here and now. They study what can be observed – namely the *what* and the *where* of megaregions – then typically project into the near and far future with little more than a passing acknowledgement to the antecedent work on megaregions and urban history more broadly. Our point is that megaregional research needs to look back as much as it looks forward, with the geography of megaregions seen more as an outcome than the beginning of something new. That said it is important to ask what type of historical perspective is necessary, and this is our second point. Nostalgic references to Gottmann, Geddes and Mumford are common in megaregional research but what the contributors to this book reveal is a much broader tradition of megaregional research, providing valuable empirical insights, conceptual elements and theoretical provocations to animate and renew analyses of the megaregions. Indeed, this leads neatly on to a third point. What is revealing is that although many will agree with the need to position the current focus on megaregions within a much longer trajectory of megaregional research, there are very different views on what that historical trajectory should constitute: for Zhang (2015) it involves going back at least two millennia; Schafran (2015) to the late nineteenth century; while for Wachsmuth (2015) and Fleming (2015) the 1960s and 1970s hold the key. So as much as we advocate a more historical approach to researching megaregions, we caution that in so doing we need to consider why authors revisit certain points in history to make certain arguments in relation to current events. It is not simply a case of knowing when and who they select, but why and how they are selected.

This leads to the fourth and final point of why we need to adopt a more historical perspective in megaregional research. One answer is to ensure as researchers we do not repeat the same mistakes (Harrison, 2007; Schafran, 2015). But a second, more progressive, answer is the merits of periodization, an idea being brought to bear in Neil Brenner's latest writings on the spatial reorganization of economic and political power in globalization. For Brenner (2009, p. 134), periodization represents 'one of the most challenging and exciting frontiers' for research in global urban studies. This is because periodization confronts the necessary task of moving beyond temporally defined scaled moments of capitalist growth – that is, those claims to a 1990s 'regional', early-2000s 'city-regional' or late-2000s 'megaregional' *scalar fix* – which are presented as though they are internally coherent and consistent narratives of economic and political logic for how capitalism is organized in the current phase of globalization, to look in much more detail at how these spatial developments vary across time and space (see also Harrison and Hoyler, 2014). It is for this reason that our introductory chapter began by identifying how the megaregion has been prominent in different world regions at different points in history. We showed how the megaregion discourse was pervasive in Europe during the late 1980s and through the 1990s, in southeast Asia during the 1990s, before coming alive across North America in the mid-2000s, and is now seen emerging in Australia and Africa. The timing of this book is significant because it comes at a time when despite this long-held interest in the term and its associated concept in urban and regional studies, the megaregion is arguably of 'global' significance for the very first time in its history. Yet, that being said, one of the key findings from this book has been to show how its global significance and appeal does not necessarily equate to omnipresence.

10.3 CODA: MEGAREGIONS AS GLOBALIZATION'S NEW URBAN FORM?

The megaregional urban form is not going to disappear any time soon. The question is whether the megaregion concept will survive with it. This is the dilemma, as we see it, arising from this book. The problem, as many of the contributions attest, is the megaregional thesis is built around a partial, largely economistic, reading of megaregions which has a tendency to neglect important temporal and political aspects of developments in megaregional form and function. To this end, one of the main outcomes of the book is to argue the case for a more deeply politicized and historicized account of megaregions. To be clear, our argument is not that megaregional research should somehow become less economic, rather that singular economistic readings of megaregional development are insufficient to account for globalization's urban form, and need to be complemented by the more political and historical investigations we advocate here. Indeed, one purpose of this book is to create space for debating megaregions in a more challenging and robust way, one which serves to refine, question and, if necessary, debunk some of the claims made about megaregions from a purely geoeconomic perspective.

Let us be clear, we do not wish to see a withering away of megaregions in critical urban inquiry, but if the megaregion concept is to remain central to intellectual and practical developments in urban studies and urban policy it needs to be a more robust concept and framework. To do this we need to move beyond the theoretical myopia and exaggerated claims to newness which currently surround megaregions. We argue that this requires researchers to focus on the *who*, the *how* and the *why* of megaregions rather more than the *what* and the *where* of megaregions. Indeed, one of the main contributions of this book has been to extend research from questions of definition, identification and delimitation to questions of agency (who or what is constructing megaregions), process (how are megaregions being constructed) and specific interests (why are megaregions being constructed). More broadly, we believe the megaregional story detailed in this book is one which can illuminate certain aspects of currently topical debates around urban futures and the future of the urban. In our final statements we want to briefly touch on three broader contours of global urban studies that the content of this book contributes to.

The first contour relates to the production of new theory in urban studies. Part of a special issue on the future of city-regions, international urbanist, Ananya Roy (2009), argued the need for 'new geographies of theory' and 'new conceptual vectors' to understand the 21st century metropolis, and evolving forms of globalized urbanization more broadly. It is time, she argues, to 'blast open theoretical geographies, to produce a new set of concepts in the crucible of a new repertoire of cities' (Roy, 2009, p. 820). This call to arms has certainly been taken forward in the intervening years, yet, for all that we agree with Roy's sentiments we cannot help but feel the call for *new* concepts is not always the most desirable outcome. Actually what we need are more robust concepts, something which does not preclude the production of new concepts but also does not exclude renewing existing concepts. The latter is certainly not as glamorous as minting new concepts, but, as the story of megaregions illustrates, it might prove to be a necessary antidote to the theoretical myopia and exaggerated claims to newness and conceptual innovation present in some accounts purporting to explain globalization's new urban form.

The second contour relates to methodology and approaches to doing global urban research. It is certainly the case that urban scholars are leaving no stone unturned in the pursuit of new theory production, but what, we ask, can be said about the current state of empirical research (and the methodological approaches we possess) for conceptualizing globalized urbanization? We believe that focusing on questions of agency (who or what is constructing megaregions), process (how are megaregions being constructed) and specific interests (why are megaregions being constructed) offers one important way forward in complementing and/or challenging the current assumptions and beliefs which surround megaregions. We are particularly encouraged by the potential afforded by periodization, but this requires researchers to divert their attention away from the examples of outstanding success to begin considering how the individual trajectories of megaregions compare and how megaregions relate to one another.

The third contour is the issue of temporality. For our part we are encouraged by what we see as something of a 'historical turn' in global urban studies. What we observe is a much closer reading of urban history and an onus on explaining current urban developments by positioning cities in globalization into a much longer trajectory of urban development, expansion and change (see, for example, Brenner and Schmid, 2014; Scott and Storper, 2014; Taylor et al., 2010; Taylor, 2013; Wachsmuth, 2014). Not only is this approach revealing important continuities and discontinuities in urban development, it is noticeable how many claims to newness are in fact not altogether new but the rediscovery and bringing forward of a previous idea or approach.[4]

In conclusion, we want to confront the main question raised by this book: namely, is the megaregion globalization's new urban form? Spatially, there is no denying the trend is towards more megaregional formations in globalization. Yet, as we have sought to demonstrate in this book, focusing on the temporal aspects of megaregional development reveals no essential connection between megaregions and globalization. What it demonstrates is how we are in a temporally defined scaled moment where the focus is on megaregions as we seek to understand the dynamics of capitalist growth. In the current moment the megaregion concept is of global significance and relevance to academics, political leaders and policymakers alike. This is not to say that the megaregion concept will necessarily remain so in the future. Put bluntly, what this book argues is that the megaregion concept will only remain the focus of attention for as long as social actors find it useful in advancing their own specific interests (cf. Mayer, 2008). We should not forget that only ten years ago, Taylor and Lang (2004) did not include 'megaregion' in their list of 50 terms accounting for globalization's new urban form. This shows how quickly momentum can gather around a particular spatial imaginary, but also acts as a warning for how quickly it could subsequently disappear. Indeed, Glass offers a useful summation of what for us is the key factor in determining the longevity of the mega-region (or any other spatial imaginary) in framing changing urban form in globalization, across space and time:

> [T]he political sovereignty of proposed spaces such as the megaregion can never be completed – the authority of the megaregion as a viable political space, including its value to continue through time – must be continually reasserted, or else new geographical projects and imaginaries will co-opt the semblance of legitimacy which the megaregion as geographical imaginary has constructed. (Glass, 2015, p. 129)

What this reaffirms is our key point. Megaregionalism is as much a political project as it is a story about capitalist processes. For as long as social actors see value – in other words, an ability to exert influence over other centres of social power by using this framing of megaregions to advance their own specific interests – it will continue to be promoted both intellectually and practically. However, if and when a point arises where another spatial imaginary can challenge, overtake, or replace the megaregion in best serving this purpose, the appeal of the megaregion will almost inevitably wane. It is critical to understand that the appearance and/or disappearance of the megaregion concept will not result from some radical change to the spatial form of globalized urbanization, nor will it result from a fundamental shift in the economic logic of agglomeration economics, rather it will result from changes in the political authority of megaregions as a politically viable space of engagement for key social actors. This line of thinking brings us back to the sentiments expressed by August Hecksher (1964) some 50 years ago in the foreword to Jean Gottmann's classic text *Megalopolis: The Urbanized Northeastern Seaboard of the United States*. To this day the megaregion remains a powerful imaginary for exploring globalization's new urban form; nevertheless, we need to be very careful how we choose to use it because it is very easy for misconceptions to take root.

NOTES

1. Despite the US–Mexico border recording the highest number of legal crossings of any land border in the world it is also one of the most protected.
2. We interpret Schafran's (2014, 2015) distinction between 'megaregional spaces' and 'spaces of the megaregion' as closely mirroring Cox's (1998) distinction between the 'spaces of engagement' and 'spaces of dependence'.
3. You might imagine that these questions are more appropriate to ask in relation to

megaregional spaces with the least legitimacy, but we would argue they are equally relevant across *all* megaregional spaces.

4. The latest example of this is 'planetary urbanization' (Brenner, 2013) which reimagines
the idea of *ecumenopolis* (meaning 'universal city', or a city made of the whole world) put
forward by the Greek architect and urban planner Constantinos Doxiadis in the 1960s
(Doxiadis, 1961; Doxiadis and Papaioannou, 1974).

REFERENCES

Bozick, T. (2013), 'Hampton Roads, Richmond could be "megaregion"', *Daily Press*, 26 December.

Brenner, N. (2009), 'Open questions on state rescaling', *Cambridge Journal of Regions, Economy and Society*, **2** (1), 123–139.

Brenner, N. (ed.) (2013), *Implosions/Explosions: Towards a Study of Planetary Urbanization*, Berlin: Jovis.

Brenner, N. and C. Schmid (2014), 'The "urban age" in question', *International Journal of Urban and Regional Research*, **38** (3), 731–755.

Connor, K. (2013), 'CaliBaja aims to create economic mega-region', *San Diego Source – The Daily Transcript*, 29 October.

Cour, J.-M. and S. Snrech (1998), *Preparing for the Future: A Vision of West Africa in the Year 2020*, Paris: OECD.

Cox, K. (1998), 'Spaces of dependence, spaces of engagement and the politics of scale, or: looking for local politics', *Political Geography*, **17** (1), 1–23.

Davis, M. (2006), *Planet of Slums*, London: Verso.

Doxiadis, C.A. (1961), *Ecumenopolis: Toward the Universal City*, Athens: Athens Technological Organization.

Doxiadis, C.A. and J.G. Papaioannou (1974), *Ecumenopolis: The Inevitable City of the Future*, New York: W & W Norton.

Fleming, B. (2015), 'Towards a megaregional future: analysing progress, assess-ing priorities in the US megaregion project', in J. Harrison and M. Hoyler (eds), *Megaregions: Globalization's New Urban Form?* Cheltenham, UK and Northampton, MA, USA: Edward Elgar, pp. 200–229.

Florida, R. (2014), 'The dozen regional powerhouses driving the U.S. economy', *The Atlantic Cities*, 12 March.

Florida, R., T. Gulden and C. Mellander (2008), 'The rise of the mega-region', *Cambridge Journal of Regions, Economy and Society*, **1** (3), 459–476.

Glaeser, E. (2011), *Triumph of the City: How Our Greatest Invention Makes Us Richer, Smarter, Greener, Healthier and Happier*, Oxford: Pan Macmillan.

Glass, M.R. (2015), 'Conflicting spaces of governance in the imagined Great Lakes megaregion', in J. Harrison and M. Hoyler (eds), *Megaregions: Globalization's New Urban Form?* Cheltenham, UK and Northampton, MA, USA: Edward Elgar, pp. 119–145.

Gleeson, B. (2012), 'The urban age: paradox and prospect', *Urban Studies*, **49** (5), 931–943.

Gottmann, J. (1961), *Megalopolis: The Urbanized Northeastern Seaboard of the United States*, New York: The Twentieth Century Fund.

Harrison, J. (2007), 'From competitive regions to competitive city-regions: a new orthodoxy, but some old mistakes', *Journal of Economic Geography*, **7** (3), 311–332.

Harrison, J. (2013), 'Configuring the new "regional world": on being caught between territory and networks', *Regional Studies*, **47** (1), 55–74.

Harrison, J. and A. Growe (2014), 'When regions collide – in what sense a new "regional problem"?', *Environment and Planning A*, forthcoming.

Harrison, J. and M. Hoyler (2014), 'Governing the new metropolis', *Urban Studies*, **51** (11), 2249–2266.

Harrison, J. and M. Hoyler (2015), 'Megaregions: foundations, frailties, futures', in J. Harrison and M. Hoyler (eds), *Megaregions: Globalization's New Urban Form?* Cheltenham, UK and Northampton, MA, USA: Edward Elgar, pp. 1–28.

Harvey, D. (2010), *The Enigma of Capital*, London: Profile Books.

Hecksher, A. (1964), 'Foreword', in J. Gottmann, *Megalopolis: The Urbanized Northeastern Seaboard of the United States*, Cambridge, MA: MIT Press, pp. vii–viii.

Hesse, M. (2015), '*Mega*urban regions: epistemology, discourse patterns, big urban business', in J. Harrison and M. Hoyler (eds), *Megaregions: Globalization's New Urban Form?* Cheltenham, UK and Northampton, MA, USA: Edward Elgar, pp. 29–50.

Hidalgo, A. (2014), 'London and Paris: we could soon be part of the same conurbation', *The Guardian*, 23 January.

Hoyler, M., T. Freytag and C. Mager (2006), 'Advantageous fragmentation? Reimagining metropolitan governance and spatial planning in Rhine-Main', *Built Environment*, **32** (2), 124–136.

Jessop, B. (2012), 'Cultural political economy, spatial imaginaries, regional economic dynamics', CPERC Working Paper [English language version of a paper that appears in German in Brand, O., P. Eser and S. Dörhöfer (eds) (2013), *Ambivalenzen regionaler Kulturen und Identitäten*, Münster: Westfälisches Dampfboot], Lancaster University, available at http://www.lancaster.ac.uk/cperc/docs/Jessop%20CPERC%20Working%20Paper%202012-02.pdf (accessed 10 February 2014).

Jessop, B., N. Brenner and M. Jones (2008), 'Theorizing sociospatial relations', *Environment and Planning* D, **26** (3), 389–401.

Lovering, J. (1999), 'Theory led by policy: the inadequacies of the "new regionalism" (illustrated from the case of Wales)', *International Journal of Urban and Regional Research*, **23** (2), 379–395.

Mayer, M. (2008), 'To what end do we theorize sociospatial relations?' *Environment and Planning D*, **26** (3), 414–419.

Mumford, L. (1968), *The City in History: Its Origins, Its Transformation, and Its Prospects*, New York: Harvest Books.

Regional Plan Association (2006), *America 2050: A Prospectus*, New York: RPA.

Regional Plan Association (2013), *Landscapes: Enabling Partnerships in the Northeast Megaregion*, New York: RPA.

Ross, C.L. (2009), 'Introduction', in C.L. Ross (ed.), *Megaregions: Planning for Global Competitiveness*, Washington, DC: Island Press, pp. 1–8.

Ross, C.L., D. Lee, E. Meijers and T. Welch (2015), *Megaregions, Prosperity and Sustainability*, London: Routledge.

Roy, A. (2009), 'The 21st-century metropolis: new geographies of theory', *Regional Studies*, **43** (6), 819–830.

Samuel, H. (2014), '"London is suburb of Paris" claims mayoral favourite', *The Telegraph*, 20 January.

Schafran, A. (2014), 'Rethinking mega-regions: sub-regional politics in a fragmented metropolis', *Regional Studies*, **48** (4), 587–602.

Schafran, A. (2015), 'Beyond globalization: a historical urban development approach to understanding megaregions', in J. Harrison and M. Hoyler (eds), *Megaregions: Globalization's New Urban Form?* Cheltenham, UK and Northampton, MA, USA: Edward Elgar, pp. 75–96.

Scott, A.J. (2012), *A World in Emergence: Cities and Regions in the 21st Century*, Cheltenham, UK and Northampton, MA, USA: Edward Elgar.

Scott, A.J. and M. Storper (2014), 'The nature of cities: the scope and limits of urban theory', *International Journal of Urban and Regional Research*, DOI: 10.1111/1468-2427.12134.

Seltzer, E. and A. Carbonell (2011), *Regional Planning in America: Practice and Prospect*, Cambridge, MA: Lincoln Institute of Land Policy.

Smas, L. and P. Schmitt (2015), 'Brave new "megaregional worlds"? Reflections from a North European perspective', in J. Harrison and M. Hoyler (eds), *Megaregions: Globalization's New Urban Form?* Cheltenham, UK and Northampton, MA, USA: Edward Elgar, pp. 146–174.

Storper, M. (1997), *The Regional World: Territorial Development in a Global Economy*, New York: Guilford Press.

Storper, M. (2013), *Keys to the City: How Economics, Institutions, Social Interaction, and Politics Shape Development*, Princeton, NJ: Princeton University Press.

Taylor, P.J. (2013), *Extraordinary Cities: Millennia of Moral Syndromes, World-Systems and City/State Relations*, Cheltenham, UK and Northampton, MA, USA: Edward Elgar.

Taylor, P.J. and R.E. Lang (2004), 'The shock of the new: 100 concepts describing recent urban change', *Environment and Planning A*, **36** (6), 951–958.

Taylor, P.J. and K. Pain (2007), 'Polycentric mega-city regions: exploratory research from Western Europe', in Regional Plan Association and Lincoln Institute of Land Policy (eds), *The Healdsburg Research Seminar on Megaregions: Discussion Papers and Summary*, Cambridge, MA: Lincoln Institute of Land Policy, pp. 59–66.

Taylor, P.J., B. Derudder, M. Hoyler and P. Ni (2013), 'New regional geographies of the world as practised by leading advanced producer service firms in 2010', *Transactions of the Institute of British Geographers*, **38** (3), 497–511.

Taylor, P.J., A. Firth, M. Hoyler and D. Smith (2010), 'Explosive city growth in the modern world-system: an initial inventory derived from urban demographic changes', *Urban Geography*, **31** (7), 865–884.

UN-Habitat (2010), 'Urban trends: urban corridors – shape of things to come?', UN-Habitat Press Release, 13 March, Nairobi: UN-Habitat.

Wachsmuth, D. (2014), 'City as ideology: reconciling the explosion of the city form with the tenacity of the city concept', *Environment and Planning D*, **32** (1), 75–90.

Wachsmuth, D. (2015), 'Megaregions and the urban question: the new strategic terrain for US urban competitiveness', in J. Harrison and M. Hoyler (eds), *Megaregions: Globalization's New Urban Form?* Cheltenham, UK and Northampton, MA, USA: Edward Elgar, pp. 51–74.

Wheeler, S.M. (2015), 'Five reasons why megaregional planning works against sustainability', in J. Harrison and M. Hoyler (eds), *Megaregions: Globalization's*

New Urban Form? Cheltenham, UK and Northampton, MA, USA: Edward Elgar, pp. 97–118.

Zhang, X. (2015), 'Globalization and the megaregion: investigating the evolution of the Pearl River Delta in a historical perspective', in J. Harrison and M. Hoyler (eds), *Megaregions: Globalization's New Urban Form?* Cheltenham, UK and Northampton, MA, USA: Edward Elgar, pp. 175–199.

Index